Maria's War

1916

MARIA'S WAR

A Soldier's Autobiography

MARIA BOCHKAREVA

with Isaac Don Levine

Russian Life
BOOKS

Originally published under the title, *Yashka: My Life as Peasant, Exile and Soldier* (1919). The original text has been brought up to date through edits, corrections, annotations, and illustrations. The original text has also been supplemented with a new preface and afterword.

Photo credits: Cover - Library of Congress digital archive, photographer unknown. Pages 2, 85, 140, Captain Donald C. Thompson. Pages 131, 196, 207 - Library of Congress digital archive. Page 261 - Library of Congress digital archive, credited to Harris & Ewing.

ISBN 978-1-880100-51-6

Library of Congress Control Number: 2016963279

Russian Information Services, Inc.
PO Box 567
Montpelier, VT 05601-0567
www.russianlife.com
orders@russianlife.com
phone 802-223-4955

CONTENTS

PREFACE

"They were going to meet death, death in battle against a foreign foe, the first women in the world to volunteer for such an end. Yet every one of them was happy, and the only fear expressed was lest the battalion should not be sent at once to the trenches."

Rheta Dorr, *Inside the Russian Revolution*

Surely the best known aspect of Maria Bochkareva's life was her formation and command of the First Women's Battalion of Death in Russia's final months of the First World War. Yet this was merely the most famous aspect of a life of unbelievable hardship, difficulty and achievement. From her childhood in poverty and two abusive marriages, to Siberian exile, imprisonment, death sentences, grueling travel, war wounds and horrific battle experiences, Bochkareva seems to have lived out the fullness of the Chinese blessing/curse: May you live an interesting life.

Certainly, it is not the sort of life one would have expected her to have, born a poor peasant, unschooled, and married at the age of 15 in a Siberian backwater. Had her husband not been arrested and sent into Siberian exile, and had she not voluntarily followed him, her life might have turned out very differently. Or perhaps not. For if there is one thing we learn from Bochkareva's memoir, she was a person of extraordinary grit and determination. Once she set her mind to something, she would not be deterred. Reading her memoir, one loses count of the number of times she skirts death or disaster, was mortally wounded, or simply surmounted what to others might have been a crippling obstacle.

That said, we of course cannot know how much Bochkareva or her literary collaborator, Isaac Don Levine, embellished her story to make it more heroic and gripping. Certainly there are times when Levine's authorial voice breaks through, or when the propaganda intent of the book (to spur American and British support for intervention in Russia) becomes rather loud – this is particularly the case in the book's final chapters.

Nonetheless, reading this volume with such caveats in mind, it offers an invaluable firsthand look into: pre-revolutionary life in peasant Russia; the role of women in a deeply mysogynistic society; the lives of soldiers in the trenches; the top echelons of power before and after the 1917 revolutions. Indeed, it seems difficult to find anyone important that Bochkareva did *not* meet during her war, from Kerensky and Rodzianko to Generals Kornilov and Alexeyev, from Western suffragettes and journalists to Lenin and Trotsky. And then, after the period of time covered by the memoir, she traveled to the US and met with President Woodrow Wilson and Teddy Roosevelt, and then on to England where she had an audience with King George, before returning to a Russia still embroiled in a bloody civil war.

There is little reason to question the basic facts of Bochkareva's narrative. (Spoiler alert: skip to the next section if you want to learn her life story through the memoir.) Born Maria (Marusya) Leontyevna Frolkova in July 1889, in the village of Nikolskoe, Novgorod *gubernia*, she was the third child in a very destitute family that, when she was six or seven, accepted a government offer of resettlement to Siberia that came with some financial support and land. The family was sent to Tomsk region, to the village of Kuskovo. But life there was far from easy, and the family continued to struggle. Maria was repeatedly abused by her father and, at 15, was married off to the 23-year-old Afanasy Bochkarev. She initially embraced her marriage as a way to escape her troubled home. But Afanasy turned out to be a drunkard who also abused her.

Having the strength and sense to leave Afanasy, Maria later became the common law wife of Yakov Buk, a butcher. Her life was set on a better path, but then, in 1912, Buk was arrested for robbery and exiled to Siberia. She followed him to Yakutsk and helped arrange for better conditions for Yakov, including the opening of a butcher shop there, by giving in to the advances of the lecherous local governor. Yet Buk kept up his criminal activity, was caught, and sent remote Amga. Maria again followed him, trying to make things work, but Yakov continued to drink and began abusing her.

It was about this time that World War I broke out, and, after Yakov tried to murder her, Maria wisely decided to leave him and escape her miserable life in Amga. Returning to Tomsk, she succeeded in joining the Russian Imperial Army. Overcoming scorn, abuse and discrimination, Maria (who adopted the nickname Yashka) soon distinguished herself in battle and began to win the hearts and loyalty of her fellow soldiers. She was twice wounded in battle and promoted to the rank of Senior Unter-Officer, roughly equivalent to a senior warden.

After the February Revolution, Bochkareva's fame led Alexander Kerensky, then the War Minister (later the head of the government), to ask her to lead a women's volunteer movement (in the memoir, Bochkareva says it was her idea). The government's intent was to use women volunteers as a way to shame men into continuing to fight against the Germans. Fraternization, apathy, and insubordination were rampant along the front lines after the February Revolution, given the incompetence and vacilation of the military leadership, the elimination of the death penalty for not obeying orders, and the generally perceived pointlessness of trench warfare.

Some two thousand women responded to Bochkareva's call, and about 300 were chosen to be trained for the Women's Battalion of Death. Bochkareva developed a reputation for severe discipline and, in the summer of 1917, her battalion distinguished itself in battle near Smorgon. She was severely wounded there and again promoted in rank, this time to sub-lieutenant.

Meanwhile, other Women's Battalions were established in Moscow, the Kuban and many cities throughout the empire. As Laurie Stoff writes, "The number of women involved in combat and combat-related activities was so significant that in August 1917, a Women's Military Congress was convened in Petrograd to coordinate women's military unions around the country."[1] But when Kerensky's summer 1917 offensives failed and the October Revolution trumped all other developments, the Women's Battalions lost their propaganda value, to say nothing of their operational purpose. As Stoff summarizes, "Of the fifteen women's military formations designated by the Ministry of War, Bochkareva's battalion was the only unit that participated in the defense of the homeland against the external enemy. The new Soviet government had little use for what they perceived to be 'bourgeois' women with guns. It issued a decree ordering all the women's military units to disband on 30 November 1917."

Arrested briefly after the revolution, and refusing (in a direct meeting with Lenin and Trotsky) to fight for the Bolsheviks (telling the two leaders they had no idea what war was), Bochkareva decided to go home to Tomsk. On her way there she was persecuted both for being a woman and an officer and suffered a serious injury when thrown from a train at Chelyabinsk.

1. "Women Soldiers in Russia's Great War," Laurie Stoff, Online at http://russiasgreatwar.org/media/military/women_soldiers.shtml, accessed 12/19/2016.

After healing at home, restless and upset at being unable to provide for her family in the difficult conditions wrought by the Civil War, she undertook a secret mission on behalf of White forces to make contact with General Kornilov in the South, in Novocherkassk. She traveled by train and cart disguised as a Sister of Mercy, and later as a common peasant. She met with Kornilov who, according to one source, tasked her with traveling to the West to rally support for aid to White forces,[2] though she makes no mention of Kornilov's request in the book, insisting (much as with the founding of the Women's Battalion) that it was her idea.

Unfortunately, after crossing back over the lines into Red territory, Bochkareva was almost captured, then turned herself in (hoping for mercy). She narrowly escaped a brutal and anonymous death before a firing squad after being recognized by a former comrade in arms. She was transported back to Moscow where she acquitted herself of all charges and gained a document allowing her free passage throughout the country, a barely credible feat that seems miraculous for those times.

In any event, Bochkareva then headed east, stopping to spend time with her family near Tomsk, and was joined by her sister on her round-the-world trip to America and the UK. The memoir ends with the pair's unlikely departure from Vladivostok aboard the *Sheridan*, on April 18, 1918.

Maria's life after the events recounted in this memoir are detailed in the Afterword, and a map showing many of the points on her life journey can be found at: bit.ly/marias-war.

GIVEN THAT MARIA Bochkareva was functionally illiterate, capturing her life story required a co-author. Her trip across the US and to the UK was made possible through support from a network of influential suffragettes who shared Bochkareva's view of the necessity of continuing the two-front war against Germany. These included Florence Harriman, Emmeline Pankhurst and the journalist Rheta Dorr (who in 1916 accompanied Bochkareva's battalion to the front lines).

In June 1918, Dorr arranged for Maria to recount her story to Isaac Don Levine, a young American journalist. By Levine's accounting, the two met for only 100 hours in her New York hotel room, and from that he crafted this as-told-to biography. The amount of detail Maria recalls and the exactness of

2. "Sergei Drokov, "Мария Бочкарева: краткий биографический очерк русского воина", http://rus-istoria.ru/component/k2/item/372-mariya-bochkareva-kratkiy-biograficheskiy-ocherk-russkogo-voina, accessed 12/19/2016.

her retelling of conversations, places and people, shows that she possessed a remarkable memory.

Levine had been born in Belarus to the family of a Zionist activist, and came to the US at the age of 18, finishing high school in Missouri. He found work as a journalist and covered the Russian revolution for *The New York Herald*, and, later, the Russian Civil War for *The Chicago Daily News*. A staunch anti-communist, he later ghost-wrote the memoir of a Soviet defector, *In Stalin's Secret Service*, and played a key role in Whittaker Chambers' unmasking of spies in the Roosevelt administration, including Alger Hiss.

Thus, one expects that Levine amplified here Bochkareva's own anti-communist views, at times polishing her statements and observations to fit with his ideological imperative, which Levine insisted was neither liberal or conservative. As he wrote half a century later, in a 1968 letter to the *New York Times*, "I am an inveterate libertarian who has never joined any conservative camp and who looks upon statism regardless of its color and upon every form of concentrated power as the blights of our age."[3]

Despite this stance, the Soviets granted Levine a tourst visa in the 1960s. He visited and published a book of his experiences, *I Rediscover Russia*, in 1964. He died in 1981, at the age of 89.

– Paul E. Richardson

---

3. "Isaac Don Levine, 89, Foe of Soviet," *New York Times*, February 17, 1981.

INTRODUCTION

In the early summer of 1917, the world was thrilled by a news item from Petrograd announcing the formation by one Maria Bochkareva of a women's fighting unit under the name of "The Battalion of Death." With this announcement, an obscure Russian peasant girl made her debut in the international hall of fame. From the depths of dark Russia Maria Bochkareva suddenly emerged into the limelight of modern publicity. Foreign correspondents sought her, photographers followed her, distinguished visitors paid their respects to her. All tried to interpret this arresting personality. The result was a riot of misinformation and misunderstanding.

Of the numerous published tales about and interviews with Bochkareva that have come under my observation, there is hardly one which does not contain some false or misleading statement. This is partly due to the deplorable fact that the foreign journalists who interpreted Russian men and affairs to the world during the momentous year of 1917 were, with very few exceptions, ignorant of the Russian language; and partly to Bochkareva's reluctance to take every adventurous stranger into her confidence. It was her cherished dream to have a complete record of her life incorporated in a book some day. This work is the realization of that dream.

To a very considerable extent, therefore, the narrative here unfolded is of the nature of a confession. When in the United States in the summer of 1918, Bochkareva determined to prepare her autobiography. Had she been educated enough to be able to write a letter fluently, she would probably have written her own life story in Russian and then had it translated into English. Being semi-illiterate, she found it necessary to secure the services of a writer commanding a knowledge of her native language, which is the only tongue she speaks. The procedure followed in the writing of this book was this: Bochkareva recited to me in Russian the story of her life, and I recorded it in English in longhand, making every effort to set down her narrative verbatim. Not infrequently I would interrupt her with a question intended to draw out some forgotten experiences. However, one of Bochkareva's natural gifts is an extraordinary memory. It took nearly a hundred hours, distributed over a period of three weeks, for her to tell me every detail of her romantic life.

At our first session, Bochkareva made it clear that what she was going to tell me would be very different from the stories about her related in the press. She would reveal her innermost self and break open for the first time the sealed book of her past. This she did, and in doing so completely discredited several widely circulated tales about her. Perhaps the chief of these is the statement that Bochkareva had enlisted as a soldier and gone to war to avenge her fallen husband. Whether this invention was the product of her own mind or was attributed to her originally by some prolific correspondent, I do not know. In any event it was a convenient answer to the eternal question of importunate journalists how she came to be a soldier. Unable to explain to the conventional world that profound impulse which really drove her to her remarkable destiny, she adopted this excuse until she had an opportunity to record the full story of her courageous life.

This book will also remove that distrustful attitude based on misunderstanding that has been manifested toward Bochkareva in radical circles. When she arrived in the United States, she was immediately hailed as a "counter-revolutionary," royalist and sinister intriguer by the extremists. That was a grave injustice to her. She is ignorant of politics, contemptuous of intrigue, and spiritually far and above party strife. Her mission in life was to free Russia from the German yoke.

Being placed virtually in the position of a father confessor, it was my privilege to commune with the spirit of this remarkable peasant-woman, a privilege I shall ever esteem as priceless. She not only laid bare before me every detail of her amazing life that memory could resurrect, but also allowed me to explore the nooks and corners of her heart to a degree that no friend of hers ever did. Maintaining a critical attitude from the beginning of our association, I was gradually overwhelmed by the largeness of her soul.

Wherein does the greatness of Bochkareva lie? Mrs. Emmeline Pankhurst called her the greatest woman of the century." "The woman that saved France was Joan of Arc – a peasant girl," wrote a correspondent in July, 1917, "Maria Bochkareva is her modern parallel." Indeed, in the annals of history since the days of the Maid of Orleans we encounter no feminine figure equal to Bochkareva. Like Joan of Arc, this Russian peasant girl dedicated her life to her country's cause. If Bochkareva failed – and this is yet problematical, for who will dare forecast the future of Russia – it would not lessen her greatness. Success in our materialistic age is no measure of true genius.

Like Joan of Arc, Bochkareva is the symbol of her country. Can there be a more striking incarnation of France than that conveyed by the image of Joan of Arc? Bochkareva is an astounding typification of peasant Russia, with all her virtues and vices. Educated to the extent of being able to scribble her own name with difficulty, she is endowed with the genius of logic. Ignorant of history and literature, the natural lucidity of her mind is such as to lead her directly to the very few fundamental truths of life. Religious with all the fervour of her primitive soul, she is tolerant in a fashion befitting a philosopher. Devoted to her country with every fibre of her being, she is free from impassioned partisanship and selfish patriotism. Overflowing with good nature and kindness, she is yet capable of savage outbursts and brutal acts. Credulous and trustful as a child, she can be easily incited against people and things.

Know Bochkareva and you will know Russia, that inchoate, invincible, agonized, striving, rising colossus in all its depth and breadth.

Intrepid and rash as a fighter, her desire to live on occasions was indescribably pathetic. In a word, Bochkareva embodies all those paradoxical characteristics of Russian nature that have made Russia a puzzle to the world. These traits are illustrated almost in every page of this book. Take away from Russia the veneer of western civilization and you behold her incarnation in Bochkareva. Know Bochkareva and you will know Russia, that inchoate, invincible, agonized, striving, rising colossus in all its depth and breadth. It must be made unmistakably clear here that the motives responsible for this book were purely personal. In its origin this work is exclusively a human document, a record of an exuberant life. It was the purpose of Bochkareva and the writer to keep the narrative down to a strict recital of facts. It is really incidental that this record is valuable not only as a biography of a startling personality, but as a revelation of certain phases of a momentous period in human history; not only as a human document, but as an historical document as well. Because Bochkareva always has been and still is strictly non-partisan and because she does not pretend to pass judgment upon events and men, her revelations are of prime importance. The reader gets a picture of Kerensky in action that completely effaces all that has hitherto been said of this tragic but typical product of the Russian intelligentsia. Kornilov, Rodzianko, Lenin and Trotsky and some other outstanding personalities of the Russian revolution appear in these pages exactly as they are in reality.

Not a single book, as far as I know, has appeared yet giving an account of how the Russian army at the front reacted to the Revolution. What was the state of mind of the Russian soldier in the trenches, which was after all the decisive factor in the developments that followed, during the first eight months of 1917? No history of unshackled Russia will be complete without an answer to this vital question. This book is the first to disclose the reactions and emotions of the vast Russian army at the front to the tremendous issues of the revolution, and is of especial value coming from a veteran peasant soldier of the rank and file.

Perhaps surpassing all else in interest is the horrible picture we get of Bolshevism in action. With the claims of theoretical Bolshevism to establish an order of social equality on earth Bochkareva has no quarrel. She said so to Lenin and Trotsky personally. But then come her experiences with Bolshevism in practice, and there follows a blood-freezing narrative of the rule of mobocracy that will live forever in the memory of the reader.

Bochkareva left the United States towards the end of July, 1918, after having attained the purpose of her visit – an interview with President Wilson. She went to England and thence to Archangel, where she arrived early in September. According to a newspaper despatch, she caused the following proclamation to be posted in village squares and country churches:

"I am a Russian peasant and soldier. At the request of the soldiers and peasants I went to America and Great Britain to ask these countries for military help for Russia.

"The Allies understand our own misfortunes and I return with the Allied armies, which have come only for the purpose of helping to drive out our deadly enemies, the Germans, and not to interfere with our internal affairs. After the war is over the Allied troops will leave Russian soil.

"I, for my own part, request all loyal free sons of Russia, without reference to party, to come together acting as one with the Allied forces, who, under the Russian flag, come to free Russia from the German yoke and to help the new free Russian army with all forces, including Russia, to beat the enemy.

"Soldiers and peasants! Remember that only a full, clean sweep of the Germans from our soil can give you the free Russia you long for."

Isaac Don Levine
November 1918

MARIA'S JOURNEY
Select locations that figure in Maria Bochkareva's life story. For the full map, visit bit.ly/marias-war

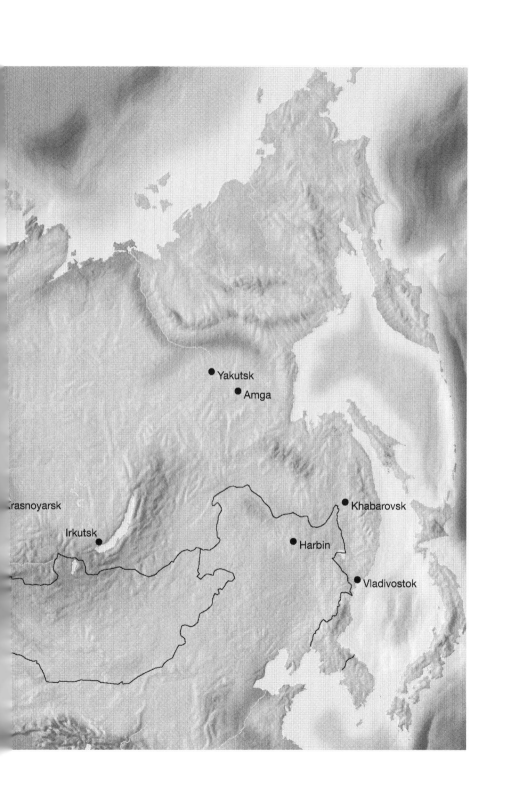

PART ONE

YOUTH

CHAPTER I
MY CHILDHOOD OF TOIL

My father, Leonti Semenovich Frolkov, was born into serfdom at Nikolsko, a village in the province of Novgorod, some two hundred miles north of Moscow. He was fifteen when Alexander II emancipated the serfs in 1861, and remembers that historic event vividly, being fond even now of telling of the days of his boyhood. Impressed into the army in the early seventies, he served during the Russo-Turkish War of 1877-78, and distinguished himself for bravery, receiving several medals. When a soldier, he learned to read and write, and was promoted to the rank of sergeant.

Returning home at the end of the war, he passed through Charonda, a fishermen's settlement on the shore of a lake, in the county of Kirilov, within thirty miles of Nikolsko.[4] No longer dressed as a *muzhik*, military in gait and bearing, with coins jingling in his pocket, he cut quite a figure in the poor hamlet of Charonda. There he met my mother, Olga, the eldest daughter of Elizar Nazarev, perhaps the most destitute inhabitant of the place.

Elizar, with his wife and three daughters, occupied a shabby hut on the sandy shore of the lake. So poor was he that he could not afford to buy a horse to carry his catch to the city, and was compelled to sell it, far below the market price, to a travelling buyer. The income thus derived was not sufficient to keep the family from hunger. Bread was always a luxury in the little cabin. The soil was not tillable. Elizar's wife would hire herself to the more prosperous peasants in the vicinity for ten kopeks a day to labor from sunrise to sunset. But even this additional money was not always to be had. Then Olga would be sent out to beg for bread in the neighboring villages.

Once, when scarcely ten years old, little Olga underwent a harrowing experience, which she could never later recall without horror. Starting home with a basketful of bread, collected from several villages, she was fatigued but happy at the success of her errand, and hurried as fast as she could. Her path

---

4. Actually, Charonda is on the shores of Lake Vozhe, in Vologda region, about 300 miles as the crow flies from Nikolsko, a small village on the Shelon River, which is about 30 miles from Novgorod.

lay through a forest. Suddenly she heard the howling of a pack of wolves. Olga's heart almost stopped beating. The dreadful sounds drew nearer. Overcome by fright, she fell unconscious to the ground.

When she regained her senses, she found herself alone. The wolves apparently had sniffed her prostrate body and gone their way. Her basket of bread was scattered in all directions, trampled in the mud. Out of breath, and without her precious burden, she arrived home.

It was in such circumstances that my mother grew to be nineteen, when she attracted the attention of Leonti Frolkov, who was then stopping in Charonda on his way home from the war. She was immensely flattered when he courted her. He even bought her a pair of shoes for a present, the first shoes she had ever worn. This captivated the humble Olga completely. She joyously accepted his marriage proposal.

After the wedding, the young couple moved to Nikolsko, my father's birthplace, where he had inherited a small tract of land. They tilled it together, and with great difficulty managed to make ends meet. My two elder sisters, Arina and Shura, were born here, increasing the poverty of my parents. My father, about this time, took to drinking, and began to maltreat and beat his wife. He was by nature morose and egotistical. Want was now making him cruel. My mother's life with him became one of misery. She was constantly in tears, always pleading for mercy and praying to God.

I was born in July 1889, the third girl in the family. At that time many railroads were being built throughout the country. When I was a year old, my father, who had once been stationed at Tsarskoye Selo, the Tsar's place of residence near the capital, decided to go to Petrograd to seek work. We were left without money. He wrote no letters. On the brink of starvation, my mother somehow contrived, with the aid of kind neighbors, to keep herself and her children alive.

When I was nearly six years old, a letter came from my father, the first he had written during the five years of his absence. He had broken his right leg and, as soon as he was able to travel, had started home. My mother wept bitterly at the news, but was glad to hear from her husband whom she had almost given up for dead. In spite of his cruelty toward her, she still loved him. I remember how happy my mother was when my father arrived, but this happiness did not last long. Poverty and misery cut it short. My father's harsh nature asserted itself again. Hardly had a year gone by when a fourth child, also a girl, arrived in our family. And there was no bread in the house.

From all parts of our section of the country, peasants were migrating that year to Siberia, where the Government allowed them large grants of land. My father wanted to go, but my mother was opposed to it. However, when our neighbor, Verevkin, who had left sometime before for Siberia, wrote glowingly of the new country, my father made up his mind to go, too.

Most of the men would go alone, obtain grants of land, till them, build homesteads, and then return for their families. Those of the peasants who took their families with them had enough money to tide them over. But we were so poor that, by the time we got to Chelyabinsk, the last station in European Russia, and the Government distribution point, we had not a penny left. At the station my father obtained some hot water to make tea, while my two elder sisters were sent to beg for bread.

We were assigned to Kuskovo, eighty miles beyond Tomsk. At every station my sisters would beg food, while father filled our tea-kettle with hot water. Thus we got along till Tomsk was reached. Our grant of land was in the midst of the taiga, the virgin Siberian forest. There could be no thought of immediately settling on it, so my father remained in Tomsk, while the rest of us were sent on to Kuskovo. My sisters went to work for board and clothing. My mother, still strong and in good health, baked bread for a living, while I took care of the baby.

One day my mother was expecting visitors. She had baked some cakes and bought a pint of vodka, which she put on the shelf. While she was at work I tried to lull the baby to sleep. But baby was restless, crying incessantly. I did not know how to calm her. Then my eyes fell on the bottle of vodka.

"It must be a very good thing," I thought, and decided to give a glass to baby. Before doing so, I tasted it myself. It was bitter, but I somehow wanted more. I drank the first cup and, the bitterness having somewhat worn off, I drained another. In this manner I disposed of the entire bottle. Drowsy and weak, I took the baby into my arms and tried to rock it to sleep. But I myself began to stagger, and fell with the child to the floor.

Our mother found us there, screaming at the top of our voices. Presently the visitors arrived, and my mother reached for the bottle, only to discover that it had been emptied. It did not take her long to find the culprit. I shall always remember the whipping I got on that occasion.

Toward winter, my father arrived from Tomsk. He brought little money with him. The winter was severe, and epidemics were raging in the country. We fell ill one by one, father, mother, then all the girls. As there was no bread in the house, and no money to buy anything, the community took care of us till the spring, housing and feeding us. By some miracle, all of us escaped death, but our clothes had become rags. Our shoes fell to pieces. My parents decided to move to Tomsk, where we arrived barefoot and tattered, finding shelter at a poor inn on the outskirts of the town.

My father would work only a couple of days a week. He was lazy. The remainder of the week he idled away and drank. My sisters served as nurse-maids, while my mother worked in a bakery, keeping the baby and me with her. We slept in the loft of a stable, with the horses stamping below us. Our bed was of straw laid on the floor, which consisted of unshaven planks thrown across logs. Soon the baker's wife began to object to feeding an extra mouth, which belonged to me. I was then over eight years old.

"Why don't you send her to work? She can earn her own bread," she argued.

My mother would draw me to her breast, weep and beg for mercy. But the proprietress became impatient, threatening to throw us all out.

Finally my father came to see us, with the good tidings that he had found a place for me. I was to care for a five-year-old boy, in return for my board and eighty-five kopeks a month.

"If you do well," my father added," you will by and by receive a ruble."

Such was the beginning of my career in life. I was eight and a half years old, small and very thin. I had never before left my mother's side, and both of us wept bitterly at parting. It was a grey, painful, incomprehensible world into which I was being led by my father. My view of it was further blurred by a stream of tears.

I took care of the little boy for several days. One afternoon, while amusing him by making figures in the sand, I myself became so engrossed in the game that I quarrelled with my charge, which led to a fight. I remember feeling keenly that I was in the right. But the child's mother did not inquire into the matter. She heard his screams and whipped me for it.

I was deeply hurt by the undeserved whipping administered by a strange woman.

"Where was my mother? Why did not she come to avenge me?"

My mother did not answer my cries. Nobody did. I felt miserable. How wrong was the world, how unjust. It was not worthwhile living in such a world.

My feet were bare. My dress was all in rags. Nobody seemed to care for me. I was all alone, without friends, and nobody knew of the yearning in my heart. I would drown myself, I thought. Yes, I would run to the river and drown myself. Then I would go up, free of all pain, into the arms of God. I resolved to slip out at the first chance and jump into the river, but before the opportunity presented itself, my father called. He found me in tears.

"What's the matter, Manka?" he asked.

"I am going to drown myself, papa," I answered sadly.

"Great Heavens! What's happened, you foolish child?"

I then poured out my heart to him, begging to be taken to my mother. He caressed me and talked of my mother's distress if I left my place. He promised to buy me a pair of shoes, and I remained.

But I did not stay long. The little boy, having seen his mother punish me, began to take advantage of me, making my life quite unbearable. Finally, I ran away and wandered about town till dark, looking for my mother. It was late when a policeman picked me up crying in the street and carried me to the police station. The officer in charge of the station took me to his home for the night.

His house was rather large. I had never been in such a house before. When I awoke in the morning it seemed to me that there were a great many doors in it and all of them aroused my curiosity. I wanted to know what was behind them. As I opened one of the doors, I beheld the police-officer asleep on a bed, with a pistol by his side. I wanted to beat a hasty retreat, but he awoke. He seized the pistol and, still dazed from sleep, threatened me with it. Frightened, I ran out of the room.

> *I had never been in such a house before. When I awoke in the morning it seemed to me that there were a great many doors in it and all of them aroused my curiosity.*

My father, meanwhile, had been informed of my flight and had gone to the police station in search of me. He was referred to the police officer's home. There he found me, weeping in the porch, and took me to my mother.

My parents then decided to establish a home. All their capital amounted to six rubles. They rented a basement for three rubles a month. Two rubles my father invested in some second-hand furniture, consisting of a lame table and benches, and a few kitchen utensils. With a few kopeks from the last ruble in her purse my mother prepared some food for us. She sent me to buy a kopek's worth of salt.

The grocer's shop of the street was owned by a Jewess named Nastasia Leontievna Fuchsman. She looked at me closely when I entered her shop, recognizing that I was a stranger in the street, and asked me :

"Whose are you?"

"I am of the Frolkovs. We have just moved into the basement in the next block."

"I need a little girl to help me. Would you like to work for me?" she asked. "I'll give you a ruble a month, and board."

I was overjoyed and started for home at such speed that by the time I got to my mother I was quite breathless. I told her of the offer from the grocerywoman.

"But," I added," she is a Jewess."

I had heard so many things of Jews that I was rather afraid, on second thoughts, to live under the same roof with a Jewess. My mother calmed my fears on that score and went to the grocer's shop to have a talk with the proprietress. She came back satisfied, and I entered upon my apprenticeship to Nastasia Leontievna.

It was not an easy life. I learned to wait on customers, to run errands, to do everything in the house, from cooking and sewing to scrubbing floors. All day I slaved without ceasing, and at night I slept on a box in the passageway between the shop and the house. My monthly earnings went to my mother, but they never sufficed to drive the spectre of starvation away from my home. My father earned little but drank much, and his temper became more and more harsh.

In time, my wages were raised to two rubles a month. But as I grew I required more clothes, which my mother had to supply me from my earnings. Nastasia Leontievna was exacting and not infrequently punished me. But she also loved me as though I had been her own daughter, and always tried to make up for harsh treatment. I owe a great deal to her, as she taught me to do almost everything, both in her business and in housework.

I must have been about eleven when, in a fit of temper, I quarrelled with Nastasia Leontievna. Her brother frequented the theatre and constantly talked of it. I never quite understood what a theatre was like, but it attracted me, and I resolved one evening to get acquainted with that place of wonders. I asked Nastasia Leontievna for money to go there. She refused.

"You little *muzhichka*,[5] what do you want with the theatre?" she asked derisively.

"You d—d Jewess!" I retorted fiercely, and ran out of the shop. I went to my mother and told her of the incident. She was horrified.

"But now she won't take you back. What shall we do without your wages, Marusia? How shall we pay the rent? We shall have to go begging again." And she began to cry.

After some time my employer came after me, rebuking me for my quick temper.

"How could I have known that you were so anxious to go to the theatre?" she asked. "All right, I'll give you fifteen kopeks every Sunday so that you can go."

I became a regular Sunday occupant of the gallery, watching with intense interest the players, their strange gestures and manners of speech.

Five years I worked for Nastasia Leontievna, assuming more important duties as I grew older. Early in the morning I would rise, open the shutters,

---

5. Diminutive of *muzhik*, man, peasant.

knead the dough, and sweep or scrub the floors. I finally grew weary of this daily grind and began to think of finding other work. But my mother was ill and my father worked less and less, drinking most of the time. He grew more brutal, beating us all unmercifully. My sisters were forced to stay away from home. Shura married at sixteen, and I, fourteen years old, became the mainstay of the family. It was often necessary to get my pay in advance in order to keep the family from starving.

The temptation to steal came to me suddenly one day. I had never stolen anything before, and Nastasia Leontievna repeatedly pointed out this virtue in me to her friends.

"Here is a *muzhichka* who doesn't steal," she would say. But one day, on unpacking a barrel of sugar delivered at the shop, I found seven sugar-loaves instead of the usual six. The impulse to take the extra loaf of sugar was irresistible. At night I smuggled it stealthily out of the shop and took it home. My father was dismayed.

"What have you done, Marusia? Take it back immediately," he ordered. I began to cry and said that the sugar was not really Nastasia Leontievna's, that the error had been made at the refinery. Then my father consented to keep it.

I returned to the shop and went to bed, but my eyes would not close; my conscience troubled me." What if she suspects that a loaf of sugar was missing? What if she discovers that I have stolen it?" And a feeling of shame came over me. The following day I could not look straight into Nastasia Leontievna's eyes. I felt guilty. My face burned. At every motion of hers my heart quivered in anticipation of the terrible disclosure. Finally she noticed that there was something the matter with me.

"What's wrong with you, Marusia?" she questioned, drawing me close to her. "Are you not well?"

This hurt even more. The burden of the sin I had committed weighed heavier and heavier. It rapidly became unbearable. My conscience would not be quieted. At the end of a couple of restless days and sleepless nights I decided to confess. I went into Nastasia Leontievna's bedroom when she was asleep. Rushing to her bed, I fell on my knees and broke into sobs. She awoke in alarm.

"What's happened, child? What is it?"

Weeping, I told the story of my theft, begging forgiveness and promising never to steal again. Nastasia Leontievna calmed me and sent me back to bed, but she could not forgive my parents. Next morning she visited our home, remonstrating with my father for his failure to return the sugar and punish me. The shame and humiliation of my parents knew no bounds.

Sundays I spent at home, helping my mother in the house. I would go to the well, which was a considerable distance away, for water. My mother baked bread all the week and my father carried it to the market, selling it at ten kopeks a loaf. His temper was steadily getting worse, and it was not unusual for me to find my mother in the yard in tears after my father had come home drunk.

I was now fifteen and began to grow dissatisfied with my lot. Life was stirring within me and quickening my imagination. Everything that passed by and beyond the narrow little world in which I lived and labored called me, beckoned to me, lured me. The impressions of that unfamiliar world which I had caught in the theatre had taken deep root in my soul and had kindled in me new ardors and desires. I wanted to dress nicely, to go out, to enjoy life's pleasures. I wanted to be educated. I wanted to have enough money to secure my parents for ever from starvation and to be able to lead for a time, for a day even, an idle life, without having to rise with the sun, to scrub the floor or to wash clothes.

Ah! what would I not have given to taste the sweetness, the joy, that life held. But there seemed to be none for me. All day long I slaved in the little shop and kitchen. I never had a spare ruble. Something revolted within me against this bleak, purposeless, futureless existence.

CHAPTER II
MARRIAGE AT FIFTEEN

Then came the Russo-Japanese War. And with it, Siberia, from Tomsk to Manchuria, teemed with a new life. It reached even our street, hitherto so lifeless and uneventful. Two officers, the brothers Lazov, one of them married, rented the quarters opposite Nastasia Leontievna's shop. The young Madame Lazov knew nothing of housekeeping. She observed me at work in the shop, and offered me work in her home at seven rubles a month.

Seven rubles a month was so attractive a sum that I immediately accepted the offer. What could not one do with so much money? Why, that would leave four rubles for me, after the payment of my mother's rent. Four rubles! Enough to buy a new dress, a coat, or a pair of fashionable shoes. Besides, it gave me an opportunity to release myself from the bondage of Nastasia Leontievna.

I took entire charge of the housekeeping at the Lazovs. They were kind and courteous, and took an interest in me. They taught me how to behave at table and in society, and took care that I appeared neat and clean.

The younger Lazov, Lieutenant Vasily, began to notice me, and one evening invited me to take a walk with him. In time Vasily's interest in me deepened.

We went out together many times. He made love to me, caressing and kissing me. Did I realize clearly the meaning of it all? Hardly. It was all so new, so wonderful, so attractive. It made my pulse throb at his approach. It made my cheeks flame with the heat of my young blood.

Vasily said he loved me. Did I love him? If I did, it was more because of the marvellous world into which he was to lead me, than on account of himself. He promised to marry me. Did I particularly want to marry him? Scarcely. The prospect of marriage was more enticing to me because of the end it would put to my life of drudgery and misery than on account of anything else. To become free, independent, possessed of means, was the attractive prospect that marriage held for me.

I was fifteen and a half when Vasily seduced me by the promise of marriage. We lived together for a short while, when orders came to the Lazovs to leave for a different post. Vasily informed me of the order.

"Then we shall have to get married quickly, before you go," I declared. But Vasily did not think so.

"That's quite impossible, Marusia," he said.

"Why?" I inquired sharply, something rising in my throat, like a tide, with suffocating force.

"Because I am an officer, and you are only a plain *muzhichka*. You understand, yourself, that at present we can't marry. Marusenka, I love you just as much as ever. Come, I'll take you home with me; you'll stay with my parents. I'll give you an education, then we will get married."

I became hysterical, and throwing myself at him like a ferocious animal, I screamed at the top of my voice: "You villain. You deceived me. You never did love me. You are a scoundrel. May God curse you."

Vasily tried to calm me. He tried to approach me, but I repulsed him. He cried, he begged, he implored me to believe that he loved me, and that he would marry me. But I would not listen to him. I trembled with rage, seized by a fit of uncontrollable temper. He left me in tears.

I did not see Vasily for two days. Neither did his brother nor sister-in-law. He had disappeared. When he returned, he presented a pitiable sight. His haggard face, the appearance of his clothes, and the odor of vodka told the story of his two-days' debauch.

"Ah, Marusia, Marusia," he lamented, gripping my arms." What have you done, what have you done? I loved you so much. And you would not understand me. You have ruined my life and your own."

My heart was wrung with pity for Vasily. Life to me then was a labyrinth of blind alleys, tangled, bewildering. It is now clear to me that Vasily did love me genuinely, and that he had indulged in the wild orgy to forget himself and drown the pain I had caused him. But I did not understand it then. Had I loved him truly, it might all have been different. But a single thought dominated my mind. "He had promised to marry me and failed." Marriage had become to me the symbol of a life of independence and freedom.

The Lazovs left. They gave me money and gifts. But my heart was like a deserted ruin in the winter, echoing with the howls of wild beasts. Instead of a life of freedom, my parents' basement awaited me. And deep in my bosom lurked a dread of the unknown...

I returned home. My sisters had already noticed a different air about me. Perhaps they had seen me with Vasily at one time or another. Whatever the cause, they had their suspicions, and did not fail to communicate them to my mother. It required little scrutiny for her to observe that from a shy little girl I had blossomed forth into a young woman. And then there began days and nights of torture for me.

My father quickly got wind of what had happened at the Lazovs. He was merciless and threw himself upon me with a whip, nearly lashing me to death, accompanying each blow with epithets that burned into me more than the lashes of the whip. He also beat my mother when she attempted to intervene on my behalf.

My father would come home drunk almost every day, and immediately take to lashing me. Often he would drive me and my mother barefoot out of the house, and sometimes we shivered for hours in the snow, hugging the icy walls.

Life became an actual inferno. Day and night I prayed to God that I might fall ill and die. But God remained deaf. And still I felt that only illness could save me from the daily punishment. "I must get ill," I said to myself. And so I lay on the oven at night to heat my body, and then went out and rolled in the snow. I did it several times, but without avail. I could not fall ill.

Amid these insufferable conditions, I met the new year of 1905. My married sister had invited me to take part in a masquerade. My father would not hear, at first, of my going out for an evening, but consented after repeated entreaties. I dressed as a boy, this being the first time I ever wore a man's clothes. After the dancing, we visited some friends of my sister's, where I met a soldier, just returned from the front. He was a common *muzhik*, of rough appearance and vulgar speech, and at least ten years older than myself. He immediately began to court me. His name was Afanasy Bochkarev.

It was not long afterwards that I met Bochkarev again in the house of a married sister of his. He invited me to go out for a walk, and then suddenly proposed that I should marry him. It came to me so unexpectedly that I had no time for consideration. Anything seemed preferable to the daily torments of home . If I had sought death to escape my father, why not marry this boorish *muzhik*? And I consented without further thought.

My father objected to my marrying since I was not yet sixteen, but without avail. As Bochkarev was penniless, and I had no money, we decided to work together and save. Our marriage was a hasty affair. The only impression of it that remains with me is my feeling of relief at escaping from my father's brutal hands. Alas! Little did I then suspect that I was exchanging one form of torture for another.

On the day following our marriage, which took place in the early spring, Afanasy and I went down to the river to hire ourselves as day laborers. We helped to load and unload lumber barges. Hard work never daunted me, and I would have been satisfied, had it only been possible for me to get along with Afanasy otherwise. But he also drank, while I did not, and intoxication invariably brutalized him. He knew of my affair with Lazov, and would use it as a pretext for punishing me.

"That officer is still in your head," he would shout. "Wait, I'll knock him out of it." And he would proceed to do so.

Summer came. Afanasy and I found work with an asphalt business. We made floors at the prison, university and other public buildings. We paved some streets with asphalt. Our work with the firm lasted about two years. Both of us started at seventy kopeks a day, but I rose to the position of assistant foreman in a few months, receiving a ruble and fifty kopeks a day. Afanasy continued as a common laborer. My duties required considerable knowledge in the mixing of the various elements in the making of concrete and asphalt.

Afanasy's low intelligence was a sufficient trial, but his heavy drinking was a greater source of suffering to me. He made a habit of beating me, and grew to be unendurable. I was less than eighteen years old, and nothing but misery seemed to be in store for me. The thought of escape dug itself deeper and deeper into my mind. I finally resolved to run away from Afanasy.

My married sister had moved to Barnaul, where she and her husband worked as servants on a river steamer. I saved some twenty rubles, and determined to go to my sister, but I needed a passport. Without a passport one could not move in Russia, so I took my mother's.

On the way, at a small railway station, I was held up by a police officer.

"Where are you going, girl?" he asked brusquely, eyeing me with suspicion.

"To Barnaul," I replied, with a sinking heart.

"Have you a passport?" he demanded.

"Yes," I said, drawing it out of my bag.

"What's your name?" was the next question.

"Maria Bochkareva."

In my confusion I had forgotten that the passport was my mother's, and that it bore the name of Olga Frolkova. When the officer unfolded it and glanced at the name, he turned on me fiercely:

"Bochkareva, ah, so that is your name?"

It dawned upon me then that I had committed a fatal mistake. Visions of prison, torture and eventual return to Afanasy flashed before me." I am lost," thought, falling upon my knees before the officer to beg for mercy, as he ordered me to follow him to headquarters. In an outburst of tears and sobs, I told him that I had escaped from a brutal husband, and since I could not possibly obtain a passport of my own, I was forced to make use of my mother's. I implored him not to send me back to Afanasy, for he would certainly kill me.

My simple peasant speech convinced the officer that I was not a dangerous political, but he would not let me go. He decided that I should go with him. "Come along, you will stay with me, and tomorrow I will send you to Barnaul. If you don't, I'll have you arrested and sent by *etape*6 back to Tomsk."

I was as docile as a sheep. This was my first contact with the authorities, and I dared not protest. If I had any power of will, it must have been dormant. Had I not found the world full of wrong since my childhood? Was not this one of the ordinary events of life? We *muzhiks* were created to suffer and endure. They, the officials, were created to punish and maltreat. And so I was led away by the guardian of peace and law, and made to suffer shame and humiliation...

I was then free to go to Barnaul, and I resumed my journey. When I arrived there, my sister quickly found employment for me on the steamship. The work was comparatively easy, and my life rapidly took a happier turn. It was an immense relief to be away from my drunken, brutal husband.

But the relief was short-lived. Afanasy came to my mother after my disappearance to inquire concerning my whereabouts. She showed surprise upon hearing of my flight, and denied all knowledge of my destination. He returned to our house again and again. One day in his presence the postman delivered a letter from Shura. He seized it, and through it learned that I was in Barnaul.

One morning, as I was standing on the deck of the ship, which was anchored in the harbor, my eyes suddenly fell on a figure approaching the wharf. It was a familiar figure. In another moment I recognized it as that of Afanasy. My blood froze and my flesh crept as I realized what was coming.

"Once fallen into his hands my life would be one of continuous torture," I thought. "I must save myself."

But how could I escape? If I were on land I might still have a chance. Here all avenues are closed. There he is already approaching the gate to the wharf. He is stopping to ask a question of a guard, who nods affirmatively. Now, he is walking a little faster. His face wears a grin that strikes terror into my heart.

---

6. A prison convoy.

I am trapped... But no, just wait a moment, Afanasy. Don't be sure of your triumph yet. I rush to the edge of the deck, cross myself and jump into the deep waters of the Ob. Ah, how thrilling it is to die! So I have outwitted Afanasy, after all. It's cold, the water is cold. And I am going down, down... I am glad. I am triumphant. I have escaped from the trap... into the arms of death.

I awoke, not in heaven, but in the hospital. I was observed jumping into the river, dragged out unconscious, and revived.

The authorities questioned me as to the cause of my attempted suicide, and drew up a protocol. I told them of my husband, of his brutality, and the utter impossibility of living with him.

Afanasy was waiting in the anteroom, to see me. My attempt at suicide had seriously upset him. It aroused a sense of shame in him. Touched by my story, the authorities went out and angrily rebuked him for his maltreatment of me. He admitted his guilt, and swore that he would be gentle to me in the future.

He was then admitted to the ward in which I lay. Falling on his knees, be begged my forgiveness, repeating his oath to me and professing his love for me in the most affectionate terms. His entreaties were so moving that I finally consented to return home with him.

For a while Afanasy was truly a different man. In spite of his coarse habits, I was deeply touched by his efforts to be kind. However, that did not last long. We resumed our life of drudging toil. And vodka resumed its grip on him. Once drunk, be became just as brutal again.

Gradually life with Afanasy grew as insufferable as it had been before my escape. That summer I turned nineteen, and I saw ahead of me nothing but a long series of dreary years. Afanasy wanted me to take to drink. I resisted, and that infuriated him. He made it a habit to torment me daily. He would hold a bottle of vodka to my face, and scoffing at me for my efforts to lift myself above my condition, he would endeavour by blows and kicks to force the bitter drink down my throat. One day he even stood over me with a bottle of vodka for three whole hours, pinning me down to the ground so that I was unable to move a muscle. Still I refused to give in.

Winter came. I baked bread for a living. On Sundays I went to church to pray to God to release me from my bondage. Again the thought of escaping took root in my mind. The first requisite was, of course, a passport, so I went secretly to a lawyer for advice, and he undertook to obtain one for me legally. But ill-luck attended me. When the police constable called to deliver the passport to me, Afanasy was at home. My scheme was discovered and my hopes were dashed to the ground. Afanasy hurled himself at me and bound me hand

and foot, deaf to my entreaties and cries. I thought my end had come. In silence he carried me out of the house and tied me to a post.

It was cold, very cold. He flogged me, drank, and flogged me again, cursing me in the vilest terms.

"That's what you get for trying to escape," he bawled, holding the bottle to my mouth." You won't escape any more. You will drink or you will die!"

I was obdurate and implored him to leave me alone. He continued his flogging, however, keeping me for four hours tied to the post, till I finally broke down and drank the vodka. I became intoxicated, staggered out into the street, and fell on the pavement in front of the house. Afanasy ran after me, cursing and kicking me. We were quickly surrounded by a crowd. My neighbors, who knew of his cruelty to me, came to my help. Afanasy was roughly handled, so roughly, indeed, that he left me in peace for some time afterwards.

Christmas was drawing near. I had saved, little by little, fifty rubles. Every kopek of that money had been earned by extra toil during the night. It was all the earthly possession that I had, and I guarded it jealously. Somehow, Afanasy got wind of its hiding place and stole it. He spent it all on drink.

I was mad with fury upon discovering the loss. What the money meant to me in the circumstances is difficult to describe. It was my blood, my sweat, a year of my youth. And he, the beast, squandered it in one orgy. The least I could do to my torturer was to kill him.

In a frenzy, I ran to my mother, who was struck by the expression of my face. "Marusia, what ails you?"

"Mother," I gasped, "let me have an axe. I am going to kill Afanasy."

"Holy Mother, have mercy!" she exclaimed, raising her hands to Heaven, and falling on her knees, she implored me to come to my senses. But I was too frantic with rage. I seized an axe and ran home.

Afanasy returned, drunk, and began to taunt me with the loss of my precious savings. I was white with wrath and cursed him from the depth of my heart. He gripped a stool and threw it at me. I caught up the axe.

"I will kill you, you blood-sucker!" I screamed.

Afanasy was stupefied. He had not expected that from me. The desire to kill was irresistible. Mentally, I already gloated over his dead body and the freedom that it would bring me. I was ready to swing the axe at him...

Suddenly the door flew open and my father rushed in. He had been sent by my mother.

"Marusia, what are you doing?" he cried out, gripping my arm. The break was too abrupt, my nerves collapsed, and I fell unconscious to the floor. Upon awakening I found the police in the house, and I told them everything. Afanasy was taken to the police station, while the police officer, a very kindhearted man, advised me to leave the town to get away from him.

I got my passport, but my money was gone. I could not afford to buy a ticket to Irkutsk, where Shura had moved from Barnaul. Determined to go at all costs, I boarded a train without a ticket. The conductor discovered me on the way, and I cried and begged him to allow me to proceed. He proposed to hide me in the baggage car and take me to Irkutsk, upon his own conditions. Enraged, I pushed him violently from me.

"I will put you off at the next station," he shouted at me, running out of the car. And he kept his word.

Nearly all the distance to Irkutsk was yet before me, and I wanted to get there without selling myself for the price of a ticket. There could be no thought of going back. I had to get to Irkutsk. I boarded the next train, and stealthily crouched under a seat, as it moved out of the station.

Ultimately I was discovered, but this conductor was an elderly man and yielded to my tears and entreaties. I told him of my experience with the first conductor and of my total lack of money. He allowed me to proceed, and whenever an inspector boarded the train, he would signal to me to hide under the seat. Sometimes I would spend several hours at a stretch there, concealed by the legs of some kind passengers. In this manner I journeyed for four days, finally reaching my destination – Irkutsk.

CHAPTER III
A LITTLE HAPPINESS

I arrived in Irkutsk penniless. All I possessed was what I wore. I went to look for my sister, who was in poor circumstances and ill. Her husband was out of work. One could not expect an enthusiastic welcome under such conditions. I lost little time in seeking employment, and quickly found a place as a dishwasher at nine rubles a month. It was revolting work, in a filthy den patronized by drunkards. The treatment I received at the hands of the clients was so unbearable that I left at the end of the first day.

On the third day I found work in a laundry, where I had to wash hundreds of articles daily. From five in the morning till eight in the evening I was bent over the washtub. It was bitter drudgery, but I was forced to stay at it for several weeks. I lived with my sister in one small room, paying her rent. Presently I began to feel pains in my back. The hard work was telling on me. I resolved to leave the laundry, although my sister was against my doing so. I had no money saved.

Having had experience of concrete work, I applied for employment to an asphalt contractor. He was kind enough to give me a trial as an assistant foreman on a job he was doing at the Irkutsk prison. I was to take charge of ten men and women laborers.

When I began I was met by an outburst of mirth on all sides. "Ha, ha," they laughed, "a *baba* holding a foreman's place!"[7]

I paid no heed to the ridicule and went about my business quietly and gently. The men obeyed, and as they saw that I knew what I was about, began even to gain a respect for me. I was given for a first test the preparing of a floor. Stretching myself on the ground with the rest of the party, planning and working, I managed to finish my task a couple of hours ahead of my scheduled time, and marched the men triumphantly out of the building, to the utter amazement of the other foremen. My employer was in high glee.

---

7. *Baba* is short for *babushka* and usually derogatory.

"Look at this *baba*!" he said." She will have us men learning from her pretty soon. She should wear trousers."

The following day I was put in charge of twenty-five men. As they still regarded me as a queer novelty, I made a little speech to them, telling them that I was a plain peasant worker, only seeking to earn my bread. I appealed to their sense of fairness to cooperate with me. Sending for some vodka and sausages I treated them and won their good will completely. My men called me "Manka" affectionately, and we got along splendidly. I was such a curiosity that the contractor himself invited me to his home for tea. His wife, who was a very kind soul, told me that her husband had been praising me to her very much.

The great test, however, came several days later. I had to prove my ability in preparing asphalt and applying it. We were all at work at four o'clock in the morning. As the quality of asphalt depends on the proportions of the elements used, the men were waiting with some amusement for my orders. But I gave them without hesitation, and when the contractor arrived at six o'clock he found the kettles boiling and the laborers hard at work, pouring the asphalt on the gravel.

Like a pendulum, always in motion, I would begin my daily grind before dawn, returning home after sunset, only to eat and go to bed to gain strength for another day of cheerless toil.

This work has to be done without relaxation, amid awful heat and suffocating odors. For a whole year I stayed at it, working incessantly, with no holidays and no other rest. Like a pendulum, always in motion, I would begin my daily grind before dawn, returning home after sunset, only to eat and go to bed to gain strength for another day of cheerless toil.

Finally I broke down. I caught cold while working in a basement, and became so weak that I was taken to the Kuznetzov Hospital, where I was confined to bed for two months. When I recovered and had rested for about a week, I returned to my job, but found it occupied by a man who had been especially brought from European Russia. Besides, there wasn't much work left for the firm in Irkutsk.

My sister and her husband moved back to Tomsk about this time, and my situation grew desperate. I looked for a place as a domestic servant, but, having no references, I found it impossible to obtain one. The little money I had finally gave out. My only friends in the town were the Sementovskys, neighbors of my sister. I lived with them, but they were poor themselves, and so, for days at a time, I would go without food, my only sustenance consisting of tea.

One day I applied at an employment agency and was informed, after being asked if I would agree to leave town, that a woman had been there looking for a servant, and offered to pay twenty-five rubles a month. I instantly expressed my willingness to go to her. She appeared in the afternoon, young, beautiful, elegantly dressed, her fingers and neck adorned with dazzling jewels. She was very kind to me, inspected me carefully, and asked if I was married.

"I have been," I replied, "but I escaped from my husband about two years ago. He was such a brutal drunkard." I was then in my twenty-first year.

The lady, whose name was Anna Petrovna, gave me ten rubles to pay the rent that I owed. I met her at the station, where she was accompanied by several men friends, and we started together for Sretensk, in a second-class carriage. I had never been in one before in my life. Nothing occurred on the way. I was well fed and nicely treated by her. She spoke to me of their business, and I got the idea that her husband kept a shop. Upon our arrival at Sretensk we were met by a man and two young women. The man was introduced to me as her husband, and the two women as her foster daughters. We drove home, where I was given a neat little room.

I was getting uneasy. Things looked suspicious. "Where is the shop?" I inquired." In the market," was the answer. Anna Petrovna took me by the arm and caressingly suggested:

"Marusenka, will you dress up nicely? We shall have guests tonight." And she handed me some very dainty and light garments, not at all befitting a servant. I was amazed, and objected emphatically. "I never wore such extravagant clothes, Anna Petrovna. I am a plain working girl," and I blushed deeply. I was both ashamed and afraid. I had a premonition of evil. And when she handed me a very low-necked gown I became thoroughly frightened.

But Anna Petrovna was persuasive and persistent, and I was finally persuaded to put it on. It was so transparent that my cheeks burnt with shame. I refused to leave my room, but was coaxed by Anna Petrovna into following her. As I crossed the threshold I saw several girls sitting in company with men, drinking beer. A young man was standing apart, evidently anticipating our appearance. He moved toward us. Anna Petrovna had apparently promised me to him.

Stars were shooting before my eyes. "A house of shame!" The thought pierced my mind and made me furious. I lost all my submissiveness and meekness. Seizing my clothes, I tore them madly into shreds, stamping with my feet, cursing, shrieking and breaking everything that I could get hold of. I caught up several bottles of beer and shattered them into fragments on the floor.

This outbreak lasted but a moment. Everybody in the room was too stupefied to move before I ran out of the house, wrapped only in a shawl. I hastened to the police station at a pace that made people in the streets think that I must be mad. Arriving there I made my complaint to the officer in charge.

To all appearance he was little touched by my story. While I prayed for mercy and relief, on my knees before him, he was regarding me with amusement. He drew me to him and proposed that I should go to live with him! I was shocked and overwhelmed. He, whose duty it was to protect me, was clearly in alliance with white slave traders.

"You are all scoundrels and murderers!" I cried out in anguish." You ought to be ashamed to take advantage of a defenseless girl."

He grew angry and ordered me to be locked up for the night. The policeman who took me away also made advances to me, and I had to slap him to keep him away. The cell was cold, dark and dirty. I had left my shawl upstairs. Enraged against the authorities, I broke all the windows and hammered continuously at the doors and walls, till I was set free in the morning.

But my troubles had only begun. I had no place to go. For two days I wandered about the town day and night. I was starved and worn out. Then I knelt on the bank of the river and prayed for half an hour. I prayed devoutly, pouring out my whole soul. It seemed to me that the Lord had heard my plea, and I felt relieved.

I resolved to return to Anna Petrovna after my prayer. I thought she had been so kind at first that if I begged her to let me work for her as a servant she would agree. Before entering her house I went into the little grocer's shop nearby, and posing as the new servant of Anna Petrovna, who was a customer of the place, got a small bottle of essence of vinegar. I then entered the house and was well received. However, the solicitude for my safety angered me, and I resented Anna Petrovna's caresses. I locked myself up in my room, getting ready to poison myself with the essence.

As I was saying my last prayers there was a knock at the door." Who is it?" I asked sharply. The reply was: "I am the young man whom you saw two days ago in the parlour. I want to help you. I realize that you are not a girl of that sort. Pray, open the door and let me talk to you."

I naturally thought that this was another trap and answered wrathfully: "You are a villain! You are all villains! What do you want with me? What have I done to deserve torture and starvation? If I fall into your hands, it will be only when I am dead. I am going to drink this poison and let you gloat over my corpse."

The man got excited. He ran out into the yard, raised an alarm, and dragging several people with him, shouted that I had threatened to take poison. A large crowd collected round the house, and he forced the window of my room from the outside and jumped in. Seizing the glass of essence, he threw it out of the window, cursing Anna Petrovna and her house. He made every effort to calm me, expressing his admiration for my courage and virtue. His professions of sincerity and friendship were so convincing that I yielded to his invitation to go with him to the home of his parents.

My savior, who was a handsome young man of about twenty-four, was Yakov Buk. He was a man of education, having studied at a high school for some time. His father was a butcher. I was well received by his family, fed, dressed and allowed to rest. They were kind and hospitable people. Yakov, or Yasha, as he was called by his intimates, took especial care of me. He loved me, and it was not long before he declared that he could not live without me.

I was also attracted towards him. He knew of my previous marriage and proposed that we should live together by civil agreement, without the sanction of the Church, a very common mode of marriage in Russia of late years, because of the difficulty of obtaining a divorce. I consented to his proposal, on condition that he tell me the reason for his living in a small barn in the back yard, apart from the family. He agreed.

"When I was twenty," he began, "my father was engaged in the business of supplying meat to several army regiments. He was a partner in a firm, and was assisted by my brothers and myself. Considering me the most industrious and reliable of his sons, he entrusted me once with ten thousand rubles to go to buy cattle. Most of the money did not belong to him.

"On the train I was drawn into a game of cards, deliberately got up by a gang of rascals for the purpose of fleecing innocent passengers like myself. I lost all my money and my clothes to boot. Dressed in rags, with two rubles, presented to me by the gamblers, in my pocket, I alighted at the Chinese frontier in a suicidal state of mind. There I became acquainted, at an inn, with some Chinese brigands who were members of a band operating in the neighborhood. One of them was the chief of the band.

"I told him my story, adding that I would do anything to save my father from disgrace and bankruptcy. He proposed that I should join his band in a raid on an incoming train which was carrying fifty thousand rubles. I was aghast at the suggestion. But then I had a vision of my parents turned out of their house, of their property sold at auction, and of themselves forced to go begging. It rent my heart. There was nothing to do but to accept the offer. I was led by the chief into a field and there introduced to most of the robbers. I was the only white man in the band.

"In the evening we armed ourselves with daggers, pistols and rifles and started for the railway line, where we lay in wait for the train. The thought that I had turned highwayman nearly froze my blood. It was such a violence to my own nature.

"The train was to pass at one in the morning. I prayed to God that He would save me somehow from this experience. Suddenly a body of Cossacks appeared in the distance, racing in our direction. The authorities had been on the track of this band for a long time. Every man in the gang threw down his weapons and ran into the forest. I, too, ran for all I was worth.

"The Cossacks pursued us, and I was caught. As I was a Russian and a new member of the organization, I succeeded by persistent denials of any knowledge of the band in creating doubt in the minds of my captors as to my participation in the projected raid. But I was arrested, and sent to the Irkutsk prison, where I was kept for a whole year. There I came in contact with many politicals and was converted to their ideas. Finally, for lack of evidence I was set free.

"I returned home covered with disgrace. My father had arrived at an understanding with his partner whereby he was to pay back in monthly instalments the sum I had gambled away. He would not let me enter the house, but my mother defended me. There was a quarrel, which ended in an agreement that I be allowed to occupy this barn. But my father swore that he would disinherit me, giving my share of his estate to his other sons."

I soon had occasion to discover that Yasha was considered a suspicious character by the local police, because of his imprisonment. His kindness, too, was his misfortune. Freed or escaped prisoners would sometimes visit him secretly and he would give them his last penny, piece of bread or shirt. But I liked him all the more for that, for it was this warm heart in him that had rescued me from death. We vowed to be faithful to each other for ever. And I entered upon my duties as a housewife.

The barn in which we were going to live was filled with rubbish, and had never been cleaned. I applied myself industriously to making it habitable. It was not an easy task, but I finally succeeded. We received a gift of one hundred rubles from Yasha's parents, and decided to establish a butcher's shop of our own. We got some lumber and built a small shop. Then Yasha bought three cows and the two of us led them to the slaughterhouse, where I learned how to butcher. Yasha ran the shop. I was the first woman butcher in that neighborhood.

One summer day, while walking in the street, I saw some boys peddling ice-cream. I had learned how to make ice-cream during my apprenticeship with Nastasia Leontievna. It occurred to me that I could make ice-cream and sell it. Finding out from the boys how much they paid for it, I offered them better cream at a lower price and asked them to come for it the next day. I immediately returned home and bought milk from Yasha's mother, who offered to give it to me without payment upon learning the purpose for which it was intended. The ice-cream I prepared was, happily, very good, and it sold quickly. During the summer I earned two or three rubles daily by this means.

I led a life of peaceful industry with Yasha for about three years. Every morning I would get up at six o'clock and go with him to the slaughterhouse. Then all day I would spend at home. There were always many poor people, mostly women and children, stranded in our town, which was the junction of a railway and river route. They would wander about the streets, begging for bread and shelter. The greater number of them would land in our barn-home. At times they would fill it completely, sleeping in rows on the floor. Frequently they were ill. I fed them, washed them, and looked after their children.

Yasha would often remonstrate with me for working so incessantly and so hard. But I had my reward in the gratitude and blessings these women bestowed upon me. There was joy in being able to serve. In addition, I sent regularly to my mother ten rubles a month. Yasha taught me in leisure moments how to read.

My name became a household word in the neighborliood. Wherever I went I was blessed. "There goes Buk-Bochkareva!" people would point at me, whispering. Yasha's parents also grew very attached to me.

It all ended one evening in May 1912. There was a peculiar knock at the door, and Yasha went out to admit a man of about thirty, well dressed, with a beard and pince-nez, of distinguished appearance. He was pale and showed signs of agitation. He stood with Yasha in the passage-way for ten minutes, talking in a whisper. He was then introduced to me as an old friend of Yasha's. He had escaped from prison and it was our task to hide him, as his capture would mean his death. The unexpected guest was no less a person than the revolutionary who was responsible for the death of a notorious Governor of Siberia.

Yasha proceeded to remove our bed from its corner. He next removed a board in the lower part of the wall, revealing, to my great astonishment, a deep cavity in the ground underneath. Our visitor was invited to make himself comfortable there. The board was replaced and the bed restored to its former position. Yasha and I went to bed.

We had barely put out the light when there was heard a thumping of many feet around the house, followed by loud knocks at the door. It was the police! My heart was in my mouth, but I feigned sleep while Yasha opened the door. He had previously given me his revolver to hide and I concealed it in my bosom.

The search continued for nearly two hours. I was dragged out of bed, and everything in the house was turned upside down.

We denied any knowledge of a political fugitive, but the sheriff took Yasha along with him. However, he was released a couple of hours later. Upon his return Yasha let the man out of the secret hole, supplied him with peasant clothes and food, harnessed our horse, and drove away with him before dawn, instructing me to answer to all inquiries by saying that he had gone to buy cattle.

On the outskirts of the town a policeman, emerging from some drinking den in a semi-drunken condition, observed Yasha driving by. He attached little significance to the fact at the time, but when he reported for duty in the morning and learned of the fugitive, he said that he had seen Yasha leave the town with a stranger. I was doing some washing when the house was again surrounded by police.

"Where is your husband?" the sheriff inquired fiercely." Gone to buy cattle," I replied.

"Get ready to come with me!" he shouted angrily. I pleaded innocence, but in a terrible voice he informed me that I was under arrest.

I was taken to the detective bureau, where a middle-aged man, who talked very gently, and seemed very mindful of my comfort, entered into a conversation with me and even invited me to tea, which invitation I refused. He went about his work very craftily, and I was nearly caught when he asked me if I had also met the young man who had arrived at our house at nine o'clock the night before.

His information was quite correct, but I obstinately refused to admit the truth. I declared that I knew nothing of the young man he spoke of, but my examiner was patient. He was generous in his praise of my help and devotion to the poor. Promising me inmunity, he urged me to tell the truth.

I would not yield, and his patience finally wore out, and he struck me furiously with a rubber whip a couple of times. I was enraged and bestowed on him some epithets that led to my being locked up in a cell where two drunken street women were confined. They were of the most abonimable sort, cursing on everybody. They persecuted me unceasingly. It was a horrible night that I passed there. The stench alone was sufficient to drive one mad. I was greatly relieved when morning arrived, and I was taken to the office for another examination.

I repeated my denials. There followed threats of long imprisonment, coaxings, rebukes and attempts to extort a confession from me, and I learned that Yasha had been arrested on his way back, before reaching home, so that he did not know of my own arrest. I was detained for seven days, at the end of which the authorities, having been unable to obtain anything from me, set me free.

Yasha was still in jail, and I started out to visit various officials and bureaus in his behalf. The chief of police of the province was then in town, stopping in the house of a friend of ours. I invoked the aid of the latter for the purpose of obtaining an interview with him, and finally I was admitted to the presence of a largely built man wearing the uniform of a colonel. I fell on my knees before him and protested my husband's innocence, praying for mercy. I was so unnerved that he helped me to rise and ordered some water for me, promising to investigate the case and to secure that justice was done.

I went next to the jail, hoping to see Yasha. But there I was informed that he had been sent to Nerchinsk, about five miles from Sretensk. I was not long in making an effort to catch up with him. Taking with me a hundred rubles, I caught the next train to Nerchinsk, just as I was, and, immediately upon my arrival there, sought an audience with the Governor, and was told to await my turn in the line. When my turn came, the Governor, reading my name from the list, asked:

"Well, what is your case?"

"My husband, your Excellency, Yasha Buk," I replied.

"Your husband, eh? How is he your husband il' your name is Bochkareva?"

"By civil agreement, your Excellency."

"We know these civil marriages," he remarked scoffingly." There are many like you in the streets," and he dismissed my case. He said it in the hearing of a room full of people. My blood rushed to my face, and I was bitterly hurt. It was with difficulty that I got a card of admission to the prison, but how profound was my grief upon being informed that Yasha had spent there only one night and had been sent on to Irkutsk.

I had barely enough money with me to buy a fourth class ticket to Irkutsk, and hardly any of the necessaries for a journey, but I did not hesitate to take the next train westward. It took three days to reach the Siberian capital. I stopped again with the Sementovskys, who were glad to welcome me. I made my way to the Irkutsk prison, only to discover that Yasha had been taken to the Central Distribution Prison at Alexandrovskoye, two miles from the railway station of Usolye. There was little time to lose. I left the same day for Usolye, whence I had to walk to Alexandrovskoye.

It was late in the autumn of 1912. I started out with little food, and was soon exhausted. It was not an easy task to get to Alexandrovskoye. The road lay across a river and through an island, connected by ferries.

On the way I made the acquaintance of a woman, Avdotia Ivanovna Kitova, who was also bound for the prison. Her husband was there too, and she told me why. He was drunk when the dog catcher came to take away his favorite dog, and he shot the dog catcher; now he was sentenced to exile, and she had decided to go along with him, with her two children, who were in Irkutsk.

At the Central Prison I received another shock. I could not be admitted without a pass. I did not know that it was necessary to have a pass, I declared. But the warden in charge, a wizened old man, with a flowing white beard, shouted angrily at me, "No! No! Get out of here. It's against the law; you can't be admitted. Go to Irkutsk and come back with a pass, and we will let you in."

"But I have journeyed nearly seventy miles to see him." I pleaded, in tears. "I am worn out and hungry. Allow me to see him just for five minutes – only five short minutes. Is there no mercy in your heart for a weak woman?"

With this I broke down and became hysterical. The harsh little warden, and his assistants in the office, became frightened. Yasha was brought in for a brief interview. The few minutes that we were allowed to pass in each other's presence gave us new strength. He told me of his experiences, and I told him of mine, and we decided that I should go to the Governor-General, Knyazev, to entreat his mercy.

It was not till late evening that I started back to the railway station. I reached the river at dusk and managed to catch a ferry to the island. But it was dark when I landed there, and I lost my way trying to cross the island to the other ferry.

I was cold, hungry, exhausted. My feet were swollen from wandering for several hours in a frantic effort to find the right path. When at last I got to the other side it must have been about midnight. I saw the lights across the water and called with all my remaining strength for the ferry. But there was no response. Only the wind, shrieking through the woods behind me, echoed my cries. I kept calling all night, but in vain.

When it dawned I gathered my last energies, stood up and called out again. This time I was observed, and a canoe was sent after me. Unfortunately, it was in the charge of a boy. I was too ill to move, and he could not carry me to it. I had to creep on all-fours to the boat. With the boy's aid, I finally found myself in the canoe. It took him a long time to ferry me across, and I was in a state of collapse by the time we reached the other side. I was taken to the Kuznetzov Hospital in Irkutsk again, where I lay dangerously ill for nearly two months. During this time I lost all my hair and half my weight.

After my visit to Yasha, he naturally told his prison mates of it, being proud of my loyalty to him, but when days and weeks passed by, and I did not return, his comrades began to tease him about me.

"A fine *baba* is yours. You may indeed be proud of her," they would torment him. "She has found some other husband. A lot of use she has for you, a prisoner. They are all alike, yours and ours." Yasha took such jesting very much to heart. He was in complete ignorance of my whereabouts and finally made up his mind that I had betrayed him.

As soon as I was released from the hospital, I went to the Governor-General, in whose office I was told that Yasha had been sentenced to four years' exile. Obtaining a pass, I went to Alexandrovskoye to see him. But Yasha would not see me. Believing his comrades' taunts, confirmed by my two months' absence, he resolved that he had done with me. I was naturally at a loss to account for this abrupt change, and wept bitterly. Some of his acquaintances, who had been brought downstairs, saw me crying and described to him my wasted appearance. Then he came down.

Visitors were not allowed to come in contact with the prisoners at Alexandrovskoye. There were two steel gratings in the office, separated by a distance of a couple of feet. The prisoner was kept behind one grating, while the persons who came to see him were placed behind the other. They could not touch each other.

This was the manner in which I was permitted to meet Yasha. We both cried like children, he, at the sight of my thinness, realizing that he had wronged me in suspecting me of faithlessness. It was a pathetic scene, this meeting behind bars. Yasha told me that he would not be exiled before May. As I offered to accompany him into exile, it was necessary for me to spend the several intervening months at some work. I also had to get permission to join Yasha in exile.

I found work with the same asphalt firm, but now as a common laborer, earning only fifty kopeks a day. At intervals I would go to Alexandrovskoye to see Yasha. It happened once that I was working at a job in the Irkutsk prison, and it was not long before the prisoners knew that I had a husband in Alexandrovskoye, for there was a complete secret system of communication between the two prisons. On the whole, I was well treated by the convicts.

One evening, however, while at work in the hall, a trusty, catching me in a corner, attacked me. I fought hard, but he knocked me down. My cries were heard by the laborers of my party and several prisoners. Soon we were surrounded by a crowd, and a quarrel ensued between those who defended me and the friends of the trusty. An assistant warden and some guards put an end to it, drawing up a protocol of my complaint to have the trusty tried in court for assault.

As the day of the trial drew near, Yasha was urged by his fellow-prisoners to influence me to withdraw my charge. He told me that the law of prison communal life demanded that I should comply with the request to drop my complaint. I knew that my refusal might mean Yasha's death, and when I was called in court to testify against the trusty, I declared that there had been no assault and that I had no complaints to make. The case was dismissed, and my act enhanced Yasha's reputation among the inmates of both prisons.

The winter passed. Toward Easter of 1913 I succeeded in obtaining permission to have myself arrested and sent to Alexandrovskoye, in anticipation of my exile with Yasha. I was put in the women's building, in which were detained a number of women criminals. What I endured at their hands is almost beyond description. They beat me, but I knew that complaining would make my lot more bitter. When supper was served to us the matron asked me if I had been badly treated. I said no, but she must have known better, for, turning to the women, she told them not to iU-usc me.

My reply to the matron somewhat' improved my relations with my prison-mates, but they forced me, nevertheless, to wait on them and do their dirty work. In addition to these sufferings, the food was putrid. The bunks in which we slept were dirty. Eight of us were in one tiny cell. I saw Yasha only once a week, every Sunday. I spent two months in this voluntary imprisonment, but it seemed like two years to me, and I looked forward eagerly and impatiently to the day of our starting on the open road to exile.

CHAPTER IV
SNARED BY A LIBERTINE GOVERNOR

May had come. The Lena had opened and become navigable. The heavy iron doors of the prison were unlocked and hundreds of inmates, including myself and Yasha, were mustered out in the yard to prepare for exile.

Every winter the huge prison at Alexandrovskoye would gather within its walls thousands of unfortunate human beings, murderers, forgers, thieves, students, officers, peasants and members of the professional classes, who had transgressed against the tyrannical regime. Every spring the gloomy jail would open its doors and pour out a stream of half-benumbed men and women into the wild Siberian forest and the uninhabited regions bordering on the Arctic.

All through the spring and summer this river of tortured humanity would flow through Alexandrovskoye into the snow-bound north, where they languished in unendurable cold and succumbed in large numbers in the land of the six months' night. Tens of thousands of them lie scattered from the Ural mountains to Alaska in unmarked graves...

So finally we were to breathe some fresh air. There was much stir and bustle before our party was formed. It consisted of about a thousand persons, including twenty women. Our guard was composed of five hundred soldiers. We were to go on foot to Kachug,[8] near the source of the Lena, a distance of about one hundred and thirty-three miles. Our baggage was loaded on wagons.

We travelled about twenty-two miles in the first day, according to schedule, stopping for the night at an exile-station on the edge of a village. There are many such stations on the Siberian roads – large wooden buildings of barn-like construction, with iron doors and grated windows. Empty inside, save for double tiers of bunks, they are surrounded by high fences, with a sentry-box at every corner. They offer no opportunity for escape.

We supped on food we had brought from the prison, and turned in for the night. Our party was divided into groups of ten, each group choosing a trusty

---

8. Kachug sits near the source of the Lena. It is the starting point of navigation and lies on the road to Irkutsk.

charged with the purchasing of food. Beginning with the second day, each of us received an allowance of twenty kopeks.

There were about one hundred politicals in the party, the remainder being a mixed assemblage of criminals. These two classes of prisoners did not get on well together, and there was a continuous feud. Men and women were packed together, and, some of the latter behaved outrageously. The filth, the vermin-infested bunks, the unimaginable stench, the frequent brawls, made our journey insufferably hideous.

Further, there was a privileged group among us consisting of the long-sentence convicts, who wore chains and were always given priority by the unwritten law of the criminal world. They always had the first use of the kettles to prepare their food. Until they had finished, none of us dared approach the fire. Their word was law. They were always given the precedence. Even the soldiers and officers respected their privileges. One of them was chief of the party, and if he pledged himself, in return for more freedom for all of us, that there would be no escapes, his word would be taken without question by the Commander of the Guard, and it was never broken.

The weather was fine the first three days. We travelled twenty miles the second day and the same distance the third day, but then it began to pour, and the roads became almost impassable. The mud was frightful, but we had to walk our scheduled twenty miles. Many in our party fell ill. We looked forward to the next exile-station with eager expectation, so soaked were we and so tired. We longed for a roof and a dry floor, and nothing else. We forgot our hunger, we did not feel the vermin that night, for as soon as we reached the station we dropped into a leaden sleep.

We had a two-days' rest upon our arrival at Kachug, and were allowed to bathe in the Lena, our chief making himself responsible for our conduct. We found a small party waiting to join us at Kachug. A member of this new group was recognized by some of the exiles as one who was said to have betrayed his comrade in a raid, and was dragged for trial before the entire body.

Here I witnessed a remarkable scene, the trial of a criminal by criminals. There was as rigid a code of morals in the underworld as in any legitimate government, and just as relentless a prosecution. It was announced that there would be a trial and the privileged criminals in chains were chosen as judges. The accusers were called upon to state their charges, in the hearing of the whole party. They related how the accused man had betrayed a comrade in a robbery some time ago.

There were cries of, "Kill him! Kill him! The traitor! Kill him!" This was the usual punishment for any one found guilty. It was the custom of the authorities to watch the proceedings and never interfere with the carrying out of a sentence. As the mob was closing in on the accused, and my heart was sinking within me, the judges called for order and demanded that the man be given a hearing too. White and trembling, he got up to tell his story in detail.

"There were two of us," he began, "in the scheme to rob a banker. It was decided that I should force my way into the house through a window, hide there and signal to my confederate at the opportune moment. I found that the banker had gone for the evening to a club, and concealed myself in a closet, waiting for his return. My comrade kept guard, without receiving any sign from me, for a couple of hours.

"When the banker returned, he sent his valet to fetch something from the closet in which I was hidden. The valet discovered me, and raised an alarm, and some servants ran out to call for help just at the moment when my comrade was about to enter the house. He was caught. I managed to escape through the window and the garden. I am innocent, comrades. I have been a criminal for many years, and I have a clean, honorable record."

He then proceeded to enumerate the most striking accomplishments of his career, the chiefs under whom he had worked, and the robbers with whom he had been associated in the past.

He must have mentioned some very important personages, as immediately a number of voices were raised in his favor. Some got up and spoke in high terms of the connections of the accused, while others scoffed at him. The deliberations lasted for several hours, resulting in the acquittal of the man.

The entire party, at the conclusion of the rest at Kachug, was taken on board a huge roofed barge. A thousand people in one hole! The prison at Alexandrovskoye, the exile-stations, were paradise in comparison with this unimaginable den. There was no air and no light. Instead of windows there were some small openings in the roof. Many fell ill, and were left lying there uncared for, some of them dying. We were so crowded that we slept almost on top of one another, inhaling the foulest of odors. Every morning we were allowed to come out on the deck of the barge, which was towed by a tug.

In our group was the woman Kitova, with her husband and two children. We cooked and ate our food together, suffering much at the hands of the criminals. There were some quiet people among the latter, and they suffered from the whims of the leaders and their lackeys.

There was one such case of a man who happened to cross the path of an old criminal. The latter did not like the way he looked at him, and the poor man was beaten and, without any ceremony, thrown overboard and drowned. We were all locked up for it inside the barge and were denied the privilege of going out on the deck. It was the most cruel of punishments, worse than a long term in prison.

We changed barges on the way, spending about two months on the water, having journeyed about two thousand miles upon arriving at Yakutsk at the end of July. We were beached at night, but it was almost as light as day, though much colder.

Our joy at landing was indescribable. The local politicals all came out to welcome us. We were marched to the Yakutsk prison, where our roll was called. Here the women were separated from the men, and those who voluntarily accompanied their husbands were set free.

I then went to the office to inquire about the fate of Yasha, and was told that it was probable that he would be sent farther north. I was cared for by the local politicals, who sheltered me and gave me new clothing and money with which to purchase food and cook dinners for Yasha.

Yakutsk is such a distant place that the prisoners there are allowed considerable freedom. I was kindly treated by the officials when I took the dinner-pail to Yasha, and was permitted to remain with him as long as I desired, even in privacy.

Shortly afterwards Yasha was informed that he had been assigned to Kolymsk, within seven miles of the Arctic ocean, where the snow never melts and the winter never relaxes its grip. The news was a terrible shock to us. To be buried alive in some snow-bound hut! What for? To live like beasts in that uninhabitable region from which only few ever emerge alive!

There was still one ray of hope. Governor Kraft, of Yakutsk, had the reputation of being a very kind man, and he might reassign Yasha if I begged him to do so. Yasha had been advised to appeal to the Governor, and he sent me on this mission.

The Governor's office was in his home. He received me very kindly, even shook my hand, and invited me to be seated. He was a tall, erect, black-bearded man of middle-age, and he showed every consideration for me as I told my story. I proposed to him to open a sanitary butcher's shop in Yakutsk if he allowed Yasha to remain there, as the local butchers' shops were inconceivably filthy.

He at first refused to consider my suggestion, but then, apparently on second thoughts, bade me follow him into his private room, where he seated me at a table, and, filling two glasses with wine, invited me to drink with him. I refused, wondering what could be the reason for this extreme friendliness. He drew nearer to me, laid his hands on my coat and removed it. Before I recovered from my astonishment he seized my hand and kissed it. No man had ever before kissed my hand, and I had an idea that it was an action that could only imply immoral intentions. Startled and indignant, I jumped to my feet.

"I will give you a thousand rubles, room for a butcher's shop in the market, and keep your husband in Yakutsk, if you will agree to belong to me," the Governor declared, trying to calm me.

I lost my self-control. "Scoundrels! beasts! you men are all alike!" I shouted. "All! all! all! High and low, you are all depraved." Seizing my coat, I ran out of the house, leaving the Governor speechless.

I rushed to my lodging, locked myself in a room and wept all night. My errand had failed, and I was now faced with the choice between a living death for Yasha and selling myself. I had visions of Kolymsk, a settlement consisting of several scattered huts, inhabited by natives, lost in the vast expanse of the ice-bound steppe, and buried for months under mountains of snow. I could almost hear the howling of the Arctic winds, and the frightful growling of the polar bears.

I pictured Yasha in the midst of it, cut off from human companionship, slowly languishing in the monotony of inactivity. Then my thoughts would revert to the other alternative. To live and work with Yasha in outward happiness, and stealthily, in the night, to go to this degenerate Governor! And what if Yasha learned of my secret visits? How should I explain? And of what avail would any explanations be to him? No, it was impossible, impossible! Ah, what a terrible night it was! From visions of the frozen banks of the Arctic waters, my imagination would carry me to the revolting embraces of Governor Kraft, in a fruitless search for a way out.

Morning finally came and found me completely worn out. When my friends questioned me as to the result of my call on the Governor, I replied that he had refused my appeal. In low spirits I went to see Yasha. He quickly noticed my downcast appearance and inquired into the cause.

"I saw the Governor, and he would not change your place of exile," I informed him dejectedly.

Yasha flared up. "You appealed to the Governor, eh? The Governor never yet refused an appeal of this sort from a woman, I am told. He is the kindest of men. The warden here just told me that the Governor has long felt the need of a first-class butcher's shop in the town, and would never let us go if properly appealed to. I hear that you did not plead with sufficient warmth. You want to get rid of me, eh? You want to have me sent to Kolymsk to die, so that you can remain here alone and carry on with some other man."

Yasha's words pained me deeply. He had always been very jealous, but the strain of the imprisonment and the journey had made him more irritable.

Besides, it was evident that some one from the Governor's office had informed him that I had not sufficiently exerted myself in his behalf. I did not dare to tell him the truth, for that would have meant certain exile to Kolymsk, and I still hoped against hope.

"Yasha," I implied, "how can you say such things of me? You know how I love you, and if you go to Kolymsk I shall go with you. I have been to the Governor, and entreated him."

"Then go again. Fall on your knees before him and beg harder. He is said to be such a kind man that he will surely have mercy. Otherwise, we are lost. Think of our destination, a land without sun, a colony of three or four huts, spread over a space of about ten miles, that is Kolymsk. No horses, no business, no trades! It is not a land for the living. Go and implore the Governor, and he may take pity."

I looked at Yasha, and my heart was filled with anguish. He was only twenty-seven, but his hair was already turning grey. He looked pale and exhausted. I could not keep myself from breaking into sobs. Yasha was touched, and, placing his arm around me, apologized for his insinuation, assuring me of his devotion and appreciation of my endeavours to sustain him in his trials. I left him, with the understanding that I would call on the Governor again.

"To go or not to go," was the thought that tormented me on the way from Yasha. I learned that the Governor was notorious as a libertine. He had married into the family of a high-placed bureaucrat for the sake of a career, and his wife was a hunch-back, spending most of her time abroad. Plucking up courage, I went to the Governor again, hoping to win his favor by a passionate plea for Yasha. As I entered the office I saw the clerks wink to one another significantly. I could scarcely keep my self-control, trembling in anticipation of another meeting with the Governor. As I was admitted into his study he stood up and smiled benevolently, saying :

"Ah, so finally you have come, my dear. Now, don't be afraid; I won't harm you. Calm yourself, and be seated," and he helped me to a chair.

"Have pity on us, sir. Permit Yasha to remain here," I sobbed.

"Now, now, don't cry," he interrupted me. "I will. He shall stay."

My heart was full of gratitude, and I threw myself on the floor at his feet, thanking and blessing him for his kindness. Then it occurred to me that Yasha would be overjoyed to hear the news, and I rose to go, telling the Governor of my purpose.

"You need not tire yourself by rushing to the prison. I will have the message telephoned to the warden, with instructions to inform your husband immediately," the Governor said, "and you may rest here a little while."

I was overflowing with thankfulness. He poured some wine into a glass and insisted that I should drink it to refresh myself. I had never tasted wine before, and this particular wine was of a very strong quality. I felt a wave of warmth creep over me. It was so sweet and languorous. The Governor then filled my glass again and, also one for himself, invited me to drink with him. I made an effort to resist, but was too weak to withstand his persuasion. After the second glass it was much easier for the Governor to make me empty the third. I became drowsy and dull, unable to move. I had a sense of the Governor removing my clothes, but was too helpless to protest, let alone to offer physical I resistance. He embraced me, kissed me, but I remained I inert. I then had a sensation of being picked up by him and carried to a couch. Very dimly I seemed to realize it all, and, collecting my last strength, I attempted to struggle, but felt as if I had been drugged...

I awoke about four in the morning and found myself in unfamiliar, luxurious surroundings. For a few moments I could not understand where I was, and thought that I was dreaming. There was a strange man near me. He turned his face, and I recognized him as the Governor. I suddenly remembered everything. He made a motion to embrace me, but I cried out, jumped up, dressed myself hastily and ran from the house as if pursued.

Day was just breaking. The town was still wrapped in sleep, and a low mist merged the city with the river. It was early autumn. There was peace everywhere but in my heart; there, the elements were raging, and life grappled with death for supremacy. "What shall I say to Yasha? What will our friends think of me? A prostitute!" pierced my mind poignantly. "No, that must never happen. Death is my only escape."

I wandered about the streets for a while, until I found a grocer's shop open, and I purchased there thirty kopek's worth of essence of vinegar. Entering my lodging, I was met by the question:

"Where have you been? Maria Leontievna, where did you sleep last night?" My appearance in itself was enough to arouse suspicion. Without answering, I rushed into my room and locked the door. After offering my last prayers, I resolutely drank up all the poison, and was soon writhing in agony.

At the same time, about ten in the morning, Yasha was released from prison and given five hundred rubles for the establishment of a butcher's shop. In high spirits, he made his way to my lodging, completely unaware of what had befallen me. It was only when he arrived at the house that he observed an unusual commotion. The door of my room had been broken in when my moans were heard. The poison had scorched my mouth and throat as if with a flame, and I was found unconscious on the floor, and only recovering my senses after I had been removed to the hospital. Around me stood Yasha, some nurses, and a physician who was pouring something down my throat. I could not speak, although I understood all that was going on in the room. I had lost so much blood, the doctor explained to Yasha, in reply to his anxious questions, that my recovery was very doubtful. "Only a person of unusually powerful constitution could emerge alive from such an ordeal," he added.

For two weeks I hovered between life and death, suffering agonizing pains, writhing in breathless convulsions that choked my breathing. I was fed only on milk, introduced into my throat through a tube. For a month I was incapable of speech, at the end of which time I was out of danger, but I had to spend another month in the hospital before I regained my normal health.

Yasha could not, at first, understand the reason for my act. The Governor was so kind, so generous. He had not only commuted his sentence, but had given us five hundred rubles for a shop. Could there be anything more noble? He finally arrived at the conclusion that the trials of the last year had resulted in a temporary mental derangement, which was responsible for my attempt at suicide. I did not disillusion him, although I was tempted to do so whenever he praised the Governor.

Upon leaving the hospital, we opened the butcher's shop and immediately began to do good business. For several months we led a peaceful life. Then one afternoon the Governor suddenly called at our shop, ostensibly to inquire how we were prospering. He stretched out his hand to me, but I turned away.

The Governor left, and Yasha raged at me for my inexplicable conduct. Had I gone mad? I must have, to be capable of refusing to greet our benefactor, the kindest of men! I was sullen and silent, but Yasha would not be satisfied. He demanded an explanation. There was nothing left for me to do but to make a clean breast of it, which I did.

The truth was such a shock to him that it threw him into convulsions. He struck me with something and felled me to the floor. His face turned chalk-white, the veins stood out on his temples, and he was trembling all over. He seemed utterly prostrated by the horror of this nightmare. The Governor's liberality was now explained. The five hundred rubles, the commutation of his sentence, it had all been dearly paid for by his beloved.

My attempted suicide now appeared to him in its true light. He would take vengeance. He would kill the Governor, he swore, yes, he would murder that most despicable of villains. I hugged his feet and begged him not to attempt to carry out his threat. He paid no heed to my prayers, and talked of the hollowness of his life if he did not avenge me.

He set off on his fateful errand, all my efforts to bar his way having failed. When he appeared at the Governor's office and requested an audience, giving his name, the clerks immediately suspected him of some sinister design. The secretary reported to the Governor that Buk, the butcher, desired an audience, but that his manner roused suspicion. The Governor ordered that he should be detained and searched. A long, sharp knife was found on him, and he was arrested, orders being given for his exile on the following day to Amga, a hamlet about one hundred and thirty miles from Yakutsk. I had only twenty-four hours to dispose of the shop, and was compelled to hand it over to a local political, with the understanding that he would pay us for it a few months later.

It was Easter Eve, 1914, when we started out in a cart, driven by a Yakut, for Amga. The mud was the worst I have ever come across. The horses sank so deep, and the wheels of the vehicle stuck so often, that frequently we had to alight and help in extricating them. We spent Easter Day in a native's hut on the road, in which children, women and animals lived together. There is always a fire in the center of these huts, the smoke being allowed to escape through a hole in the roof. The cows were milked in the hut, and the filth was beyond words. After supping on some bread and a sort of tea, which was unfit for human consumption, we went to sleep. The following day we resumed our journey to Amga.

CHAPTER V
ESCAPE FROM EXILE

We spent about six days on the road to Amga. It was a town with a mixed population. Half of its homes were tiny cabins, built by Russian exiles, many of whom had married Yakut women, as the latter were physically attractive and were proud to be the wives of white men. The natives ill-treated their wives, and were lazy, so that the women usually labored to support their families. Some of the Yakuts were very wealthy, owning as many as a thousand head of deer and cattle. Men, women and children alike dressed only in fur. They made their bread of a coarse flour, ground by hand.

There were about fifteen political exiles in Amga. Five of these were university graduates, and one of them was Prince Alexander Gutemurov, who had been arrested eight years before, and had turned grey in exile.

I was the first Russian woman to come to Amga, and the joy of the small colony of politicals knew no bounds. As the Yakut women never wash clothes, the filth in which the white men lived was unspeakable, and their unkempt appearance testified eloquently to the c nditions in which they lived. They were at the mercy of vermin, and offered little resistance to epidemics. Clean food and drinkable milk could not be had at any price.

Money was cheap at Amga. The Prince, for instance, received a monthly allowance of one hundred rubles, but he could not get a bath for a thousand.

I immediately took charge of the situation, and the small cabin which I rented at two rubles a month soon became the social center of the colony. I had benches made as well as a table and a bed. I obtained flour at the general shop owned by Karyakin, who had been exiled there for a murder in 1904, and now did a very flourishing trade. I baked real Russian bread, cooked a regular Russian meal, and made Russian tea, inviting all the politicals to dinner.

It was a feast fit for the gods to them, and those of them who were single asked me to board them regularly. I not only boarded them, but I washed and repaired their clothes as well. I had a hut turned into a bathhouse, and it was not long before the politicals looked human again. My duties in the house demanded all my time and energy, but I was happy in being able to give help. The men regarded me as their mother, and never tired of praising me.

I planted a garden, and sowed some grain, as land was given by the community for the asking, there being few settlers in spite of the natural riches of the district. The rivers in Northern Siberia are full of fish, and there is no end to the wealth of timber. Less than 150 miles from us gold mines were being worked. On the strength of our having owned the butcher's shop in Yakutsk, we were able to buy a horse on credit and also to borrow some money.

My popularity with the politicals irritated Yasha. He grew jealous of their kindness, now suspecting one man of courting me, and now another. As he had nothing to do, he nursed his jealousies till they grew in his imagination. He took to playing cards, which is very popular with the Yakuts, who like to gamble. This led gradually to his becoming a confirmed gambler. He would leave home for some neighboring Yakut settlement and frequently stay away for several days, spending all his time in gambling. Finally it became a habit with him. He would disappear, and reappear suddenly, only in different moods.

When he had won he would return all smiles, with money jingling in his pockets, bringing me some presents, and displaying great generosity to all. But that was not the usual case. Most frequently he lost, and then he would come back home gloomy and dejected, nervous and irritable, ready to pick quarrels and give provocation. His temper was especially roused whenever he found some political in the house. Consumed by jealousy, he would taunt me, and not infrequently resort to blows.

"Yasha, have you lost your senses?" I would say. "Do you need some money? You know I am always glad to help you out," and I would have resort to my small savings, knowing that he had lost his last penny. But that would not alleviate my suffering. It was with relief that I looked forward to his departures, and with apprehension that I saw him return.

At the end of about three months, we obtained permission to visit Yakutsk for the purpose of collecting the money due to us for the butcher's shop, but the man to whom we had made over the business now denied that he owed us any money, claiming to have paid fully at the time of our exile to Amga. There was a violent quarrel, but no money. As I had surrendered the shop to him on trust, we could not substantiate our claims and oust him from his possession of the premises. There was nothing to be done but to return with empty hands, with the burden of the debts we had incurred at Amga weighing heavily on our shoulders. I was faced with the dreary prospect of hard and continuous toil, in order to pay what we owed.

One summer day a new party of exiles arrived at Amga. One of them was a young man of about twenty. Yasha took a fancy to him and proposed that he should remain in our house as my assistant. Knowing Yasha's jealousy, I objected.

"Yasha," I argued, "what are you doing? You know how jealous you become when you find one of the colony in the house, and now you want me to keep this young man here, while you will be away most of the time. You are only making trouble for me, I don't want him, I need no help. Please don't burden me with him."

"Marusia," Yasha replied, tenderly, "I swear that I won't be jealous any more. I won't, dear. Forgive me for all the pain I have caused you."

Yasha's words did not entirely pacify me, but he overruled my objections, promising to be reasonable in the future. The same afternoon a Yakut called for him, and they left together to go to a gambling place. The young man remained with me. Nothing occurred the first day or two. Then, one night, I was awakened by the young man bending over me. I repelled him, appealing to his sense of shame, but as he persisted in his advances, I struck him violently, jumped out of bed, and seizing a chair and shouting at the top of my voice, drove him out of the house.

It was about one o'clock in the morning. Prince Gutemurov was returning home from an evening with a friend and saw me drive the young man out into the night. The latter, however, harbored a deep feeling of vengeance against me. He resolved to await Yasha's return, on the road outside the village, and tell him a false version of the story!

"A fine wife you have," he addressed Yasha, derisively, as soon as the latter appeared.

"What do you mean?" questioned Yasha excitedly. The young man replied that the night before I had come to him, but, being a loyal friend to Yasha, he drove me away and left the house with the purpose of meeting him and informing him of the incident. Yasha only had sufficient self-control to thunder out, "Swear, are you telling the truth?"

The young rascal answered, "Certainly it's the truth."

When Yasha appeared on the threshold I observed immediately with horror that he was in a ferocious mood, but was suppressing his fury. That made him the more dangerous. He spoke slowly, picking his words deliberately, words which struck terror to my soul.

"You are a faithless woman. You always have been faithless, deceiving me continually, but you are caught now, and you won't escape. It's fortunate that

Dmitri is a decent young fellow and repelled your advances. You can say your last prayers, you base creature."

While speaking thus, Yasha proceeded in a cold, business-like, purposeful manner to make a noose to hang me. It was this calm about Yasha's actions, expressive of his terrible earnestness, that made me tremble all over.

"Yasha, I am innocent, Yasha," I sobbed, throwing myself at his feet and kissing them. "I swear that I am innocent," I cried. "Have mercy! think what you are doing! I tell you I am innocent!"

Yasha went on with his preparations undisturbed.

He attached the rope to a hook on the ceiling and tested the noose.

"Yasha, come to your senses," I implored, hugging his legs.

He pushed me aside, placed a stool under the rope and ordered me, in a terrible voice, to stand up on it.

"Now say your last prayers," he repeated.

He then placed the noose around my neck and jerked the stool from under my feet. In an instant it tightened about my throat, I wanted to cry out but could not, the pressure against the crown of my head was so terrific that it seemed about to crack open. Then I lost consciousness.

As the noose was tightening around my neck Yasha came to himself and hastened to loosen it. I dropped, lifeless, to the floor. In response to his calls for help several politicals, among whom were a couple of medical students, came running to the house. They made every effort to revive me, succeeding only after long and persistent attempts. When I opened my eyes, the whole colony was at my bedside. Pressed for an explanation of his inhuman act, Yasha told Dmitri's story.

He then placed the noose around my neck and jerked the stool from under my feet. In an instant it tightened about my throat, I wanted to cry out but could not...

Then Prince Gutemurov revealed what he had seen the previous night, on his way home. Yasha was overwhelmed. He fell on his knees and begged my forgiveness, cursing Dmitri and promising to make short work of him. But Yasha could not find him. Dmitri learned of the disclosure and disappeared forever from Amga.

Soon afterwards, another incident occurred which further embittered my life with Yasha. In his absence Vasily, a political, came and told me that the authorities were in receipt of an order to arrest and send him to Irkutsk to be tried on a new charge, which carried with it the death-sentence. It was a regular practice of the Tsar's government to recall exiles for second trials on some additional bit of evidence.

Vasily asked me to lend him our horse, Malchik, to help him escape. Knowing how attached Yasha was to the horse, I refused Vasily's request. But he persisted in imploring me, claiming that Prince Gutemurov had seen the order for the arrest, and that the sheriff was already on his tracks.

"But how could the horse be returned?" I asked Vasily, touched by his continuous pleading. He replied that he would leave it with a certain Yakut friend of ours, some hundred versts away, and I finally yielded, although not without misgivings. As soon as he left with Malchik my anxiety grew into alarm. I hurried to Prince Gutemurov to verify Vasily's story. How thunder-struck I was upon learning from the Prince that he knew of no order to arrest Vasily, and that he had not even seen him. It was clear that I had been swindled and that I would never see the horse again.

"My God," I thought, "what will happen upon Yasha's return and his discovery that Malchik is gone?"

The fear of death rose up before me, the impression of my recent escape from hanging still fresh in my mind. I trembled at the thought of Yasha, with the feeling of an entrapped animal seeking an escape. But there seemed to be no remedy.

It was August 1914. Rumors of the great conflict were just reaching the remote Siberian provinces. The order for mobilization came, and there was great excitement, even in the death-bound Arctic settlements, as if suddenly a new life had been infused into that land of monotony. Upon the heels of the call to arms came the Tsar's Manifesto, abolishing the scourge of our national life – vodka, and with it a gigantic wave of popular enthusiasm, sweeping the steppes, valleys, and forests of vast Russia, from Petrograd and Moscow, across the Ural mountains and Siberia, to the borders of China, and the Pacific coast.

There was something sublime about the nation's response. Old men, who had fought in the Crimean War, in the Turkish Campaign of 1877-78, and The Russo-Japanese War, declared that they never saw such exaltation of spirit. It was a glorious, inspiring, unforgettable moment in one's life. My soul was deeply stirred, and I had a dim realization of a new world coming to life, a purer, a happier and a holier world.

And when Vasily robbed me of our horse, and I was filled with the dread of Yasha's fury, intensified by my helplessness in the face of this misfortune, the thought, "WAR!" suddenly flashed into my mind.

"Go to war to help save the country!" a voice within me called.

To leave Yasha for my personal comfort and safety was almost unthinkable. But to leave him for the field of unselfish sacrifice, that was a different matter. And the thought of going to war penetrated deeper and deeper into my whole being, giving me no rest.

When Yasha returned, Prince Gutemurov and several other friends were in the house ready to defend me. He had already learned from the natives, on his way home, that Vasily had escaped on our horse. He could not believe that I would have given his favorite horse to anybody without his permission, and he therefore suspected that I had an intrigue with Vasily, and that I had dispatched him to make preparations for an elopement. He made a violent scene, attacking me savagely, with showers of blows. My friends tore him away, which only infuriated him the more. This inability to give vent to his rage made him act like one demented.

His temper was clearly becoming a danger, which called for a remedy. A physician came to Amga only once a month. As Yasha considered himself in good health, there could be no question of suggesting to him that he should consult the physician. It was, therefore, agreed among my friends that Prince Gutemurov should take a walk about the village with the doctor when he arrived, pass by our house as if by accident, and that I should greet them with an invitation to come in for tea. Everything went smoothly. The physician was introduced to Yashka and immediately remarked upon his pallor and his bloodshot eyes.

"What ails you?" he asked Yasha, "you seem to have fever. Let me examine you."

The result of the examination was the advice to Yasha to go to a hospital for treatment, which he, of course, scoffed at. Privately, the doctor informed Prince Gutemurov that Yasha's nerves had broken down and that he was dangerous to live with, as he might kill me for some trivial cause. The physician urged that I should leave him at once. But I hesitated. Another quarrel, however, was not long in coming. Yasha actually made another attempt to kill me, but was stopped by our comrades. The cup was full. I decided to escape.

Day and night my imagination carried me to the fields of battle, and my ears rang with the groans of my wounded brethren. The impact of the mighty armies was heard even in uncivilized northern Siberia. There were rumors in the air, rumors of victory and of defeat, and in low voices people talked of torrents of blood and of rivers of maimed humanity, streaming back from the front, and already overflowing into the Siberian plains. My heart yearned to be there, in the seething caldron of war, to be baptized in its fire and scorched in its lava. The spirit of sacrifice took possession of me. My country called me. And an irresistible force from within impelled me.

I only awaited the opportunity when Yasha should be away for several days. It arrived one September day. Some Yakuts called for Yasha. As soon as he left I cut off my hair, dressed in men's clothes and provided myself with two loaves of bread. I had no money to speak of, as I took none of the colony into my confidence.

It was evening when I stealthily hurried out of Amga and took the road to Yakutsk. I had before me a journey of over 130 miles. I ran at such a pace that night, since I could not expect to travel in the daytime without being recognized, that I covered thirty-three miles before dawn.

Several times I met Yakuts, and answered their greetings in their native dialect, with which I had grown familiar. In the dark they must have taken me for a Yakut. Otherwise, the journey was uneventful. The road was dry, the weather calm, and only the stars lit my way, while the loud throbbing of my heart echoed my footsteps.

When day broke I stopped beside a stream and breakfasted on bread and cold water. I then made a bed of twigs in a hole by the road, lay down, covered myself with branches and went to sleep for the day, awoke when evening came, offered my prayers to God, dined on some more bread and water, and resumed my journey. It took me six nights of walking to arrive at Yakutsk, living only on bread and water, and sleeping in hidden nooks by the road during the day.

There was a new Governor in Yakutsk. Baron Kraft had gone to western Europe to join his wife at some health resort, was stranded there after the outbreak of the war, and later died a prisoner in the hands of the enemy. The new Governor received me well, and granted my request to be sent home, to Tomsk, at the expense of the Government. He even offered me a convoy for protection.

My escape was a success, but my heart would not rejoice. The image of Yasha, stricken with grief, frantically searching for me, calling to me, rose before my eyes, and demanded an account from my conscience. Was it right, was it just, to leave poor Yasha all alone in forlorn Amga? Had I not vowed to remain eternally faithful to him? Was it not my bounden duty to stand by him to the end? Should I not return to him, then and give up this wild fancy of going to war?

I hesitated. Was it not true, on the other hand, that Yasha had become a professional gambler? Was not life with him a perilous adventure? Devotion to Yasha, a voice within me argued, did not mean perishing with him, but an effort to save him. Indeed, to get Yasha out of that wilderness was an idea which suddenly gripped my imagination. And how could I ever expect to find a better opportunity to do so than by distinguishing myself in war and then petitioning the Tsar in his behalf?

So there I was again in the magic circle of war. I asked an acquaintance to write a letter for me to Yasha. Apologizing for my strange departure, I informed him that I was going to Tomsk to enlist as a soldier, leave for the front, and win distinction for bravery, then petition the Tsar to pardon him, so as to enable us to resume our peaceful life in Sretensk.

It was a plan with which Destiny, which held no more peace for me, played havoc. The war was to continue as many years as I had expected it to last months, shrouding Russia in darkness, sowing revolution, bearing thunder and lightning in its wings, spreading famine and chaos and seeds of a new world order. In those stormy years, Yasha was to retreat to the far background of my life, then vanish altogether. But all my heart was with him that autumn day of 1914, when I turned my eyes toward the bleak North for the last time, as I boarded the barge that was to carry me to Irkutsk, thence to Tomsk, and thence to war.

PART TWO

WAR

CHAPTER VI
I ENLIST BY THE GRACE OF THE TSAR

I spent nearly two months traveling homeward from Yakutsk, by water, rail and foot. The war was everywhere. The barge on the Lena was filled with recruits. In Irkutsk the uniform was much in evidence, and every now and then a regiment of soldiers would march through the streets on the way to the station, arousing one's martial spirit. My convoy left me upon my arrival there, and I had to appeal to the authorities for funds to continue my journey.

My heart was beating furiously when I reached Tomsk, after an absence of about six years. Tears dimmed my eyes as I walked the familiar streets. Here, in this two-storied house, I had first learned the fickleness of man's love. That was ten years ago, during the Russo-Japanese War, when I was only fifteen years old. There, in that dilapidated little shop, where I can see the figure of Nastasia Leontievna bent over the counter, I spent five rears of my early youth, waiting on customers, scrubbing loors, cooking, washing and sewing. That long apprenticeship, under the stem eyes of Nastasia Leontievna, served me in good stead in later years, I must admit.

The smoking chimney yonder belongs to the house in which I was married, some eight years ago, only to gain experience at first hand of man's brutality. And here, in this basement, my father and mother have been dwelling for seventeen years.

I swung open the door. My mother was baking bread and did not turn immediately. How old she had grown! How bent her shoulders, how white her hair! She turned her head and stared at me for a second. A lump rose in my throat, rendering me speechless.

"Maria!" she exclaimed, rushing toward me and locking me in her arms.

We wept, kissed each other, and wept again. My mother offered prayers to the Holy Mother and swore that she would never let me leave her side again. The bread was almost burned to charcoal, having been forgotten in the oven in the excitement of my return. My father came in, and he also was greatly aged. He greeted me tenderly, the years having softened the harshness of his nature.

I paid some visits to old friends. Nastasia Leontievna was overjoyed to see me. The sister of Afanasy Bochkarev, my first husband, also welcomed me cordially, in spite of the fact that I had escaped from her brother. She realized well enough how brutal and rough he was. She told me that Afanasy had been called in the first draft, and that it was reported that he was among the first prisoners taken by the Germans. I have never heard of him again.

I rested for about three days. The news from the front was exciting. Great battles were raging. Our soldiers were retreating in some places and advancing in others. I longed for wings to fly to their help. My heart yearned and ached.

"Do you know what war is?" I asked myself.

"It is no work for a woman. You must make sure before starting out, Marusia, that you won't disgrace yourself. Are you strong enough in spirit to face all the trials and dangers of this colossal war? Are you strong enough in body to shed blood and endure the privations of war? Are you firm enough at heart to withstand the temptations that will come to you, living among men? Search your soul for a brave and truthful answer."

And I found strength enough in me to answer "yes" to all these questions. I suppressed the hidden longing for Yasha in the depths of my being, and made the fateful decision. I would go to war and fight till death, or, if God preserved me, till the coming of peace. I would defend my country and help those unfortunate ones on the field of slaughter who had already made their sacrifices for their country.

It was November 1914. With my heart steeled in the decision I had made, I resolutely approached the headquarters of the Twenty-Fifth Reserve Battalion stationed in Tomsk. Upon entering a clerk asked me what I wanted.

"To see the Commander," I replied.

"What for?" he inquired.

"I want to enlist," I said.

The man looked at me for a moment and burst out laughing. He called to the other clerks." Here is a *baba* who wants to enlist!" he announced jokingly, pointing at me. There followed a general uproar. "Ha! ha! ha!" they chorused, forgetting their work for the moment. When the merriment subsided a little I repeated my request to see the Commander, and his adjutant came out. He must have been told that a woman had come to enlist, for he addressed me gaily, "What is your wish?"

"I want to enlist in the army, your Excellency," I answered.

"To enlist, eh? But you are a *baba*," he laughed." The regulations do not permit us to enlist women. It is against the law."

I insisted that I wanted to fight, and begged to see the Commander. The adjutant reported me to the Commander, who ordered that I should be shown in.

With the adjutant laughing behind me, I blushed and became confused when brought before the Commandor. He rebuked the adjutant and inquired what he could do for me. I repeated that I wanted to enlist and fight for the country.

"It is very noble of you to have such a desire. But women are not allowed in the army," he said. "They are too weak. What could you, for instance, do in the front line? Women are not made for war."

"Your Excellency," I insisted, "God has given me strength, and I can defend my country as well as a man. I have asked myself before coming here whether I could endure the life of a soldier, and found that I could. Cannot you place me in your regiment?"

"My dear," the Commander declared gently, "how can I help you? It is against the law. I have no authority to enlist a woman, even if I wanted to. You can go to the rear, enlist as a Red Cross nurse or in some other auxiliary service."

I rejected his proposal. I had heard so many rumors about the women in the rear that I had come to despise them. I therefore insisted on my determination to go to the front as a regular soldier. The Commander was deeply impressed by my obstinacy, and wanted to help me. He suggested that I should send a telegram to the Tsar, telling him of my desire to defend the country, of my moral purpose, and beg him to grant me special permission to enlist.

The Commander promised to draw up the telegram himself, with a recommendation of his own, and to have it sent from his office. He warned me, however, to consider the matter again, to think of the hardships I should have to bear, of the soldiers' attitude toward me, and the universal ridicule that I should provoke. But I did not change my mind. The telegram was sent at my expense, costing eight rubles, which I obtained from my mother.

When I disclosed to my family the nature of my visit to the Commander of the Twenty-Fifth Battalion, they burst into tears. My poor mother cried that her Maria must have gone out of her senses, that it was an unheard of, impossible thing. Who ever heard of a *baba* going to war? She would allow herself to be buried alive before letting me enlist. My father supported her. I was their only hope now, they said. They would be forced to starve and go begging without my help. And the house was filled with sobs and lamentation, the two younger sisters and some neighbors joining in.

My heart was rent in twain. It was a cruel, painful choice that I was called upon to make, a choice between my mother and my country. It had cost me so much to steel myself to that new life, and now, when I was seemingly near the goal, my long-suffering mother called upon me to give up this ideal that possessed me, for her sake. I was tormented and agonized by doubt. I realized that I must make a decision quickly, and, with a supreme effort and the help of God, I resolved that the call of my country came before the call of my mother.

After some time had passed, a soldier came to the house.

"Is Maria Bochkareva here?" he questioned.

He came from headquarters with the news that a telegram had arrived from the Tsar, authorizing the Commander to enlist me as a soldier, and that the Commander wanted to see me.

My mother did not expect such an answer. She grew frantic. She cursed the Tsar with all her might, although she had always revered him as the Little Father. "What kind of a Tsar is he?" she cried, "if he takes women to war? He must have lost his senses. Who ever heard of a Tsar calling women to arms? Hasn't he enough men? Goodness knows, there are myriads of them in Mother Russia."

She seized the Tsar's portrait on the wall, before which she had crossed herself every morning, and tore it to bits, stamping them on the floor, with imprecations and anathema on her lips. Never again would she pray for him, she declared. "No, never!"

The soldier's message had an opposite effect on me, and I was in high spirits. Dressing in my best clothes, I went to see the Commander. Everybody at headquarters seemed to know of the Tsar's telegram, smiles greeting me everywhere. The Commander congratulated me and read its text in a solemn voice, explaining that it was an extraordinary honor which the august Emperor had conferred on me, and that I must make myself worthy of it. I was so happy, so joyous, so excited. It was the most blissful moment of my life.

The Commander called in his orderly and instructed him to obtain a full soldier's outfit for me. I received two complete undergarments made of coarse linen, two pairs of foot-rags, a laundry-bag, a pair of boots, one pair of trousers, a belt, a regulation blouse, a pair of epaulets, a cap with the insignia on it, two cartridge pockets and a rifle. My hair was clipped short.

There was an outburst of laughter when I appeared in full military attire, as a regular soldier of the Fourth Company, Fifth Regiment. I was confused and somewhat bewildered, being hardly able to recognize myself. The news of a woman recruit had preceded me at the barracks, and my arrival there was the signal for riotous mirth. I was surrounded on all sides by raw recruits who stared at me incredulously, but some were not satisfied with mere staring, so rare a novelty was I to them. They wanted to make sure that their eyes were not deceived, so they proceeded to pinch me, jostle me and brush against me.

"Get out, she isn't no *baba*," remarked one of them.

"Indeed, she is," said another, pinching me.

"She'll run like the devil at the first German shot," joked a third, provoking roars of laughter.

"We'll make it so hot for her that she'll run before even getting to the front," threatened a fourth.

Here the Commander of my company interfered, and the men dispersed. I was granted permission to take my things home before settling permanently at the barracks. I asked to be shown how to salute. On the way home I saluted every uniform in the same manner. Opening the door of the house, I halted on the threshold. My mother did not recognize me.

"Maria Leontievna Bochkareva here?" I asked sharply, in military fashion. Mother took me for some messenger from headquarters, and answered, "No."

I threw myself on her neck. "Holy Mother, save me!" she exclaimed. There were cries and tears which brought my father and little sister on the scene. My mother became hysterical. For the first time I saw my father weep, and again I was urged to come back to my senses and give up this crazy notion of serving in the army. The landlady and old Nastasia Leontievna were called to help dissuade me from my purpose.

> *My mother grew angry and, crying out at the top of her voice, she shouted: "You are no longer my daughter! You have forfeited your mother's love."*

"Think what the men will do to a solitary woman in their midst," they argued." Why, they'll make a prostitute of you. They will kill you secretly, and nobody will ever find a trace of you. Only the other day they found the body of a woman along the railroad track, thrown out of a troop-train. You have always been such a sensible girl. What has come over you? And what will become of your parents? They are old and weak, and you are their only hope. They always said that when Marusia came back, they would end their lives in peace. Now you are shortening their days, driving them to their graves in sorrow."

For a little while I hesitated again. The fierce struggle in my bosom between the two conflicting calls was renewed. But I held by my decision, remaining deaf to all entreaty. Then my mother grew angry and, crying out at the top of her voice, she shouted:

"You are no longer my daughter! You have forfeited your mother's love."

With a heavy heart I left the house for the barracks. The Commander of the Company did not expect me, and I had to explain to him why I could not pass that night at home. He assigned to me a place in the general sleeping-room, ordering the men not to molest me. On my right and on my left were soldiers, and that first night in the company of men will ever stand out in my memory. I did not close my eyes once during the night.

The men were, naturally, unaccustomed to such a strange creature as my self and took me for a woman of loose morals who had made her way into the ranks for the sake of carrying on her illicit trade. I was, therefore, compelled constantly to fight off intrusions from all sides. As soon as I made an effort to shut my eyes I would discover the arm of my left-hand-neighbor round my neck, and would restore it to its owner with a push. While keeping an eye on his movements, however, I offered an opportunity for my neighbor on the right to get too near to me, and I would savagely kick him in the side. All night long my nerves were taut and my fists busy. Toward dawn I was so exhausted that I nearly fell asleep, when I discovered a hand on my chest, and before the man realized my intention, I struck him in the face. I continued to rain blows till the bell rang at five o'clock, the hour for rising.

Ten minutes were given us to dress and wash, tardiness being punished by a rebuke. At the end of ten minutes the ranks formed and every soldier's hands, ears and foot-rags were inspected. I was in such haste to be in time that I put my trousers on inside out, provoking roars of laughter.

The day began with a prayer for the Tsar and country, following which every one of us received the daily allowance of two-and-a-half pounds of bread and a few cubes of sugar from our respective squad commanders. There were four squads to a company. Our breakfast consisted of bread and tea and lasted half an hour.

At the mess I had an opportunity to get acquainted with some of the more sympathetic soldiers. There were ten volunteers in my company, and they were all students. After eating, there was roll-call. When the officer reached my name he read: "Bochkareva," to which I answered, "Aye." We were then taken out for instruction, since the entire regiment had been formed only three days before. The first rule that the training officer tried to impress upon us was to pay attention, and to watch his movements and actions. Not all the recruits could do it easily. I prayed to God to enlighten me in the study of a soldier's duties.

It was slow work to establish proper relations with the men. The first few days I was such a nuisance to the Company Commander that he wished me to ask for dismissal. He hinted as much on a couple of occasions, but I continued to mind my own business and never reported the annoyances I endured from the men. Gradually I won their respect and confidence. The small group of volunteers always defended me. As the Russian soldiers call each other by nicknames, one of the first questions put to me by my friends was what I would like to be called.

"Call me Yashka," I said, and that name stuck to me ever after, saving my life on more than one occasion. There is so much in a name, and "Yashka" was the sort of name that appealed to the soldiers and always worked in my favor. In time it became the nickname of the regiment, but not before I had been tested by many additional trials and found to be a comrade, and not merely a woman, by the men.

I was an apt student and learned almost to anticipate the orders of the instructor. When the day's duties were completed and the soldiers gathered into groups to while away an hour or two in games or storytelling, I was always asked to take part. I came to like the soldiers, who were good-natured fellows, and to enjoy their sports. The group which Yashka joined would usually prove the most popular in the barracks, and it was sufficient to secure my co-operation in some scheme to make it a success.

There was little time for relaxation, however, as we went through an intensive training course of only three months before we were sent to the front. Once a week, every Sunday, I would leave the barracks and spend the day at home, my mother having reconciled herself to my enlistment. On holidays I would be visited by friends or relatives. On one such occasion my sister and her husband called. I had been detailed for guard duty in the barracks that day. While on such duty a soldier is forbidden to sit down or to engage in conversation. I was entertaining my visitors when the Company Commander passed.

"Do you know the rules, Bochkareva?" he asked.

"Yes, your Excellency," I answered.

"What are they?"

"A soldier on guard duty is not allowed to sit down or engage in conversation," I replied. He ordered me to stand for two hours at attention at the completion of my guard duty, which took twenty-four hours. Standing at attention, in full military equipment, for two hours is a severe task, as one has to remain absolutely motionless under the eyes of a guard, and yet it was a common punishment.

During my training I was punished in this manner three times. The second time it was really not my fault. One night I recognized my squad commander in a soldier who annoyed me, and I dealt him as hard a blow as I would have given to any other man. In the morning he placed me at attention for two hours, claiming that he had accidentally brushed against me.

At first there was some difficulty in arranging for my bathing. The bath-house was used by the men, and so I was allowed one day to visit a public bath-house. I thought it a good opportunity for some fun. I came into the women's room, fully dressed, and there was a tremendous uproar as soon as I appeared. I was taken for a man. However, the fun did not last long. In an instant I was attacked from all sides and only narrowly escaped serious injury by crying out that I was a woman.

In the last month of our training we engaged in almost continuous rifle practice. I applied myself zealously to acquiring skill in handling a rifle and won an honorable mention for good marksmanship. This considerably enhanced my standing with the soldiers and strengthened our feeling of comradeship.

Early in 1915 our regiment received orders to prepare to proceed to the front. We received a week's leave. The soldiers passed these last days in drink and revelry and gay parties. One evening a group of boys invited me to go along with them to a house of ill repute.

"Be a soldier, Yashka," they urged me laughingly, scarcely expecting me to accept their invitation.

A thought flashed through my mind.

"I will go with them, and learn the soldier's life, so that I may understand his soul better." And I expressed my willingness to go. Perhaps curiosity had something to do with my decision. It was greeted with an explosion of mirth. Noisily we marched through the streets, singing and laughing, until we came to our destination.

My knees began to tremble as the party was about to enter the house. I wanted to turn back and flee. But the soldiers would not let me. The idea of Yashka going with them to such a place took a strong hold on their imagination. Soldiers, before going to the front, were always welcome in the haunts of vice, as they spent their money freely. Our group was, therefore, promptly surrounded by the women of the place, and one of them, a very young and pretty girl, picked me out as her favorite to the boundless mirth of my companions. There was drinking, dancing and a great deal of noise. Nobody suspected my sex, not even my youthful sweetheart, who seated herself in my lap and exerted all her charms to entice me. She caressed me, embraced me and kissed me. I giggled, and my comrades gave vent to peals of laughter. Presently I was left alone with my charmer.

Suddenly the door swung open and an officer entered. Soldiers were forbidden to leave their barracks after eight o'clock, and our party had slipped out in the dark when we were supposed to be asleep.

"Of what regiment are you?" the officer asked, abruptly, as I rose to salute.

"The Fifth Reserve Regiment, your Excellency," I replied ruefully.

While this was going on the boys in the other rooms were notified of the officer's presence and made their escape through windows and all available doors, leaving me to take care of myself.

"How dare you leave your barracks?" he thundered at me, "and frequent such places so late at night. I shall order you to the military prison for the night." And he commanded me to report there immediately.

It was my first acquaintance with the military jail. It is not a very comfortable place in which to spend a night. In the morning I was called before the prison commandant, who questioned me sternly. Finally, I could contain myself no longer and broke out into laughter.

"It was all a mistake, your Excellency," I said.

"A mistake, eh? What the devil do you mean, a mistake? I have a report here," he cried out angrily.

"I am a woman, your Excellency," I laughed.

"A woman!" he roared, opening his eyes wide, and surveying me. In an instant he recognized the truth of my words. "What the devil!" he muttered. "A woman indeed : A woman in a soldier's uniform!"

"I am Maria Bochkareva, of the Fifth Regiment," I explained. He had heard of me.

"But what were you, a woman, doing in that place?" he inquired.

"I am a soldier, your Excellency, and I went along with some of my comrades to investigate for myself the places where the soldiers pass their time."

He telephoned to the Commander of my regiment to inquire into my record and told him where and why I was detained. A titter ran through the offices when they learned of Yashka's adventure. The soldiers already knew from their comrades of the night's escapade, and with great difficulty suppressed their merriment, not wanting to attract the attention of the officers. But now there was a general outburst of laughter. When I arrived it reached such a pitch that men were actually rolling on the floor, holding their sides. I was punished by two hours at attention, the third and last time during my training. For a week afterwards the regiment talked about nothing but Yashka's adventure, nearly every soldier making a point of accosting me with the question: "Yashka, how did you like it there?"

The date of our departure was fixed. We received complete new outfits. I was permitted to go home to spend the last night, and it was a night of tears and sobs and longings. The three months I had spent in Tomsk as a soldier were, after all, remote from war. But now that I felt so near to that great experience, it awed me. I prayed to God to give me courage for the new trials that were before me, courage to live and die like a man.

There was great excitement in the barracks the following morning. It was the last that we were to spend there. In complete marching equipment we marched to the Cathedral where we were sworn in again. There was a solemn service. The church was filled with people, and there was an enormous crowd outside. The Bishop addressed us. He spoke of how the country was attacked by an enemy who sought to destroy Russia, and appealed to us to defend gloriously the Tsar and the Motherland. He prayed for victory for our arms and blessed us.

A spiritual fervour was kindled in the men. We were all so buoyant, so happy, so forgetful of our own lives and interests. The whole city poured out to accompany us to the station, and we were cheered and greeted all along the route. I had never yet seen a body of men in such high spirits as we were that February morning. Woe to the Germans that might have encountered us that day. Such was Russia going to war in those first months of the struggle. Hundreds of regiments like our own were streaming from east, north and south to the battlefields. It was an inspiring, uplifting, unforgettable sight.

My mother felt none of the exaltation with which I was filled. She walked along the street, beside my line, weeping, appealing to the Holy Mother and all the saints of the Church, to save her daughter.

"Wake up: Marusia," she cried, "What are you doing?" But it was too late. The ardor of war possessed me entirely. Somewhere deep in my heart my beloved mother's wailings found an echo, but my eyes were dimmed with tears of joy. It was only when I bade my mother goodbye, hugging and kissing her for what she felt was the last time, and boarded the train, leaving her on the platform prostrate and frantic with grief, that my heart sank and I trembled from head to foot. My resolution was on the point of giving way when the train moved out of the station.

I was going to war.

CHAPTER VII
MY FIRST EXPERIENCE OF NO MAN'S LAND

Our train was composed of a number of vans and one passenger car. These vans, in which the soldiers sleep, have two bunks on each side, and are called *teplushkas*.[9] There are no windows in a *teplushka*, as it is really only a converted luggage van. The passenger car was occupied by the four officers of our regiment, including our new Company Commander, Grishaninov. He was a short, jolly fellow and soon won his men's love and loyalty.

There was plenty of room to spare in the passenger car and the officers took it into their heads to invite me to share it with them. When the invitation cam , the soldiers all shook their heads in disapproval. They suspected the motives of the officers and thought that Yashka would fare as well among them as among their superiors.

"Bochkareva," said Commander Grishaninov, when I entered his car, "would you prefer to be stationed in this carriage? There is plenty of room."

"No, your Excellency," I replied, saluting. "I am a plain soldier, and it is my duty to travel as a soldier."

"Very well," declared the commander, chagrined. And I returned to my *teplushka*.

"Yashka is back. Good fellow, Yashka!" the men welcomed me enthusiastically, bestowing some strong epithets on the officers. They were immensely pleased at the idea that Yashka preferred their company in a *teplushka* to that of the officers in a spacious passenger coach, and made a comfortable place for me in a corner.

We were assigned to the Second Army, then commanded by General Gurko, with headquarters at Polotsk.[10] It took us two weeks to get there from Tomsk. General Gurko reviewed us at Army Headquarters and complimented

---

9. From the Russian word *teplo* (warm).

10. Polotsk is in the northern part of Belarus, near the border with Latvia. The Second Army fought on the Northwest Front from July 1914-August 1915, then on the Western Front until early 1918, when it was disbanded. From January to June 1915, it was commanded by Vasily Iosifovich Gurko.

the commander upon the regiment's fitness. We were then assigned to the Fifth Corps. Before we started, the news spread that there was a woman in our regiment. Curiosity was at once aroused. Knots of soldiers gathered about my *teplushka*, peeping through the door and cracks in the sides to verify with their own eyes the incredible news. Then they would swear, emphasizing their words by spitting, to having witnessed the inexplicable phenomenon of a *baba* going to the trenches. The attention of some officers was attracted by the crowd, and they came up to find out what the excitement was about. They reported me to the Commandant of the station, who immediately sent for Colonel Grishaninov, demanding an explanation. But the Colonel could not satisfy the Commandant's doubts and was instructed not to send me with the men to the fighting line.

"You can't go to the trenches, Bochkareva," my Commander addressed me upon his return from the Commandant. "The General won't allow it. He was very much concerned about you and could not understand how a woman could be a soldier."

For a moment I was shocked. Then the happy thought occurred to me that no General had the authority to overrule an order of the Tsar.

"Your Excellency!" I exclaimed to Colonel Grishaninov, "I was enlisted by the grace of the Tsar as a regular soldier. You can look up His Majesty's telegram in my record."

This settled the matter, and the Commandant withdrew his objections. We had to walk about thirteen miles to Corps Headquarters. The road was in a frightful condition, muddy and full of ruts. We were so tired at the end of seven miles that a rest was ordered. The soldiers, although they were tired out, made a dry seat for me with their overcoats. We then resumed our journey, arriving for supper at Headquarters, and were billeted for the night in a stable. We slept like the dead, on straw spread over the floor.

General Valuyev was then Commander of the Fifth Corps. He reviewed us in the morning and was extremely satisfied, assigning us to the Seventh Division, which was situated some miles distant. The Commander of the Division, whose name was Walter,[11] was of German blood and a thorough rascal. We were quartered, during the night, in the woods, behind the fighting line.

In command of the reserves was a Colonel named Shtubendorf,[12] also of German blood, but a decent and popular officer. When informed that a woman was in the ranks of the newly-arrived regiment, he was amazed.

---

11. Possibly Major General Leonid Vladimirovich Walter (1872-19??).

12. Alexei Ottovich Shtubendorf (1877-1959) was a hero of the First World War and son of the esteemed

"A woman!" he cried out, "she can't be permitted to remain. This regiment is going into battle soon, and women were not made for war."

There was a heated discussion between him and Commander Grishaninov, which ended in an order for my appearance before them. I was subjected to a searching inquiry and passed it well. Asked if I wanted to take part in the fighting, I replied affirmatively. Muttering his astonishment, Colonel Shtubendorf allowed me to remain until he had looked into the matter further.

A big battle was raging at this time on our section of the front. We were told to be ready for an order to move at any moment to the front line. Meanwhile, we were sheltered in dugouts. My company occupied ten of these, all bomb-proof, though not in first-class condition. They were cold and had no windows. As soon as day broke, we busied ourselves with cutting windows, building fire-places, repairing the dilapidated ceilings of timber and sand, and general house-cleaning. The dugouts were constructed in rows, the companies of odd numbers being assigned to the row on the right, while those of even numbers went to the left. There were notice-boards along the road and each company had a sentinel on duty.

Our position was five miles behind the first line of trenches. The booming of the guns could be heard in the distance. Streams of wounded, some in vehicles and others on foot, flowed along the road. We drilled during most of the second day under the inspection of Colonel Shtubendorf. He must have kept a close eye on me, for at the end of the drilling he called me, praised my efficiency, and granted me permission to stay in the ranks.

On the third day came the order to move to the trench lines. Through mud and under shell-fire we marched forward. It was still light when we arrived at the firing-line. We had two killed and five wounded. As the German positions were on a hill, they were enabled to observe all our movements. We were therefore instructed by field telephones not to occupy the trenches until after dark.

"So this is war," I thought. My pulse quickened, and I caught the spirit of excitement that pervaded the regiment. We were all expectant, as if in the presence of a solemn revelation. We were eager to get into the fray and to show the Germans what we, the soldiers of the Fifth Regiment, could do. Were we nervous?

General Otto Eduardovich Shtubendorf. He fought for the Whites in the Civil War, then emigrated to Estonia, where he was arrested in 1940 by the NKVD, released at the request of the Germans, whence he fled to Germany, where he later died.

Undoubtedly, but it was not the nervousness of cowardice, rather was it the restlessness of young blood. Our hands were steady, our bayonets fixed. We exulted in our adventure.

Night came. The Germans were discharging a volume of gas at us. Perhaps they noticed an unusual movement behind the lines, and wished to annihilate us before we entered the battle. But they failed. Over the wire came the order to put on our masks. Thus were we baptized in this most inhuman of all German war inventions. Our masks were not perfect. The deadly gas penetrated some and made our eyes smart and water. But we were soldiers of Mother Russia, whose sons are not unaccustomed to half-suffocating air, and so we withstood the irritating fumes.

Midnight passed. The Commander went through our ranks to inform us that the hour had come to move into the trenches and that before dawn we should take the offensive. He addressed us with words of encouragement and was heartily cheered. The artillery had been thundering all night, the fire growing more and more intense every hour. In single file we moved along a communication trench to the front line. Some of us were wounded, but we remained dauntless. All our fatigue seemed to have vanished.

The deadly gas penetrated some and made our eyes smart and water. But we were soldiers of Mother Russia, whose sons are not unaccustomed to half-suffocating air, and so we withstood the irritating fumes.

The front trench was a mere ditch, and as we lined up along it our shoulders touched. The positions of the enemy were less than three-quarters of a mile away, and the space between was filled with groans and swept by bullets. It was a scene full of horrors. Sometimes an enemy shell would land in the midst of our men, killing several and wounding more. We were sprinkled with the blood of our comrades and spattered by the mud.

At two in the morning, the Commander appeared in our midst. He seemed nervous. The other officers came with him and took their positions at the head of the men. With drawn swords they prepared to lead the charge. The Commander had a rifle.

"Climb out!" he shouted.

I crossed myself. My heart was filled with grief for the bleeding men around me and stirred by a fierce desire for revenge upon the Germans. My mind was a kaleidoscope of many thoughts and visions. My mother, death, mutilation, various petty incidents of my life filled it. But there was no time for thinking.

Russian troops awaiting the command to go over the top.

I climbed out with the rest of the men, to be met by a volley of machine-gun fire. For a moment there was confusion. So many of our number had fallen, like ripe wheat cut down by a gigantic scythe wielded by the invisible arm of Satan himself. Fresh blood was dripping on the cold corpses that had lain there for hours or days, and the moans were heart-rending.

Amid the confusion, the voice of our Company Commander was raised.

"Forward!"

And forward we went. The enemy had seen us go over the top, and he let loose Hell. As we ran forward, we kept firing. Then the order came to lie down. The bombardment grew even more concentrated.

Alternately running for some distance and then lying down, we reached the enemy's barbed wire entanglements. We had expected to find them demolished by our artillery, but, alas! they were untouched! There were only about seventy left of our Company of two hundred and fifty.

Whose fault was it? This was an offensive on a front of thirteen miles, carried out by three army corps. And the barbed wire was uncut! Perhaps our artillery was defective! Perhaps it was the fault of someone higher up! Anyhow, there we were, seventy out of two hundred and fifty. And every fraction of a second was precious. Were we doomed to die here in a heap without even coming to grips with the enemy? Were our bodies to dangle on this wire tomorrow, and the day after, to provide food for the crows and strike terror into the hearts of the fresh soldiers who would take our places in a few hours?

As these thoughts flashed through our minds, an order came to retreat. The enemy let a barrage down in front of us. The retreat was even worse than the advance. Only forty-eight of our Company got back to our trenches alive.

About a third of the two hundred and fifty were dead. The greater number of the wounded were in No Man's Land and their cries of pain and prayers for help or death gave us no peace.

The remnant of our Company crouched in the trench, exhausted, dazed, incredulous of their escape from injury. We were hungry and thirsty and would have welcomed a dry and safe place in which to recover ourselves. But there we were, smarting under the defeat by the enemy's barbed wire barrier, with the heart-breaking appeals for help coming from our comrades. Deeper and deeper they cut into my soul. They were so plaintive, like the voices of hurt children.

In the dark it seemed to me that I saw their faces, the familiar faces of Ivan and Peter and Sergei and Mitya, the good fellows who had taken such tender care of me, making a comfortable place for me in that crowded *teplushka*, or taking off their overcoats in cold weather and spreading them on the muddy road to provide a dry seat for Yashka. They called me. I could see their hands outstretched in my direction, their wide open eyes straining in the night in the hope of rescue, the deathly pallor of their faces. Could I remain indifferent to their cries? Was it not my bounden duty as a soldier, a duty as important as that of fighting the enemy, to render aid to stricken comrades?

I climbed out of the trench and crawled under our wire entanglements. There was a comparative calm, interrupted only by occasional rifle shots, when I would lie down and remain motionless, as though I were a corpse. There were wounded within a few feet of our line. I carried them one by one to the edge of our trench where they were picked up and carried to the rear. The saving of one man encouraged me to continue my efforts till I reached the far side of the field. Here I had several narrow escapes. A sound, made accidentally, was sufficient to attract several shots, and I only saved myself by at once lying flat upon the ground. When dawn broke in the East, putting an end to my expeditions through No Man's Land, I had saved about fifty lives.

I had no idea at the time of what I had accomplished. But when the soldiers whom I had picked up were brought to the relief station and asked who rescued them, about fifty replied, "Yashka." This was communicated to the Commander, who recommended me for an Order of the 4th Degree, "for distinguished valour shown in the saving of many lives under fire."

Our kitchen had been destroyed the previous night by the enemy's fire, and we were very hungry. Our ranks were replenished by fresh drafts, and our artillery again boomed all day, playing havoc with the enemy's wire fences. We guessed that it meant another order to advance the following night, and our expectations proved correct. At about the same hour as the previous morning we climbed out and started to run towards the enemy's position. Again a rain of shells and bullets, again scores of wounded and killed, again smoke and gas and blood and mud. But we reached the wire entanglement and it was down and torn to pieces this time. We halted for an instant, emitting an inhuman "Hurrah! Hurrah!" that struck terror into those Germans that were still alive in their half-demolished trenches, and with fixed bayonets rushed forward and jumped into them.

As I was about to descend into the ditch, I suddenly observed a huge German taking aim at me. Hardly did I have time to fire when something struck my right leg, and I had a sensation of a warm liquid trickling down my flesh. I fell. My comrades had put the enemy to flight and were pursuing him. There were many wounded, and cries of "Save me, Holy Jesus!" came from every direction.

I suffered little pain and made several efforts to get up and reach our trenches. But every time I failed. I was too weak. There I lay in the darkness of the night, within fifty feet of what had been, twenty-four hours before, the enemy's position, waiting for dawn and relief. To be sure, I was not alone. Hundreds, thousands of gallant comrades were scattered on the field for miles.

It was four hours after I was wounded before day arrived and with it our stretcher-bearers. I was picked up and carried to a first-aid station a mile and a half in the rear. My wound was bandaged, and I was sent on to the Division Hospital. There I was placed on a hospital train and taken to Kiev.

It was about Easter of 1915 when I arrived in Kiev. The station there was so crowded with wounded from the front that hundreds of stretchers could not be accommodated inside and were lined up in rows on the platform outside. I was picked up by an ambulance and taken to the Eugene Lazaret,[13] where I was kept in the same ward with the men. Of course, it was a military hospital, and there was no woman's ward.

I was there all through the spring of 1915. The nurses and physicians took good care of all the patients in the hospital. My swollen leg was restored to its normal condition, and it was a restful two months that I passed in Kiev. At the end of that period I was taken before a military medical commission, examined, pronounced in good health, provided with a ticket, money and a certificate, and sent to the front again.

My route now lay through Molodechno, an important railway terminus. When I arrived there in the early part of July, I was sent to the Corps Headquarters by wagon, and thence I proceeded on foot to my Regiment.

My heart throbbed with joy as I drew nearer to the front. I had been eager to get back to my comrades. They had endeared themselves to me so much that I

---

13. Лазарет (*lazaret*) in Russian means a mobile hospital in military units or prisons.

loved my Company as much as my own mother. I thought of the comrades whose lives I had saved and wondered how many of them had returned to the fighting line. I thought of the soldiers whom I had left alive and wondered if they were still among the living. Many familiar scenes came up in my imagination as I marched along under the brilliant rays of the sun.

A common *muzhik* soldier.

As I approached the regimental headquarters a soldier saw me in the distance and, turning to his comrade, he pointed towards me.

"Who can that be?" he asked, thoughtfully. The partner scratched his neck and said :

"Why, he looks familiar."

"Why, it's Yashka!" exclaimed the first, as I moved nearer. "Yashka! Yashka!" they shouted at the top of their voices, running toward me as fast as they could.

"Yashka is back! Yashka is back!" the news was passed along to men and officers alike. There was such spontaneous joy that I was overwhelmed. Our regiment was then in reserve, and soon I was surrounded by hundreds of old friends. There was kissing, embracing, handshaking. The men capered about like children, shouting, "Look who's here! Yashka!" They had been under the impression that I was disabled and would never return. They congratulated me upon my recovery. Even the officers came out to shake hands with me, some even kissing me, and all expressing their gratification at my recovery.

I shall never forget the welcome I received from my comrades.

They carried me on their shoulders, shouting, "Hurrah for Yashka! Three cheers for Yashka!" Many of them wanted me to visit their dugouts and share with them the food parcels they had received from home. The dugouts were really in a splendid state, clean, furnished, well protected. I was reassigned to my old company, the Thirteenth, and was now considered a veteran.

Our company was shortly detailed to act as the protecting force to a battery of artillery. Such duty was regarded by the men as a holiday, for it made possible a genuine rest in healthful surroundings. We spent between two and three weeks with the battery and were then moved to Sloboda, a town in the vicinity of Lake Narach, about twenty-seven miles from Molodechno.[14] Our positions were in a swampy region, full of mud-holes and marshes. It was impossible to construct and maintain regular trenches there. We, therefore, built a barrier of sand-bags, behind which we crouched, knee deep in water. It was impossible to endure such conditions for any length of time. We were compelled to snatch brief intervals of sleep standing, and even the strongest constitutions quickly broke down. We were relieved at the end of six days and sent to the rear to recuperate. Then we had to relieve the men who had taken our places.

Thus we continued to hold the line. As the summer neared its end and the rains increased, the water would rise and at times reach our waists. It was important to maintain our front intact, although for several miles the ground was so boggy as to be practically impassable. The Germans, however, made an attempt in August to outflank the marshes, but they failed.

Later we were shifted to another position, some distance away. There was comparative quiet on our front. Our main work consisted in sending out raiding parties and keeping a keen watch over the enemy's movements from our advanced listening-posts. We slept in the morning and stayed wide-awake all night.

I was assigned to numerous observation parties. Usually four of us would be detailed to a listening-post, located sometimes in a bush, another time in a hole in the ground, behind the stump of a tree, or some similar obstacle. We crawled to our post so noiselessly that not only the enemy but even our own men would not know our hiding places, which were on an average fifty feet apart. Once at the post, our safety and duty demanded absolute immobility and caution. We had to strain our ears to catch any unusual sound, and communicate it from post to post. Besides, there was always a chance of an enemy patrol or post being in close proximity without our knowing it. Every two hours the holders of the posts were relieved.

One foggy night, while on guard at a listening post, I detected a dull noise. It sounded like a raiding party, and I took it at first for our own, but there was no answer to my sharp query for the password. It was impossible to see in the mist. We opened fire, and the Germans flattened themselves on the ground and waited.

---

14. Northeast of Minsk and near the present day border with Lithuania. In May-September 1915, German forces pushed Russian forces on the Northwest Front back from their forward position in Poland (including from Warsaw), to present day Belarus, along a front that in this region was about midway between Vilnius and Minsk.

There they lay for almost two hours, until we had forgotten the incident. Then they crawled toward our post and suddenly appeared in front of us. There were eight of them. One threw a grenade, but missed our hole, and it exploded behind us. We fired, killing two and wounding four. The remaining two escaped.

When the Company Commander received an order to send out a scouting party, he would call for volunteers. Armed with hand grenades, about thirty of the best soldiers would go out into No Man's Land to test the enemy's strength by drawing his fire, or to alarm him by heavy bombing and shooting. Not infrequently, scouting parties from both sides would meet. Then there would be a regular battle. It sometimes happened that one party would let an enemy party pass in front, and then attack it from the rear and capture it.

The fifteenth of August, 1915, was a memorable day in our lives. The enemy opened a violent fire at us at three o'clock in the morning, demolishing our barbed wire defenses, destroying some of our trenches, and burying many soldiers alive. Many others were killed by enemy shells. Altogether we lost fifteen killed and forty wounded out of two hundred and fifty. It was clear that the Germans contemplated an offensive. Our artillery replied vigorously, and the earth shook with the thunder of the guns. We sought every protection available, our nerves strained in momentary anticipation of an attack. We crossed ourselves, prayed to God, made ready our rifles, and awaited orders.

At six o'clock the Germans were observed climbing over the top and running in our direction. Closer and closer they came, and still we made no move, while our artillery rained shells on them. When they approached within a hundred feet of our line we received the order to open fire, and we greeted the enemy with such a concentrated hail of bullets, that his ranks were decimated and plunged in confusion. We took advantage of the situation and rushed at the Germans, turning them back and pursuing them along the twelve-mile front on which they had started to advance. The enemy lost ten thousand men that morning.

During the day we received reinforcements, and also new equipment, including gas masks. Then word came that we were to take the offensive the following night. Our guns began a terrific bombardment of the German positions at six in the evening. We were all in a state of suppressed excitement. Men and officers mixed together, joking about death. Many expected not to return and wrote letters to their dear ones. Others prayed. Before an offensive, the men's camaraderie would reach its height. There would be affectionate partings, sincere professions by some of their premonitions of death and the sending of messages to friends. Universal joy was displayed whenever a shell of ours tore a gap in the enemy's wire defenses or fell into the midst of his trenches.

At three in the morning the order, "Advance!" rang out. In high spirits we started for the enemy's positions. Our casualties on the way were enormous. Several times we were ordered to lie down. Our first line was almost completely wiped out, but its ranks were filled up by men from the second row. On we went till we reached the Germans and overwhelmed them. Our own Polotsk Regiment alone captured two thousand prisoners and our jubilation was boundless. We held the enemy's positions, and No Man's Land, strewn with wounded and dead, was now ours. There were few stretcher-bearers available, and a call went out for volunteers to gather in the wounded. I was among those who answered the call.

There is great satisfaction in helping a suffering human being. There is great reward in the gratitude of a man tortured with suffering whom one has saved. It gave me immense joy to be able to maintain the life in an miconscious human body. As I was kneeling over one such wounded man, who had suffered a great loss of blood, and was about to lift him, a sniper's bullet hit me between the thumb and forefinger and passed on and through the flesh of my left forearm. Fortunately I realized quickly the nature of the wounds, bandaged them, and, in spite of his protests, carried the bleeding man out of danger.

I continued my work all night, and was recommended to receive the Cross of St. George of the 4th Degree, "for bravery in defensive and offensive fighting and for rendering, while wounded, first aid on the field of battle." But I never received it. Instead, I was awarded a medal of the 4th Degree and was informed that a woman could not obtain the Cross of St. George.

I was disappointed and chagrined. Hadn't I heard of the Cross being given to some Red Cross nurses? I protested to the Commander. He fully sympathized with me and expressed his belief that I certainly deserved the Cross.

"But," he added, disdainfully, shrugging his shoulders, "it is *nachalstvo.*"[15]

My arm was painful, and I could not remain in the front line. The medical assistant of our regimental hospital had been severely wounded, and I was sent to act in his place, under the supervision of the physician. I stayed there two weeks, until my arm improved, and I attained such proficiency under the Doctor's instructions that he issued a certificate to me, stating that I could temporarily perform the duties of a medical assistant.

The autumn of 1915 passed, for us, uneventfully. Our life become one of routine. At night we kept watch, warming ourselves with hot tea, boiled on

---

15. Officialdom, leadership.

little stoves in the front trenches. At dawn we would go to sleep, and at nine in the morning the day would begin for some of us, as that was the hour for the distribution of bread and sugar. Every soldier received a ration of two and a half pounds of bread daily. It was often burned on the outside and not done on the inside. At eleven o'clock, when dinner arrived, everybody was awake, cleaning rifles and generally setting things in order. The kitchen was always some distance in the rear, and some of the men were sent to bring the dinner pails to the trenches. The dinner generally consisted of a hot cabbage soup, with some meat in it. The meat was often bad. The second dish was always kasha, Russia's popular gruel. Our daily ration of sugar was supposed to be three-sixteenths of a pound. By the time our dinner got to us it was cold, so that tea was resorted to again. After noon we received our orders, and at six in the evening supper arrived, this being the last meal, and consisting only of one course. It was either cabbage soup or kasha or half a herring, with bread. Many ate all their bread before the supper hour, or if they were very hungry, with the first meal, and were thus forced to beg for morsels from their comrades, or go hungry in the evening.

Every twelve days we were relieved and sent to the rear for a six-day rest. There we found ready for us the baths established by the Union of *Zemstvos*[16] which in 1915 had extended its activities along the whole front. Every Divisional bath was in charge of a physician and a hundred voluntary workers. Every bathhouse was also a laundry, and the men, upon entering it, left their dirty underwear there, receiving in exchange clean linen. When a company was about to leave the trenches for the rear, word was sent to the bath-house of its coming. There was nothing that the soldiers welcomed so much as the bath-house, so vermin-infested were the trenches, and so great was their suffering on this account.

I suffered more than anybody else from the vermin. I could not think at first of going to the bathhouse with the men. My skin was eaten through and through and scabs began to form all over my body. I went to the Commander to inquire how I could get a bath, telling him of my condition. The Commander listened with sympathy.

"But what can I do, Yashka?" he said." I can't keep the whole Company out to let you alone make use of the bathhouse. Go with the men. They respect you so much that I am sure they won't molest you."

---

16. *Zemstvos* were a form of local self-government put in place in the mid-nineteenth century after the Liberation of the Serfs. The Union of *Zemstvos* was a national, reformist organization seeking to act as a common voice for all local zemstvos.

I could not quite make up my mind at first. But the vermin gave me no rest, and I was nearing desperation. When we were relieved next and the boys were getting ready to march to the bath-house I plucked up courage and went up to my sergeant, declaring:

"I'll go to the bath-house, too. I can't endure it any longer."

He approved of my decision, and I followed the company, arousing general merriment. "Oh, Yashka is going with us to the bathhouse!" the men joked good naturedly. Once inside, I hastened to occupy a corner for myself and begged the men to keep away from it. They did, although they continued to laugh and poke fun at me. I was very ill at ease the first time, and as soon as I had finished my bath, I hastily put on my new underwear, dressed with all speed and ran out of the building. But the bath did me so much good that I made it a habit to attend it with the Company every two weeks. In time, the soldiers got so accustomed to it that they paid no attention to me, and were even quick to silence the jests of any new member of the Company.

CHAPTER VIII
WOUNDED AND PARALYZED

Towards winter we were moved to a place called Zelenoye Polye. There I was placed in command of twelve stretcher-bearers and served in the capacity of medical assistant for six weeks, during which I had charge of the sending of men who were ill to the hospital and of granting a few days' rest from duty to those who needed it.

Our positions ran through an abandoned country estate. The house lay between the lines. We were on the top of the hill, while the Germans occupied the low ground. We could, therefore, observe their movements and they, in turn, could watch us. If any on either side raised his head, he became the mark of some sniper.

It was in this place that our men fell victims to a superior officer's treason. There had been plenty of rumors in the trenches of pro-German officials in the army and at Court. We had our suspicions, too, and now they were confirmed in a shocking manner.

General Walter paid a visit to the front line. He was known to be of German blood, and his harsh treatment of the soldiers won for him the cordial hatred of the rank and file. The General, accompanied by a considerable suite of officers and men, exposed himself completely on his tour of inspection of our trenches without attracting a single enemy bullet! It was unthinkable to us who had to crawl on our bellies to obtain some water. And here was this General in open view of the enemy, and yet they preserved this strange silence.

The General acted in an odd fashion. He would stop at points where the barbed wire was torn open or where the fortifications were weak and wipe his face with his handkerchief, there was a general murmur among the men. The word "treason!" was uttered by many lips in suppressed tones. The officers were indignant and called the General's attention to the unnecessary danger to which he exposed himself. But the General ignored their warnings, remarking, "*Nichevo!*" (It's nothing).

Maria Bochkareva

The discipline was so rigorous that no one dared to argue the matter with the General. The officers cursed when he left. The men muttered:

"He is selling us to the enemy!"

Half an hour after his departure, the Germans opened a tremendous fire. It was particularly directed against those points at which the General had stopped, reducing their faulty defenses to ruins. We thought at first that the enemy intended to launch an offensive, but our expectations were not realized. He merely continued his violent bombardment, wounding and burying alive hundreds of men. The cries of the men were such that the work of rescue could not be delayed. While the shelling was still going on I took charge and dressed some hundred and fifty wounds. If General Walter had appeared in our midst at that moment, the men would never have let him get away alive, so intense was their feeling.

For two weeks we worked at the reconstruction of our demolished trenches and altogether extracted about five hundred corpses. I was recommended for and received a gold medal of the 2nd Degree for "saving wounded from the trenches under violent fire." Usually a medical assistant received a medal of the 4th Degree, but I was given one of the 2nd Degree because of the special conditions under which I had done my work.

We were then relieved for a month and sent ten miles to the rear, to the village of Senky, on a stream called Uzlyanka. An artillery base was located there, and when we finally reached our destination, our life was easier. But getting there was no easy task, for the road was in a frightful condition. We were utterly exhausted, and most of us fell asleep without even eating the supper that had been prepared for us.

There was no work for a medical assistant in the rear, and besides my arm had fully recovered, so I applied to the Commander for permission to return to the ranks. He granted it, promoting me to the rank of Corporal, which placed me in charge of eleven men.

Here I received two letters, one from Yasha, in reply to mine, written from Yakutsk, in which I spoke of returning to him at the conclusion of the war. I sent a letter in answer to his repeating my promise, on condition that he would change his behavior towards me and treat me with consideration and love. The other letter was from home. My mother wanted me to come back, telling me of her hardships and sufferings.

It was October. This month, spent at the artillery base, was a merry one. We were billeted in the village huts, and engaged almost daily in sports and games. It was here that I was first taught how to sign my name and copy the alphabet, I had learned to read previously, Yasha having been my first teacher.

The literature that was allowed to circulate at the front was largely made up of lurid detective stories, and the name of "Nick Carter" was not unfamiliar even to me.[17]

There were other amusements, also. I remember one day, during a downpour of rain, I sought shelter in a barn, where I found about forty officers and men, who were also sheltering there from the rain. The owner of the barn, a middle-aged *baba*, was there with her cow. I was in a mischievous mood and began to flirt with her, to the general merriment of the men. I paid her some flattering compliments and declared that she had captivated me. The woman did not recognize my sex and professed to be insulted. Encouraged by the uproar of the men, I persisted in my advances, and finally made an attempt to kiss her. The baba, infuriated by the laughter of the soldiers, seized a large piece of firewood, and with curses, threatened me and the men.

"Get out of here, you tormentors of a poor baba!" she cried.

I did not want to provoke a fight and cried to her:

"Why, you foolish woman, I am a peasant girl myself."

This only further inflamed our hostess. She took it for more ridicule and became more menacing. The officers and soldiers interfered, trying to persuade her of the truth of my words, as none of us wanted to be put out into the rain. However, it required more than words to convince her, so I was compelled to unbutton my coat.

"Holy Jesus!" the woman crossed herself. "A baba, indeed." And immediately her heart softened, and her tone changed into one of tenderness. She burst into tears. Her husband and son were in the army, she told me, and she hadn't heard from them for a long time. She gathered me into her arms, and gave me food and some milk, inquiring about my mother and mourning over her lot. We parted affectionately, and she followed me with her blessings.

It was snowing when we returned to the front line. Our position was now at Ferdinandovy Nos, between Lake Narach and Baranovichy.[18] The first night the

---

17. A dime novel detective who first appeared in the US in 1886. He was featured in a popular radio series, *Nick Carter, Master Detective* from 1943-55, three movies, and became Secret Agent Nick Carter – Killmaster, in the 1960s.

18. In the summer of 1916, this region in present day Belarus would be the site of a major battle on the northwest front, an ill-timed Russian attack that failed to follow through and support the successful Brusilov Breakthrough, due largely to the incompetence and cowardice of a few Russian generals, especially Alexei Evert. Had the attack been properly effected, Russian troops might well have broken through the weakened German lines, retaken Warsaw, and rewritten the history of the war. The Ferdinandovy Nos (Ferdinand's Nose) was a forested region so named by soldiers after the notoriously long nose of Bulgaria's King Ferdinand I, who was allied with Germany.

Commander of the Company issued a call for thirty volunteers to go scouting and investigate the strength and position of the enemy. I was among the thirty.

We started out in single file, moving forward stealthily and as noiselessly as possible. We passed by some woods, in which an enemy patrol had hidden upon hearing the crackling of the snow beneath some of our soldiers' boots. We crawled on to the enemy trenches and lay in front of his barbed wire. Our chests were flattened against the snow-drifts. We were rather uneasy, as our presence seemed strangely unnoticed. Our officer, Lieutenant Bobrov, a former school teacher, but a fighting man of the first order, suddenly caught a noise in our rear.

"There is something happening," he whispered to us.

We strained our ears, but we had scarcely had time to look round when we found ourselves surrounded by an enemy force, larger than our own. It was too late to shoot. We resorted to our bayonets, and it was a brief but savage fight.

I found myself confronted by a German, who towered far above me. There was not an instant to lose. Life or death hung in the balance.

I rushed at the German before he had time to move and ran him through the stomach with the bayonet. The bayonet stuck, and the man fell. A stream of blood gushed forth. I made an effort to pull out the bayonet, but failed. It was the first man that I had bayoneted, and it all happened with lightning-speed.

I fled toward our trenches, pursued by a German, falling several times, but always rising again and pressing on. Our wire entanglements were in a zig-zag, and I had difficulty in finding our positions. My situation was getting critical, when I discovered that I had some hand grenades with me. I threw them at my pursuer, falling to the ground to avoid the shock of the explosion, and at length I reached our trenches.

Only ten of our party of thirty returned. The Commander thanked me personally, expressing his astonishment that I should have been able to bayonet a German. Deep in my soul I also wondered.

The year 1915 was nearing its end. The winter was severe, and life in the trenches almost unbearable. Death was a welcome visitor. Even more welcome was a wound that enabled one to be sent to hospital. There were many cases of men snowed under and frozen to death. There were many more cases of frozen feet that had to be amputated. Our equipment was getting very deficient. Our supply organization was already breaking down. It was difficult to replace a worn pair of boots. Not infrequently something went wrong in the kitchen, and we were forced to suffer hunger as well as cold. But we were patient, like true children of Mother Russia. It was dreadfully monotonous, this inactivity, this mere holding of frozen ditches. We longed for battles, for one mighty battle, to win the victory and end the war.

One bitter night I was detailed to a listening post with three men. My boots were worn out. One has to keep absolutely still while on such duty. A movement may mean death. So there we lay on the white ground, exposed to the attacks of King Frost. He went about his work without delay, and thoroughly. My right foot was undergoing strange sensations. It began to freeze. I longed to sit up and rub it. But sitting up was not to be thought of. Was that a noise? I ceased to trouble about my foot; I had to strain all my nerves to catch that peculiar sound. Or was it a mere freak of the wind? My foot grew numb. It was going to sleep.

"Holy Mother, what's to be done?" I thought to myself. "My right foot is gone. The feet of the other three men are freezing, too. They just whispered that to me. If only the Commander would relieve us now! But the two hours are not yet up."

Suddenly we perceived two figures in white crawling toward us, Germans provided with appropriate costumes for a deadly mission. We fired, and they replied. A bullet pierced my coat, just scratching the skin. Then everything quieted down again, and we were soon relieved. I had barely strength to reach my trench. There, I fell, exhausted, crying, "My foot! my foot!"

But we were patient, like true children of Mother Russia. It was dreadfully monotonous, this inactivity, this mere holding of frozen ditches. We longed for battles, for one mighty battle, to win the victory and end the war.

I was taken to the hospital, and there the horrible condition of my foot was revealed. It was as white as snow, covered with frost. The pains were agonizing, but nothing terrified me as much as the physician's talk of the probable necessity of amputating it. But I made a stubborn fight, and I saved my right limb. The doctors soon put me on the road to recovery, and by persistent care succeeded in restoring my foot to its normal state.

The opening of the year 1916 found me still in hospital. Almost immediately upon my discharge, our Company was sent to the rear for a month's rest in Beloye, a village some distance behind the fighting line. We were billeted with the peasants in their homes, and we enjoyed the use of a bathhouse and slept on the peasants' ovens, in true homey fashion. We even had the opportunity of seeing moving pictures, the apparatus being carried from base to base on a motor belonging to the Union of Zemstvos. We also established our own theatre and acted a play, written by one of our artillery officers. There were two women characters in the drama, and I was chosen for the leading role. The other feminine role was played by a young officer. It was with great reluctance that I consented to take the part, and only after the urgent appeals of the Commander. I did not believe myself capable of acting, and even the thunderous applause that I won on that occasion has not changed my belief.

At Beloye many of the soldiers and officers were visited by their wives. I made many acquaintances there and some fast friendships. One of the latter was with the wife of a stretcher-bearer with whom I had worked. She was a young, pretty and very lovable woman, and her husband adored her. When our month's rest was drawing to an end and the order came for the women to leave, the stretcher-bearer borrowed the Commander's horses in order to drive his wife to the station. On his way back, he had an apoplectic stroke and died immediately. He received a military funeral, and I made a wreath and placed it on his coffin.

As we lowered his coffin into the grave the thought inevitably suggested itself to me whether I would be buried like this or my body lost and blown to the winds in No Man's Land. The same thought must have passed through several minds.

Another friend, made at the same time, was the wife of Lieutenant Bobrov, the former school teacher. Both of them helped me to learn to write and improve my reading. The peasant women of the locality were so poor and ignorant that I devoted part of my time to aiding them. Many of them were suffering from minor ailments that were in need of attention. One evening I was even called to attend a woman in childbirth, this being my first experience in midwifery. Another time I was asked to visit a very bad case of fever.

Then came the trenches again. Again intense cold, again unceasing watchfulness and irritating inactivity. But the air was full of expectation. As the winter drew to its close, rumors of a gigantic spring offensive grew more and more insistent. Surely the war cannot end without a general battle, the men argued. And when, towards the end of February, we were again taken for a two-week rest, it became clear that we were to be prepared for an offensive. We received new outfits and equipment. On March the 5th the Commander of the Regiment addressed us. He spoke of the coming battle and appealed to us to be brave and win a great victory. He told us that the enemy's defenses were very strong and that it would require a mighty effort to overcome them.

Then we started for the front. The slush and mud were unimaginable. We walked deep in water, mixed with ice. On the road we met many wounded being carried to the hospital. We also passed by a cemetery, where the soldiers who had fallen in our lines were being buried in one huge grave. We were kept in the rear for the night, as reserves, and were told to await orders to-morrow to proceed to the trenches.

March the 6th began with an unprecedented bombardment on our side. The Germans replied with equal violence, and the earth fairly shook. The cannonade lasted all day. Then an order came for us to form ranks and march into the trenches. We knew that it meant that we were to take part in the offensive.

Lieutenant Bobrov came up to me unexpectedly with these words:

"Yashka, take this and deliver it to my wife after the attack. I have had a presentiment for three days that I shall not survive this battle." He handed me a letter and a ring.

"But, Lieutenant," I objected, though I knew that protestations were of no avail at such a moment. "You are mistaken so. It will not happen. Presentiments are deceiving."

He grimly shook his head and pressed my hand.

"Not this one, Yashka," he said.

We were in the trenches already, under a veritable hail of shells. There were dead and dying in our midst. Waist-deep in water we crouched, praying to God. Suddenly a gas wave came in our direction. It caught some without their masks, and for them there was no escape. I, myself, narrowly missed this horrible death. My lips contracted and my eyes watered and burned for three weeks afterward.

The signal to advance was given, and we started, knee-deep in mud, for the enemy. In places the pools reached above our waists. Shells and bullets played havoc among us. Of those who fell wounded, many sank in the mud and were drowned. The German fire was devastating. Our lines grew thinner and thinner, and progress became so slow that our doom was certain in the event of a further advance.

The order to retreat rang out. How can one describe the march back through the inferno of No Man's Land on that night of March 7, 1916? There were wounded men submerged all but their heads, calling piteously for help. "Save me, for Christ's sake!" came from every side. From the trenches there went up a chorus of the same heartrending appeals. So long as we were alive, we could not remain deaf to the pleadings of our comrades.

Fifty of us went out to do the work of rescue. Never before had I worked in such harrowing, blood-curdling circumstances. One man was wounded in the neck or face, and I had to grip him under the arms and drag his body through the mud. Another had his side torn by a shell, and it required many difficult manoeuvres before I could extricate him. Several sank so deep that my own strength was not sufficient to drag them out.

Finally I broke down, just as I reached my trench with a burden. I was so exhausted that all my bones were aching. The soldiers got some drinking water, a very hard thing to get, and made some tea for me. Somehow they obtained for me a dry overcoat and put me to sleep in a sheltered corner. I slept about four hours, and then resumed my search for wounded comrades.

All day the artillery boomed again, as violently on the previous day. At night, our ranks having been replenished with fresh drafts, we climbed out again and rushed for the enemy. Again we suffered heavily, but our operation this time was more successful. When the Germans saw us pressing forward determinedly in their direction they came out for a counter-attack. With bayonets fixed and a tremendous "Hurrah" we hurled ourselves at them.

The Germans never did like the Russian bayonets. As a matter of fact, they dreaded them more than any other arm of warfare, and so they broke down and took to their heels. We pursued them into their trenches, and there followed a fierce scrimmage. Many of the Germans raised their hands in sign of surrender. They realized that we were in a fierce, exasperated mood. Others fought to the end, and all this time German machine guns swept their own trenches, where Teuton and Slav were mixed in combat. Then we flung ourselves upon the machine gun positions.

Our regiment captured in that attack two thousand five hundred Germans and thirty machine guns. I escaped with only a slight wound in the right leg and did not leave the ranks. Elated by our victory over the strong defenses of the first line, we swept on toward the enemy's second line. His fire slackened considerably. A great triumph was in prospect, as behind the weak second and third lines there was an open stretch of undefended territory for many miles.

Our advance line was within seventy feet of the enemy's trenches when an order came from General Walter to halt and return to our positions. It was a terrible shock to men and officers alike. Our Colonel talked to the General on the field telephone, explaining to him the situation. The General was obdurate. All of us were so incensed at this treacherous order that, had any one of us taken command at the moment, we should undoubtedly have won a great victory, as the breach in the German defenses was complete.

The conversation between the Colonel and the General ended in a quarrel. The General had not, apparently, expected us to break through the first German line. So many waves of Russian soldiers had beaten in vain against it, and with such terrific losses. It became evident to our men that it was the General's treacherous design to have as many of us slaughtered as possible.

But discipline was severe, and orders were orders. We had to go back. We were so exhausted that our bodies welcomed a rest. In those two days, the 7th and 8th of August, our ranks were refilled four times with fresh drafts. Our casualties were enormous. The corpses lay thick everywhere, like mushrooms after rain, and there were innumerable wounded. One could not take a step in No Man's Land without coming into contact with the corpse of a Russian or a German. Bloody feet, hands, sometimes heads, lay scattered in the mud.

That was the most terrible offensive in which I was engaged. It has come down into history as the Battle of Postovy.[19] We spent the first night in the German trenches we had captured. It was a night of unforgettable horrors. The darkness was impenetrable. The stench was suffocating. The ground was full of mud-holes. Some of us sat on corpses. Others rested their feet on dead men. One could not stretch out a hand without touching a lifeless body. We were hungry. We were cold. Our flesh crept in the dreadful surroundings. I wanted to get up. My hand sought support. It fell on the face of a corpse, stuck against the wall. I screamed, slipped and fell. My fingers buried themselves in the torn abdomen of a body.

I was seized with horror such as I had never experienced, and shrieked hysterically. My cries were heard in the officers' dugout, and a man was sent with an electric torch to rescue Yashka, whom they had supposed to be wounded. It was warm and comfortable in the dugout, as it had previously been used by the enemy's regimental staff. I was given some tea, and little by little I recovered my self-control.

The entrance of the dugout was of course now facing the enemy. He knew its exact position and concentrated his fire on it. Although bomb-proof, it soon began to collapse under the rain of shells. Some of these blocked the entrance almost completely with debris. Finally, a shell penetrated the roof, putting out the light, killing five and wounding several. I lay in a corner, buried under wreckage, soldiers and officers, some of whom were wounded and others dead. The groans were indescribable. As the screech of a new shell was heard overhead I believed death to be close at hand. There was no question of making an immediate effort to extricate myself and escape while the bombs were still crashing into the hole. When, with the dawn, the bombardment finally ceased, and I was saved, I could hardly believe the evidence of my own senses that I was unhurt.

---

19. Actually known as the Battle of Naroch (or Narach), for the lake in the region. It was designed to precede the major 1916 offensive and was carried out on the request of the French, in hopes of relieving the pressure they were feeling from Germany on the Western Front, at Verdun. Interestingly, two other women fighters, Yevgenia Vorontsova and Yekaterina Yepachintseva, were honored for their bravery under fire in this operation. The huge losses (over 70,000 casualties) and the eventual Russian defeat in this battle played a large part in General Alexei Evert's unwillingness to expedite the summer 1916 offensive, feeling another attack was futile.

The following day I discovered the body of Lieutenant Bobrov. His presentiment was right after all. He was an intrepid fighter, and a man of noble impulses. I fulfilled his wish, and had his ring and letter sent through the physician to his wife. Our own Regiment had two thousand wounded. And when the dead were gathered from the field and carried out of the trenches, there were long, long rows of them stretched out in the sun awaiting eternal rest in the immense common grave that was being dug for them in the rear.

With bowed heads and bleeding hearts we paid final homage to our comrades. They had laid down their lives like true heroes, without suspecting that they were being sacrificed to no purpose by a vile traitor.[20]

On March 10th, still suffering from the effects of my dreadful night among the corpses, I was sent to the Divisional Hospital for a three days' rest. I was back in the trenches on the 14th, when another advance was ordered. The German positions were not yet strongly fortified, and we captured their first line without serious losses. Then there was another few days' respite, during which our ranks were reformed.

Early in the morning of March 16th, after an ineffectual bombardment of the enemy's position by our artillery, the signal to go over the top was given. We advanced in the face of a stubborn German fire, dashing through No Man's Land only to find the enemy's wire defenses intact. There was nothing to do but retreat. It was while running back that a bullet struck me in the right leg, shattering the bone. I fell. Within a hundred feet of me ran the enemy's first line. Bullets whizzed over my head, pursuing my fleeing comrades.

I was not alone. Others were groaning not far from me. Some prayed for death. ... I grew thirsty. I had lost a great deal of blood. But I knew it was useless to move. The sun rose in the east, only to be obscured by grey clouds.

"Shall I be rescued?" I wondered." Perhaps the enemy's stretcher-bearer will pick me up soon. But no, he just fired at that soldier yonder who raised himself in an effort to move."

I pressed myself closer to the ground. I seemed to hear voices coming near. I held my breath in suspense.

"I am a German prisoner!" I thought. Then the voices died away, and again my thirst tortured me.

"Holy Mother, when will help come? Or am I doomed to lie here indefinitely until I fall into unconsciousness and die?... The sun is already in mid-heaven.

---

20. The order to stand down from the attack actually came from Evert, who also had a German sounding name. During the war, it was a common belief among soldiers and the public that there was a broad swath of military and civilian leadership with "German blood" who were working against Russia's defeat of Germany in every way possible.

My comrades are having their soup and warm tea. What would I not give for a glass of hot tea! The Germans are eating, too. I can hear the clatter of their pans. Why, I can even smell faintly the steam from their soup."

It is calm now. Only rarely a sniper's bullet crosses the field... Night, night, night... How I wish for night! "Certainly our men are not going to let all of us perish here. Besides, they must have missed me by now. They surely won't let Yashka, dead or alive, lie in the field. So there is hope."

The thought of my comrades' discovery of my absence gave me new strength. The seconds seemed hours and the minutes days, but the shadows arrived at last, creeping toward the side where the sun had disappeared. Then came darkness and rescue was not long in coming. Our brave stretcher-bearers, aided by some of the soldiers, were out on their pious mission. Cautiously, they moved nearer and nearer to the German line, and finally picked me up. Yes, it was Yashka whom they carried into our trenches.

My comrades were filled with rejoicing. "Yashka, alive! God speed you to recovery, Yashka!" I could only reply in a whisper. They took me to the first-aid station, cleansed my wound and dressed it. I suffered much. Then I was sent on to Moscow, where I lay in the Yekaterina Hospital, ward Number 20.

I was lonely in the hospital, where I spent nearly three months. The other patients would have their visitors or receive parcels from home, but nobody visited me, nobody sent anything to me. March, April, May came and went in the monotony of ward Number 20. Finally, one day in the beginning of June, I was declared fit to return to the fighting line. My regiment was just then being transferred to Lutsk front. On June 20 I caught up with it. The welcome I received surpassed even that of the previous year. Fruit and sweets were showered upon me. The soldiers were in a happy mood. The Germans had just been driven back at this sector by General Brusilov for a great many miles.[21] The country was interspersed with their evacuated positions. Here and there enemy corpses were still unburied. Our men, though overjoyed, were worn out by forced marches and the long pursuit.

It was midsummer, and the heat was prostrating. We marched on June 21 a distance of ten miles and stopped for rest. Many of our number collapsed, and we felt too worn out to go on, but the Commander implored us to keep up, promising a rest in the trenches. It was thirteen miles to the front line, and we reached it on the same day.

---

21. General Alexei Brusilov (1853-1926) was one of the first to recognize that the days of the cavalry were over, given the realities of modern warfare. His innovations led to some of Russia's greatest successes in World War I, including the Brusilov Offensive in 1916, which could well have been a breakthrough victory, had not other generals and leaders waffled at the decisive moment. After the Revolution, he joined the Bolsheviks.

As we marched along we observed on both sides of the road that crops which had not been destroyed in the course of the fighting were ripening. The fighting line ran near a village called Dubova Korchma. We found in its neighborhood a country seat hastily abandoned by the Germans. The estate was full of cattle, fowl, potatoes and other food. That night we had us a royal feast.

We occupied abandoned German trenches. It was not the time for rest. The artillery opened fire early in the evening and boomed ceaselessly throughout the night. It could mean nothing but an immediate attack. We were not mistaken. At four in the morning we received word that the Germans had left their positions and started for our side. At this moment our beloved Commander, Grishaninov, was struck to the ground. He was wounded. We attended to him promptly and despatched him to the rear. There was no time to waste. We met the advancing Germans with repeated volleys, and when they approached our positions we climbed out and charged them with fixed bayonets.

Suddenly a terrific explosion deafened me, and I fell to the ground. A German shell had come my way, a shell I shall never forget, as part of it I still carry in my body.

I felt frightful pains in my back. I had been hit by a fragment at the end of the spinal column. My agony lasted long enough to attract a couple of soldiers. Then I became unconscious. They carried me to a dressing station. The wound was so serious that the physician in charge did not believe that I could survive. I was placed in an ambulance and taken to Lutsk. I required electrical treatment, but the Lutsk Hospitals were not supplied with the necessary apparatus. It was decided to send me to Kiev. My condition, however, was so grave that for three days the doctors considered it dangerous to move me.

In Kiev, the stream of wounded was so great that I was compelled to lie in the street on a stretcher for a couple of hours before I was taken to hospital. I was informed, after an X-ray examination, that a fragment of shell was imbedded in my body and asked if I wished an operation to have it removed. I could not imagine living with a piece of shell in my flesh, and so requested its removal. Whether because of my condition or for some other reason, the surgeon finally decided not to operate, and told me that I would have to be sent either to Petrograd or to Moscow for treatment. As I was given the choice, I decided on Moscow, because I had spent the spring months of the year in the Yekaterina Hospital there.

The wound in the spine paralyzed me to such an extent that I could not move even a finger. I lay in the Moscow Hospital hovering between life and death for some weeks, resembling a log more than a human body. Only my mind was active and my heart full of pain.

Every day I was massaged, carried on a stretcher and bathed. Then the physician would attend me, probing my wound with iodine, and treating it with electricity, after which I was bathed again and my wound dressed. This daily procedure was inconceivable torture, in spite of the morphine injected into me. There was little peace in the ward in which I was placed. All the beds were occupied by serious cases, and the groans and moans must have reached to Heaven.

Four months I lay paralysed, never expecting to recover. My diet consisted of milk and kasha, with which I was fed by an attendant. On many a dreary day Death would have been a welcome visitor. It seemed so futile, so hopeless to remain alive in such a state, but the doctor, who was a Jew, and very kind-hearted, would not give up hope. He persisted in his daily treatment, praising my stoicism and encouraging me with kind words. His faith was finally rewarded.

At the end of four months I began to feel life stirring once again in my helpless body. My finger could move! What a joy that was! In a few days I could turn my head a little and stretch my arm. It was a wonderful sensation, this gradual resurrection of my lifeless members. To be able to close my fingers after four months of paralysis! It thrilled me. To be able to bend a knee that had been torpid so long! It seemed like a miracle. And I offered thanks to God with all the fervour that I could command.

One day a woman by the name of Darya Maximovna Vasilyeva came to see me. I searched my mind in vain for an acquaintance of that name as I asked that she should be brought to my bed. But as I was perhaps the only patient in the ward that had no visitors and received no parcels it may be imagined how pleased I was. She introduced herself as the mother of Stepan, of my Company. Of course, I knew Stepan well. He was a student before the war and volunteered as a junior officer.

"Stepan has just written me," Madame Vasilyeva said, "begging me to come and see you. 'Go to the Ekaterina Hospital and visit our Yashka,' he writes. 'She is lonely there, and I want you to do for her as much as you would do for me, for she saved my life once, and has been like a mother to the boys here. She is a respectable, patriotic young woman and my interest in her is simply that of a comrade, for she is a soldier, and a brave and gallant soldier.' He praised you so much, my dear, that my heart went out to you. May God bless you."

She brought me some delicacies, and we became friends immediately. I told her all about her son and our life in the trenches. She wept and wondered how I had borne it. Her affection for me grew so strong that she used to visit me several times a week, although she lived on the outskirts of the city. Her husband was assistant superintendent at a factory and they occupied a small but comfortable dwelling in keeping with their means. Darya Maximovna herself was a middle-aged woman simply dressed and of distinguished appearance. She had a married daughter, Tonechka, and another son, a youth of about seventeen, who was a student at the high-school.

My friend helped me to regain my spirits, and I made good progress towards recovery. As I gradually regained full control of my muscles and nerves, I used to tease the doctor sometimes:

"Well, doctor," I would say to him. "I am going to war again,"

"No, no," he would answer, "there will be no more war for you, my dear."

I wondered whether I really would be able to return to the front. There was that fragment of shell still in my body. The doctor would not extract it. He advised me to wait until I had completely recovered and have it removed at some future date by means of an abdominal operation, as the fragment is lodged in the omentum.[22] I have not yet had the opportunity to undergo such an operation, and I still have that piece of shell in my body. The slightest indigestion causes me to suffer from it even now.

I had to learn to walk, as if I had never mastered that art before. I was not successful at the first attempt. Having asked the doctor for a pair of crutches I tried to stand up, but fell back weak and helpless on the bed. The attendants, however, placed me in a wheelchair and took me out into the garden. This movement gave me great pleasure. Once, in the absence of my attendant, I tried to stand up alone and walk a step. It was very painful, but I maintained my balance, and tears of joy came streaming down my cheeks. I was jubilant.

It was not until a week later, however, that I was permitted by the doctor to walk a little, supported by the attendants. But I had taken only ten steps, beaming with triumph and making every effort to overcome my pain, when I collapsed and fainted. The nurses were alarmed and called the doctor who told them to be more cautious in the future. I steadily improved, however, and a couple of weeks later I was able to walk. Naturally, I did not feel sure of my legs at first; they trembled and seemed very weak. Gradually they regained their former strength and at the end of six months spent in the hospital I was again in possession of all my faculties.

---

22. A layer of peritoneum that surrounds abdominal organs.

CHAPTER IX
EIGHT HOURS IN GERMAN HANDS

The morning on which I was taken before the military medical commission I was in high spirits. It was a late December day, but my heart was aglow as I was led into the large room in which about two hundred other patients were waiting for the examination which would decide whether they were to be sent home or were considered fit to be returned to the front.

The chairman of the commission was a General. As my turn came and he reached the name of Maria Bochkareva, he thought it a mistake and corrected it to Marin Bochkarev. By that name I was called out of the crowd.

The General shouted the order that was given to every soldier awaiting discharge.

"Take off your clothes."

I walked up resolutely and threw off my clothes.

"A woman!" went up from a couple of hundred throats, followed by an outburst of laughter that shook the building. The members of the commission were too amazed for words.

"What the devil!" cried the General." Why did you undress?"

"I am a soldier, Excellency, and I obey orders without question," I replied.

"Well, well. Hurry up and dress," came the order.

"How about the examination. Excellency?" I queried, as I put my things on.

"That's all right. You are passed."

In view of the seriousness of the injury I had sustained, the commission offered me a couple of months' leave, but I declined it and requested to be sent to the front in a few days. Supplied with fifteen rubles and a railway ticket, I left the hospital and went to Darya Maximovna, who had invited me previously to stay with her for a little time. It was a short visit, lasting only three days, but a very happy one. It was so pleasant to be in a home again, to eat home food and to be under the care of a woman who became a second mother to me. With packages for myself and Stepan, and the blessings of the whole family following me, I left Moscow from the Nikolayevsky Station.[23] The train was crowded and there was only standing room.

On the platform my attention was attracted to a poor woman with a little baby in her arms, another mite on the floor and a girl of about five hanging on to her skirt. All the woman's property was packed in a single bag. The children were crying for bread, the woman tried to calm them, evidently in dread of something. It touched my heart to watch this little group, and I offered some bread to the children.

Then the woman confided in me the cause for her fear. She had no money and no ticket and expected to be put off at the next station. She was the wife of a soldier from a village in German hands and was now bound for a town three thousand versts away, where she had some relatives. I felt that something must be done for this woman, and I made an appeal to the soldiers who filled the car, but they did not respond at first.

"She is the wife of a soldier, of one like yourselves," I said. "Suppose she were the wife of one of you! For all you know, the wives of some of you here may be wandering about the country in a similar state. Come, let us get off at the next station, go to the stationmaster and ask that she may be allowed to go to her destination."

The soldiers were moved and they helped me to take the woman and her belongings off the train at the next stop. We went to the station-master, who was very kind, but explained that he could do nothing in the matter. "I have no right to give permission to travel without a ticket, and I can't distribute free tickets," he said, and he sent us to the military commandant. I went with the woman, having been deserted by the soldiers who had heard the train whistle and did not want to miss it. I waited for another train.

The commandant repeated the words of the stationmaster. He had no right to provide her with a military pass, he said.

"No right!" I exclaimed, beside myself. "She is the wife of a soldier and her husband is probably now, at this very moment, going into battle to defend the country, while you, safe and well-fed in the rear here, won't even take care of his wife and children. It is an outrage. Look at the woman. She needs medical attention, and her children are starved."

"And who are you?" sharply asked the commandant.

"I will show you who I am," I answered, taking off my medals and cross and showing him my certificate. "I have shed enough blood to be entitled to demand justice for the helpless wife of a soldier."

23. Now Leningradsky Station, the oldest of Moscow's railway stations.

But the commandant turned his back on me and went away. There was nothing to be done but to make a collection. I went to the First-Class waiting room, which was filled with officers and well-to-do passengers, took my cap in my hand and went round, begging for a poor soldier's wife. When I had finished there were eighty rubles in the cap. With this money I went to the commandant again, and handed it to him with a request that he should provide accommodation for the woman and her children. She did not know how to express her gratitude to me.

The next train came in. I never before saw one so packed. There could be no thought of getting inside a car. The only space available was on the top of a coach. There were plenty of passengers even there. With the aid of some soldiers I climbed on to the top, where I spent two days and two nights. It was impossible to get off at every station to take a walk. We had to send someone even to fetch the tea, and our food consisted of that and bread.

Accidents were not uncommon. On the very roof on which I travelled a man fell asleep, rolled off, and was killed instantaneously. I narrowly escaped a similar fate. I began to doze and drifted to the edge and had not a soldier caught me in the nick of time I should undoubtedly have fallen off. We finally arrived at Kiev.

That journey on the train was a symbol of the country's condition in the winter of 1916. The government machinery was breaking down. The soldiers had lost faith in their leaders, and there was a general feeling that they were being sent in the thousands merely to be slaughtered. Rumors flew thick and fast. The old soldiers had been killed off and the fresh drafts were impatient for the end of the war. The spirit of 1914 was no more.

In Kiev I had to obtain information as to the position of my regiment. It was now near the town of Berestechko. In my absence the men had advanced ten miles. The train from Kiev was also very crowded and there was only standing room. At the stations we sent some of the soldiers to fill our kettles with hot water. The men could seldom get in and out through the entrances, so they used the windows. The train passed through Zhitomir and Zhimerinka on the way to Lutsk. There I changed to a branch line, going to the station of Verba, within twenty miles of our position.

> *That journey on the train was a symbol of the country's condition in the winter of 1916. The government machinery was breaking down. The soldiers had lost faith in their leaders, and there was a general feeling that they were being sent in the thousands merely to be slaughtered.*

It was muddy on the road to the front. Overhead flew whole flocks of aeroplanes, raining bombs. I got used to them. In the afternoon there was a downpour, and I was thoroughly soaked. Dead tired, with water streaming from my clothes, I arrived in the evening within three miles of the first line. There was a regimental supply train camping on both sides of the road. I approached a sentry and asked:

"What regiment is billeted here?"

"The Twenty-Eighth Polotsk Regiment."

My heart leaped for joy. The soldier did not recognize me. He was a new man. But the others must have told him of me.

"I am Yashka," I said.

That was a password. They all knew the name and had heard from the veterans of the regiment many stories about me. I was taken to the Colonel in command of the supply train, a queer old man who kissed me on both cheeks and jumped about, clapping his hands and shouting, "Yashka! Yashka!"

He was kind-hearted and immediately began to look after my comfort. He promptly ordered an orderly to bring a new outfit and gave instructions for the bath used by the officers to be prepared for me. Clean and in the new uniform, I accepted the invitation to sup with the Colonel. There were several other officers at the table and all were glad to see me. The news spread that Yashka had arrived, and some soldiers could not restrain their desire to shake hands with me. Every now and then there would be a meek knock at the door and in answer to the Colonel's question, "Who's there?" a plaintive voice would say: "Excellency, may I be allowed to see Yashka?"

In time quite a number of comrades were admitted into the house. One part of it was occupied by the owner, a widow with a young daughter. I spent the night with the latter and in the morning started out to the front. Some of our companies were in reserve and my progress became a triumphal journey. I was feasted on the way and given several ovations.

I presented myself to the Commander of the Regiment, who invited me to dine that afternoon with the Regimental Staff, certainly the first case of an ordinary soldier receiving such an invitation in the history of the Regiment. At dinner, the Commander toasted me, telling the story of my work with the Regiment and wishing me many more years of such service.

At the conclusion, he pinned a cross of the 3rd Degree on my breast, and marked with a pencil three stripes on my shoulder, thus promoting me to the grade of senior non-commissioned officer.[24] The Staff crowded round

---

24. Three stripes indicated the rank of Senior Warden, or Senior Under-Officer (Старший унтер-офицер).

me, pressing my hands, praising me and expressing their good wishes. I was profoundly moved by this display of cordial appreciation and affection on the part of the officers. This was my reward for all the suffering I had undergone.

And it was a reward worth having. What did I care for a wound in the spine and four months' paralysis if this was the return that I received for my sacrifice? Trenches filled with bloody corpses held no horror for me then. No Man's Land seemed quite an attractive place in which to spend a day with a bleeding leg. The screech of shells and the whistle of bullets presented themselves like music to my imagination. Ah, life was not so bleak and meaningless, after all. It had its moments of bliss that compensated for years of torment and misery.

The commander had, in his order of the day, stated the fact of my return and promotion. He furnished me with an orderly to show me the way to the trenches. Again I was hailed by everybody as I emerged from the dugout of the Commander of the Company, who had placed me in charge of a platoon of seventy men. In this capacity I had to keep an inventory of the supplies and equipment of my men, a soldier acting as clerk under my instructions.

Our positions were on the bank of the Styr, which is very narrow and shallow at that point. On the opposite bank were the German trenches. Several hundred feet from us was a bridge across the stream which had been left intact by both sides. At our end of it we maintained a post while the enemy kept a similar watch at the opposite end. Our line was very uneven, owing to the irregularity of the river's course.

The Germans were very persistent in mine-throwing. However, the mines traveled so slowly that we could take cover before they fell on our side. My Company occupied a position close to the enemy's first line.

I had not spent a month in the trenches when a local battle occurred which resulted in my capture by the Germans. The latter had continued their mine-throwing operations for a period of about twelve days so regularly that we grew accustomed to them and were not expecting an attack. Besides, it was past the time of year for active fighting, and the cold was intense.

One morning about six o'clock, when we had turned in for our daily sleep, we were suddenly awakened by a tremendous "Hurrah!" We nervously seized our rifles and peeped through the loop-holes. Great Heavens! There, within a hundred feet of us, in front and in the rear, the Germans were crossing the Styr! Before we had time to organize resistance they were upon us, capturing five hundred of our men. I was among the number.

We were brought before the German Staff for examination. Every one of us was tormented with questions, intended to extract valuable military information. Threats were bestowed on those who refused to disclose anything. Some cowards among us, especially those of non-Russian stock, gave away important facts. As the examination was proceeding, our artillery on the other side opened up a violent bombardment of the German defenses. It was evident that the German Commander had not many reserves, as he made frantic appeals by telephone for support. It required a considerable force to keep guard over us and an even larger force to take us to the rear. As the enemy expected a Russian attack at any moment, it was decided not to remove us until help arrived.

"So I am a German prisoner," I thought. "How unexpected! There is still hope that our comrades on the other side will come to our rescue. Only, every minute is precious. They must hurry or we are lost. Now my turn is coming. What shall I tell them? I must deny being a soldier and invent some kind of a story."

"I am a woman and not a soldier," I announced as soon as I was called.

"Are you of noble blood?" I was asked.

"Yes," I answered, promptly deciding to claim that I was a Red Cross nurse, dressed in man's uniform, in order to pay a visit to my husband, an officer in the front line trenches.

"Have you many women fighting in the ranks?" was the next question.

"I don't know. I told you that I was not a soldier."

"What were you doing in the trenches then?"

"I came to see my husband, who is an officer of the Regiment."

"Why did you shoot, then? The soldiers tell that you shot at them."

"I did it to defend myself. I was afraid to be captured. I serve as a Red Cross nurse in the rear hospital, and came over to the fighting line for a visit."

The Russian fire was growing hotter every minute. Some of our shells wounded not only enemy soldiers but several of the captives. It was past noon, but the Germans were too nervous to eat their lunch. The expected reserves were not forthcoming, and there was every sign of a fierce counter-attack by our troops.

At two o'clock our soldiers went over the top and started for the German positions. The enemy Commander decided to retreat with his batch of prisoners to the second line rather than defend the front trenches. It was a critical moment. As we were lined up, the "Hurrah" of our comrades reached us. It stimulated us to a spontaneous decision.

We threw ourselves, five hundred strong, at our captors, wrested many of their rifles and bayonets and engaged in a ferocious hand-to-hand combat, just as our men rushed through the torn wire entanglements into the trenches. The confusion was indescribable, the killing merciless. I grasped five hand grenades that lay near me and threw them at a group of about ten Germans. They must have all been killed. Our entire line across the river was advancing at the same time, The first German line was occupied by our troops and both banks of the Styr were then in our hands.

Thus ended my captivity. I was in German hands for a period of only eight hours and amply avenged even this brief stay. There was great activity in our ranks for a couple of days. We fortified the newly won positions and prepared for another attack. Two days later we received the signal to advance. But again our artillery had failed to cut the German wire defenses. After pushing on under a devastating fire and incurring heavy losses, we were compelled to retreat, leaving many of our comrades wounded and dying on the field of battle.

Our Commander improvised a relief party by calling for twenty volunteers. I responded among the first. Provided with twenty red crosses which we prominently displayed, and leaving our rifles in the trenches, we went out in the open daylight to rescue the wounded. I was allowed to proceed by the Germans almost to their barbed wire. Then, as I leaned over a wounded man whose leg was broken, I heard the click of a trigger and immediately lay flat on the ground. Five bullets whistled over me, one after another. Most of them hit the wounded soldier, who was killed. I continued to lie motionless, and the German sniper was evidently satisfied that he had killed me as well. I remained in this position till night, when I crawled back to our trenches.

Of the twenty Red Cross volunteers only five returned alive.

The following day an order was issued by the Commander thanking all those soldiers who had been captured three days before and had resolved to save themselves by fighting their captors. My name appeared first on the list. Those of us who had refused to give any information to the enemy were praised in the order. One soldier, who had revealed to the Germans a great deal of important information, was executed. I was recommended for a cross of the 2nd Degree, but, being a woman, I received only a medal of the 3rd Degree.

The opening of the year 1917 found us resting two miles in the rear. There was much fun and merriment in the reserve billets. Although the discipline was as strict as ever, the relations between the officers and men had, in the course of the three and a half years of the war, undergone a complete transformation.

The older officers, trained in pre-war conditions, were no longer to be found, having died in battle or been disabled. The new junior officers, all young men taken from civil life, many of them former students and school teachers, were liberal in their views and very humane in their conduct. They mixed freely with the men in the ranks and allowed us more liberty than we had ever enjoyed. At the New Year festival we all danced together. These new relations were not entirely due to the new attitude from above. In a sense, they were generated from below by a dumb and yet potent undercurrent of restlessness.

We were reviewed before returning to the front line by General Valuyev, the Commander of the Fifth Corps. I was presented to him by the Commander. The General shook my hand warmly, remarking that he had heard many praiseworthy things of me.

Our positions were now on a hill, in the vicinity of Zelyonaya Kolonia, while the enemy was at our feet in the valley. The trenches we occupied had been in German hands some time before.

It was late in January when I made an expedition into No Man's Land at the head of a patrol of fifteen men. We crawled along a ditch that had once been a German communication trench. It ran along a very exposed part of the field and we exercised the utmost caution. As we came near to the enemy's trench line I thought I heard German conversation. Leaving ten men behind, with instructions to come to our aid in case of a fight, five of us crept forward at a snail's pace and with perfect noiselessness. The German voices grew clearer and clearer.

Finally we beheld a German listening-post. There were four of them, all seated with their backs toward us. Their rifles were scattered on the ground while they warmed their hands over a fire. Two of my men stretched their hands out, reached the rifles and removed them. It was a slow and difficult operation. The Germans chattered on unconcernedly. As I was cautiously reaching for the third rifle two of the Germans, having apparently heard a noise, made as if they were about to turn.

In an instant my men were upon them. The two were bayoneted before I was able to realize what was happening. It had been my intention to bring in the four alive. The other two Germans were safe in our hands.

In all my experience of patrol duty, and I must have taken part in at least a hundred expeditions into No Man's Land, it was the first case of a German listening post being caught in such a manner. We returned triumphantly with our prizes.

One of the prisoners was a tall, red-headed fellow, the other, who wore a pince-nez, was evidently an educated man. We took them to Regimental Headquarters, accompanied on the way by much cheering and congratulations. The Commander wanted to know the details of the capture and had them written down word for word. He congratulated me, pressing my hand, and so did all the other officers, telling me that my name would live for ever in the annals of the Polotsk Regiment. I was recommended for a gold cross of the 1st Degree and given two days' leave for rest in the village.

At the end of the two days, my Company joined me in the reserve. Strange things were occurring in our midst. In subdued voices the men repeated dark rumors about Rasputin's death.[25] Wild stories about his connections with the Court and Germany were communicated from mouth to mouth. The spirit of insubordination was growing among the soldiers, though at that time it was still kept within bounds. The men were weary, terribly weary of the war. "How long shall we continue this fighting?" and "What are we fighting for?" were on the lips of everybody. It was the fourth winter and still there was no end in sight.

Our men were genuinely anxious to solve the great puzzle that the war had become to them. Hadn't it been proved again and again that the officers at Headquarters were selling them to the enemy? Hadn't a multitude of reports reached them that the Court was pro-German? Hadn't they heard of the War Minister placed under arrest and charged with being a traitor?[26] Wasn't it clear, therefore, that the Government, the official class, was in league with the enemy? Then, why continue this carnage indefinitely? If the Government was in alliance with Germany, what prevented it from concluding peace? Was it the desire to have millions more of them slaughtered?

This was the riddle that forced itself upon the peasant mind. It was complicated by a hundred other suggestions that were injected into his brain from various channels. Depressed in spirit, discouraged and sullen in appearance was the Russian soldier in February 1917.

We returned to our positions and took up the heavy burden. It was not long before an attack was organized against the German line. Our artillery again displayed little effectiveness and again we climbed out of the trenches and swept across No Man's Land while the enemy's wire defenses were intact. It was not the first wave of Russian breasts that had beaten itself in vain against that deadly barrier, to be hurled back with grave losses without even coming to grips with the foe. But each of those waves had left its drop of bitterness in the hearts of the survivors. And it was a particularly strong draught of bitterness that this last futile attack had left in the souls of the soldiers upon our sector.

Nevertheless, in February 1917, the front was unprepared for the eruption that was soon to shake the world. The front maintained its fierce hatred for the Germans and could not conceive of a righteous peace, save through the

---

25. Grigory Rasputin, the influential and charismatic monk, was murdered in St. Petersburg on December 30, 2016.

26. General Vladimir Sukhomlinov, Minister of War, was arrested on April 20, 1916, and later accused him of abuse of power, corruption, depositing millions of rubbles at the Deutsche Bank in Berlin, and high treason, after some of his close associates were convicted of espionage on behalf of Germany.

efficient organization of a gigantic offensive against the enemy. The obstacle in the way of such an offensive was the traitorous Government. Against this Government were directed the indignation and suppressed discontent of the rank and file. But so old, so stable, so deep-rooted was the institution of Tsarism that, with all their secret contempt for the Court, with all their secret hatred for the officials of the Government, the armies at the front were not ripe yet for a conscious and deliberate rising.

PART THREE

REVOLUTION

.

CHAPTER X
THE REVOLUTION AT THE FRONT

The first warning of the approaching storm reached us through a soldier from our Company who had returned from leave at Petrograd.

"Oh, heaven!" he said. "If you but knew what is going on behind your backs! Revolution! Everywhere they talk of overthrowing the Tsar. The capital is flaming with revolution."

These words spread like wildfire among the men. They gathered in knots and discussed the significance of the report. Would it mean peace? Would they get land and freedom? Or would it mean another huge offensive before the end of the war? The arguments, of course, took place in whispers, behind the backs of the officers. The consensus of opinion seemed to be that revolution meant preparation for a general attack against the Germans in order to win a victory before the conclusion of peace.

For several days the air was charged with excitement and expectation. Everybody felt that earth-shaking events were taking place and our hearts echoed the distant rumblings of the storm. There was something reticent about the looks and manners of the officers, as if they were keeping important news to themselves.

Finally, the joyful news arrived. The Commander gathered the entire Regiment to read to us the glorious words of the first manifesto, together with the famous Order No. 1. The miracle had happened! Tsarism, which had enslaved us and flourished on the blood and sweat of the toiler, was overthrown. Freedom, Equality and Brotherhood! How sweet were these words to our ears! We were transported. There were tears of joy, embraces, dancing. It all seemed a dream, a wonderful dream. Who could have believed that the hated regime would be destroyed so easily and in our own lifetime?

The Commander read to us the manifesto, which concluded with a fervent appeal to us to hold the line with greater vigilance than ever, now that we were free citizens, and to defend our newly won liberty from the attacks of the Kaiser and his supporters. Would we defend our freedom? A multitude of throats shouted in a chorus, that passed over No Man's Land and reverberated in the German trenches, "Yes, we will!"

Would we swear allegiance to the Provisional Government, whose desire it was that we should prepare to drive the Germans out of Free Russia before returning home to divide up the land?

"We swear!" thundered thousands of men, raising their right hands, and thoroughly alarming the enemy.

Then came Order No. 1, signed by the Petrograd Soviet of Workmen and Soldiers. Soldiers and officers were now equal, it declared. All the citizens of Free Russia were henceforth equal. There would be no more discipline. The hated officers were enemies of the people and should no longer be obeyed and kept at their posts. The common soldier would now rule the army. Let the rank and file elect their best men and institute committees; let there be Company, Regimental, Corps and Army committees.

We were dazzled by this wealth of fine sounding phrases. The men went about as if intoxicated. For four days the festival continued unabated, so wild with delight were the men. The Germans could not at first understand the cause of our rejoicings. When they learned it they ceased firing.

There were meetings, meetings and meetings. Day and night the Regiment seemed to be in continuous session, listening to speeches that dwelt almost exclusively on the words of peace and freedom. The men were hungry for beautiful phrases and gloated over them.

All duty was abandoned in the first few days. While the great upheaval had affected me profoundly, and the first day or two I shared completely the ecstasy of the men, I awoke early to a sense of responsibility. I gathered from the manifestoes and speeches that what was demanded of us was to hold the line with still more energy than before. Was not this the meaning of the revolution so far as we were concerned? When I put this question to the soldiers they answered in the affirmative, but they had not the strength of will to tear themselves away from the magic circle of speechmaking and visions. Such was their dazed condition, that they seemed to me no longer sane. The front had become a veritable lunatic asylum.

One day, in the first week of the revolution, I ordered a soldier to take up duty at the listening-post. He refused.

"I will take no orders from a *baba*,'" he sneered, "I can do as I please. We have freedom now."

It was a bitter shock to me. Why, this very same soldier would have gone through fire for me a week before. And now he was sneering at me. It seemed incredible and overwhelming.

"Ha, ha," he jeered. "You can go yourself."

Flushed with vexation I seized a rifle and answered:

"Can I? I will show you how a free citizen ought to guard his freedom!"

And I climbed over the top and made my way to the listening-post where I remained on duty for the full two hours.

I talked to the soldiers, appealing to their sense of honor and arguing that the revolution imposed greater responsibilities upon the man in the ranks. They agreed that the defense of the country was the most important task confronting us. But had not the revolution brought them also freedom, with the injunction to take upon themselves the control of the army, and to abolish discipline? The men were full of enthusiasm, but obedience was contrary to their ideas of liberty. Seeing that I could not get my men to perform their duties, I went to the Commander of the Company and asked to be released from the army and sent home.

"I see no good in staying here and doing nothing," I said. "If this is war, I want to be out of it. I can do nothing with my men."

"Have you gone out of your mind, Yashka?" said the Commander. "Why, if you, who are a peasant yourself, one of them, beloved by all the rank and file, cannot remain, what can we officers do? It is our duty as soldiers to stay to the last, until the men come to their senses. I am having my own troubles, Yashka," he confided to me, in a low voice. "I cannot have my way, either. So you see, we are all in the same boat. We have just got to put up with it."

It was altogether contrary to my inclinations, but I remained. Little by little things improved. The soldiers' committees began to exercise their functions, but they did not interfere with the purely military department of our life. Those of the officers who had been disliked by the men, or whose records were typical of Tsarist officials, disappeared with the revolution. Even Colonel Shtubendorf, the Commander of the Regiment, had gone, retiring perhaps because of his German name. Our new Commander was Kudryavtsev, a popular officer.

Discipline was gradually re-established. It was not the old discipline. Its basis was no longer dread of punishment. It was a discipline founded on the high sense of responsibility that was soon instilled into the grey ranks of our army. True, there was no fighting between us and the enemy. There were even the beginnings of that fatal fraternization plague which was later to be the ruin of the mighty Russian Army. But the soldiers responded to the appeals from the Provisional Government and the Soviet in the early weeks of the spring of 1917. They were ready to carry out unflinchingly any order from Petrograd.

Those were still the days of immense possibilities. The men worshipped the distant figures in the rear who had brought them the boon of liberty and equality. We knew almost nothing of the various parties and factions. Peace was the sole thought of the men. They were told that peace could not come without defeating or overthrowing the Kaiser. Therefore, we all expected the word for a general advance. Had that word been given at that time, nothing in the world could have withstood our pressure. Nothing. The revolution had given birth to elemental forces in our hearts that defied and ever will defy description.

Then there began a procession of speech-makers. There were delegates from the army, there were members of the Duma, there were emissaries of the Petrograd Soviet. Almost every day there was a meeting, and almost every other day there were elections. We sent delegates to Corps Headquarters and delegates to Army Headquarters, delegates to a congress in Petrograd and delegates to consult with the Government. The speakers were almost all eloquent. They painted beautiful pictures of Russia's future, of universal brotherhood, of happiness and prosperity. The soldiers' eyes would light up with the glow of hope. More than once even I was caught by those eloquent and enticing phrases. The rank and file were carried away to an enchanted land by the orators and rewarded them with tremendous applause.

There were speakers of a different kind, too. These solemnly appealed for a realization of the immediate duty which the revolution imposed upon the shoulders of the army. Patriotism was their keynote. They called us to defend our country, to be ready at any moment for an attack to drive out the Germans and win the much-desired victory and peace. The soldiers responded to these calls to duty with equal enthusiasm. They swore that they were ready. Was there any doubt that they were? No. The Russian soldier loved his Mother Country before. He loved her now a hundred-fold more.

The first signs of spring arrived. The rivers had opened, the ice fields had thawed. It was muddy, but the earth was fragrant. The winds were laden with intoxicating odors. They were carrying across the vast fields and valleys of Mother Russia tidings of a new era. There was spring in our souls. It seemed that our long-suffering people and country were being restored to a new life and one wanted to live, live, live.

But there, a few hundred feet away, were the Germans. They were not free. Their souls did not commune with God. Their hearts knew not the immense joy of this wonderful spring. They were still slaves, and they would not let us alone in our freedom. They thrust themselves over the fair extent of our country and would not retire. They must be driven out before we could embark upon a life of peace. We were ready to drive them out. We were awaiting the order to leap at their throats and show them what Free Russia could do. But why was the order postponed? Why wait? Why not strike while the iron was hot?

Yet the iron was allowed to cool. There was a flood of talk in the rear; there was absolute inactivity at the front. And as hours grew into days and days into weeks there sprang forth out of this inactivity the first beginnings of fraternization.

"Come over here for a drink of tea!" a voice from our trenches would address itself across No Man's Land to the Germans. And voices from there would respond:

"Come over here for a drink of vodka!"

For several days they did not go beyond such mutual invitations. Then one morning a soldier from our ranks advanced openly into No Man's Land, announcing that he wanted to talk things over. He stopped in the center of the field, where he was met by a German and engaged in an argument. From both sides soldiers flocked to the debaters.

"Why do you continue the war?" asked our men. "We have overthrown the Tsar and we want peace, but your Kaiser insists on war. Get rid of your Kaiser and then both sides will go home."

"You don't know the truth," answered the German. "You are mistaken. Why, our Kaiser offered peace to all the Allies last winter. But your Tsar refused to make peace. And now your Allies are forcing Russia to continue in the war. We are always ready for peace."

I was with the soldiers in No Man's Land and saw how the German argument impressed them. Some of the Germans had brought vodka with them, which they gave to our soldiers. While they were returning to the positions, engaged in heated arguments over the story of the Kaiser's peace offer, Commander Kudryavtsev came out to rebuke them.

"What are you doing? Don't you know that the Germans are our enemies? They want to entrap you."

"Kill him!" a voice shouted in the crowd. "We have been deceived long enough! Kill him!"

The Commander got out of the way quickly before the crowd had caught up the shout of the ruffian. This incident, when the revolution was still in its infancy, was an early symptom of the malady to which the Russian army succumbed in months to come. It was still an easily curable malady. But where was the physician with foresight to diagnose the disease at its inception and conquer it while there was time?

We were relieved and sent to the reserve billets. There a mass meeting was organized in honor of a delegate from the Army Committee who came to address us. He was welcomed by Krylov, one of our most enlightened soldiers, who spoke well and to the point.

"So long as the Germans keep their Kaiser and obey him we will not have peace," he declared. "The Kaiser wants to rob Russia of many provinces and to enslave their populations. The German soldiers do his will just as you did the will of the Tsar. Isn't that the truth?"

"The truth! The truth, indeed! Right!" the multitude roared.

"Now," resumed Krylov, "the Kaiser liked the Tsar and was related to him. But the Kaiser does not and cannot love Free Russia. He is afraid that the German people will take a lesson from us and start a revolution in their country. He is, therefore, seeking to destroy our freedom because he wants to keep his throne. Is this plain?"

"Yes! Yes! Good! It's the truth!" shouted thousands of throats, cheering wildly for Krylov.

"Therefore," continued the speaker, "it is our duty to defend our country and our precious liberty from the Kaiser. If we don't destroy him, he will destroy us. If we defeat him, there will be a revolution in his country and the German people will get rid of him. Then our freedom will be secure. Then we shall go home and take possession of all the available land. But we can't return home with an enemy at our back. Can we?"

"No! No! No! Certainly not!" thundered the swaying mass of soldiers.

"And we can't make peace with a ruler who hates us at heart and who was the secret accomplice of the Tsar. Isn't this true?"

"True! True! True! Hurrah for Krylov!" bawled the vast gathering, applauding vigorously.

Then the delegate from the Army Committee mounted the speaker's stoop. The soldiers were in high spirits, thirsting for every word of enlightenment.

"Comrades!" the delegate began. "For three years we have bled, suffered from hunger and cold, confined in the muddy and vermin-infested trenches. Myriad of our brethren have been slaughtered, maimed for life, taken into captivity. Whose war was it? The Tsar's. He made us fight and perish while he and his associates revelled in wealth and luxury. Now the Tsar is no more. Why, then, comrades, should we continue his war? Do you want to lay down your lives again by the thousands?"

"No! No! No! We have had enough of war!" thousands of voices rang out.

"Well," continued the delegate, "I agree with you. We have had enough of war, indeed. You are told that our enemy is in front of us. But what about our enemies in the rear? What about the officers who are now leaving the front and fleeing to safety? What about the landowners who are holding fast to the large estates bestowed on them by former Tsars? What about the bourgeoisie who have sucked our blood for generations and grown rich through our sweat and toil? Where are they all now? What do they want us to do? They want you to fight the enemy here so that they, the enemies of the people, can pillage and loot in the rear! So that when you come home, if you live to come home, you will find all the land and the wealth of the country in their hands!"

"It is the truth! The truth! He's right!" interrupted the vast crowd.

"Now you have two enemies," resumed the speaker. "One is foreign and the other is of your own race. You can't fight both at once. If we continue the war, the enemy at your back will rob you of the freedom, the land and the rights that the revolution has won for you. Therefore, we must have peace with the Germans in order to be able to fight these bourgeois vampires. Isn't that so?"

"Yes! Yes! It's the truth! It's the truth! We want peace! We are tired of the war!" came in a chorus from every side."

The passions of the soldiers were inflamed. The delegate was right, they said. If they remained in the trenches they would be robbed of the land and of the fruits of the new freedom, they argued heatedly among themselves. My heart ached when I saw the effect of the orator's words. All the impression of Krylov's speech had been effaced. The very same men who so enthusiastically responded to his appeal to do their duty now applauded just as fervidly, if not more so, the appeal of the delegate for a fratricidal war. It maddened me. I could not control myself.

"You stupid fools!" I burst out. "You can be turned one minute one way and the next minute the opposite way... This is war! War, you understand, war! And in war there can be no compromise with the enemy.

"You stupid fools!" I burst out. "You can be turned one minute one way and the next minute the opposite way. Didn't you cheer Krylov when he said truly that the Kaiser was our enemy and that we must drive him out of Russia first, before we can have peace? And now you have been incited to start a civil war so that the Kaiser can simply walk over Russia and get the whole country into his power. This is war! War, you understand, war! And in war there can be no compromise with the enemy. Give him an inch and he will take a mile! Come, let us get to work. Let us fulfil our duty."

There was a commotion among the soldiers. Some expressed their dissatisfaction loudly.

"Why stand here and listen to this silly *baba*?" said one.

"Give her a blow!" shouted another.

"Kick her!" cried a third.

In a moment I was being roughly handled. Blows were showered on me from every side.

"What are you doing? Why, it's Yashka! Have you gone crazy?" I heard a friendly voice appeal to the men. Other comrades hurried to my aid and I was rescued without suffering much injury. But I decided to ask for leave to go home and get away from this war without warfare. I would not be thwarted by the Commander. No, not this time.

The following day Mikhail Rodzianko,[27] the President of the Duma, arrived at our sector. We were formed for review, and although the men were somewhat lax in discipline they made up for it in enthusiasm. Rodzianko was given a tumultuous welcome as he appeared before the crowd.

"The responsibility for Russia," he said, "which rested before on the shoulders of the Tsar and his Government now rests on the people, on you. This is what freedom means. It means that we must, of our own good will, defend the country against the foe. It means that we must all work together, forget our differences and quarrels and present a solid front to the Germans. They are subtle and hypocritical. They give you fair words, but their hearts are full of hatred. They claim to be your brothers, but they are your enemies. They seek to divide us so that it will be easier for them to destroy our liberty and country."

"True! True! Right! Right! It is so! It is so!" the throng voiced its approval.

"Free Russia will never be secure until the Kaiser's soldiers are driven out of Russia," the speaker continued. "We must, therefore, prepare for a general offensive to win a great victory. We must work together with our Allies who are helping us to defeat the Germans. We must respect and obey our officers, as there can be no army without chiefs, just as there can be no flock without a shepherd."

"Correct! Correct! Well said! It's the truth! It's the truth!" the soldiers shouted from every corner.

"Now, my friends, tell me what you think of launching an attack against the enemy?" asked the President of the Duma. "Are you ready to advance and die, if necessary, to secure our precious freedom?"

"Yes, we are! We will go!" thundered the thousands present.

---

27. Mikhail Rodzianko (1859-1924) was a colorful, conservative politician with strong ties to the Old Regime. He was Chairman of the State Duma and one of the leaders of the February Revolution of 1917, during which headed the Provisional Committee of the State Duma. He played a key role in bringing about the abdication of Tsar Nicholas II in March 1917.

Then Orlov, the chairman of the Regimental Committee, a man of education, rose to answer for the rank and file. He expressed what all of us at the front had in our minds:

"Yes, we are ready to strike. But we want those millions of soldiers in the rear, who spread all over the country, overflowing the cities, overcrowding all the railroads and doing nothing, to be sent back to the front. Let us advance all together. The time for speeches has passed. We want action, or we will go home."

Comrade Orlov was boisterously acclaimed. Indeed, he said what we all so keenly felt. It wasn't just to the men in the trenches to allow hundreds of thousands of their comrades to keep holiday in the rear without interruption. Rodzianko agreed with us. He would do his best to remedy this injustice, he promised. But, privately, in reply to the insistent questions of the officers why the golden opportunity for an offensive was being wasted, he confessed that the Provisional Government and the Duma were powerless.

"It is the Soviet, Kerensky[28] and its other leading spirits, who have the decision in such matters," he said. "They are shaping the policy of the country. I have urged them not to delay, but to order a general attack immediately."

Chairman Orlov then presented me to Rodzianko with a little speech in which he recounted my record since the beginning of the war. The President of the Duma was greatly surprised and moved.

"I want to bend the knee to this woman," he said, shaking my hand warmly. He then asked what was my feeling about conditions at the front. I gave vent to the bitterness that was in my heart.

"I can't stand this new order of things. The soldiers don't fight the Germans any more. My object in joining the army was to defend the country. Now, it is impossible to do so. There is nothing left for me, therefore, but to go away."

"But where shall you go?" he asked.

"I don't know. I suppose I shall go home. My father is old, and my mother is ailing, and they are almost reduced to begging for bread."

Rodzianko patted me on the shoulder.

"Come to me in Petrograd, little heroine, and I will see what I can do for you."

---

28. Alexander Kerensky (1881-1970) was Justice Minister and Vice Chairman of the Petrograd Soviet after the February Revolution, War Minister from May to July (allowing many of the liberalizing reforms in the army that Maria decries), and Prime Minister from July to November 1917. He led the socialist Trudoviks (workers) faction of the Socialist Revolutionary Party, and was a moderate. Overthrown by the Bolsheviks on November 7, 1917, he fled Russia and spent the rest of his life in exile, in Paris and New York City.

I joyfully accepted the invitation, and told my comrades that I should be leaving soon. I was provided with a new outfit and one hundred rubles by the Commander. The news spread that Yashka was going away and about a thousand soldiers, many of whose lives I had saved in battle, presented me with a testimonial.

A thousand signatures! They were all the names of dear comrades who were attached to me by ties of fire and blood. There was a record, on that long scroll, of every battle which we had fought and of every episode of life-saving and self-sacrifice in which I had taken part. It made my heart beat with joy and my eyes fill with tears, while deep in my soul something ached and yearned.

It was May, but there was autumn in my breast. There was autumn also in the heart of Mother-Russia. The sunshine was dazzling. The fields and the forests rioted in all the glories of spring. There was peace in the trenches, calm in No Man's Land. My country was still celebrating joyously the festival of the newly born Freedom. It was scarcely two months old, this child of generations of pain and suffering. It came into being with the first warm wind, and how deep were the forces that it aroused in us, how infinite the promises it carried! My people still entertained the wonderful illusions of those first days. It was spring, the beginning of eternal spring to them.

But my heart pined. All joy was dead in it. I heard the autumn winds howling. I felt instinctively an immense tragedy developing, and my soul went out to Mother Russia.

The entire Regiment was formed in line so that I could bid them farewell. I addressed them as follows:

"You know how I love you, how I have cared for you. Who picked you up on the field of battle? Yashka. Who dressed your wounds under fire? Yashka. Who braved with you all dangers and shared with you all privations? A *baba*, Yashka. I bore with your insults and rejoiced in your caresses. I knew how to receive them both, because I knew your souls. I could endure anything with you, but I cannot endure this any longer. I cannot bear fraternization with the enemy. I cannot bear these incessant meetings. I cannot bear this endless chain of orators and their empty phrases. It is time to act. The time for talk is gone. Otherwise, it will be too late. Our country and freedom are perishing.

"Nevertheless, I love you and want to part from you as a friend."

Here I stopped. I could not go on. My comrades gave me a hearty goodbye. They were sorry, very sorry, to lose me, they said, but of course I was entitled to my opinion of the situation. They assured me that they respected me as ever and that, when they had been at home on leave, they had always told their mothers to pray for me. And they swore that they would always be ready to lay down their lives for me.

The Commander placed his carriage at my disposal to go to the railway station. A delegate from the Regiment was leaving the same day for Petrograd, and we went together. As the horses started, tearing me away from the men, who clasped my hands and wished me luck and God-speed, something tore a big hole in my heart, and the world seemed desolate.

CHAPTER XI
I ORGANIZE THE BATTALION OF DEATH

The journey to Petrograd was uneventful. The train was crowded to overflowing with returning soldiers who engaged in arguments day and night. I was drawn into one such debate. Peace was the subject of all discussion, immediate peace.

"But how can you have peace while the Germans are occupying parts of Russia?" I broke in. "We must win a victory first or our country will be lost."

"Ah, she is for the old regime. She wants the Tsar back," murmured some soldiers threateningly.

The delegate accompanying me here advised me to keep silence if I wanted to arrive safely in Petrograd. I followed his advice. He left me at the station when we got to the capital. It was in the afternoon, and I had never been in Petrograd before. With the address of Rodzianko on my lips I went about making inquiries how to go there. I was directed to take a tram, the first I had ever ridden in.

About five in the afternoon I found myself in front of a big house. For a moment I lost courage. "What if he has forgotten me? He may not be at home and nobody will know anything about me." I wanted to retreat, but where could I go? I knew no one in the city. Plucking up my courage, I rang the bell and awaited the opening of the door with a trembling heart. A servant came out and I gave my name, with the information that I had just arrived from the front to see Rodzianko. I was taken up in a lift, a new experience to me, and was met by the secretary of the President. He greeted me warmly, saying that he had expected me, and invited me to make myself at home.

President Rodzianko then appeared, exclaiming cordially:

"My little heroine![29] I am glad you have come," and he kissed me on the cheek. He then presented me to his wife as his little heroine, pointing to my military decorations. She was very cordial and generous in her praise. "You have come just in time for dinner," she said, leading me into her dressing-room to remove the dust of the journey. This warm reception cheered me greatly.

---

29. Геройтчик (*geroitchik*) is apparently what Rodzianko said.

At the table the conversation turned to the state of affairs at the front. Asked to tell of the latest developments, I said, as nearly as I can remember:

"The agitation to leave the trenches and go home is growing. If there is not an immediate offensive, all is lost. The soldiers will disperse. It is also an urgent necessity to send back to the fighting line the troops now scattered in the rear."

Rodzianko answered as nearly as I can remember as follows:

"Orders have been given to many units in the rear to go to the front. All have not obeyed, however. There have been demonstrations and protests on the part of several troops, due to Bolshevik propaganda."

That was the first time I ever heard of the Bolsheviks. It was May 1917.

"'Who are they?" I asked.

"They are a group led by one Lenin, who has just returned from abroad by way of Germany, and Trotsky, Kollontai and other political exiles. They attend the meetings of the Soviet at the Tauride Palace, in which the Duma meets, stir up class-bitterness and demand immediate peace."

I was further asked how Kerensky then stood with the soldiers, being informed that he had just left for a tour of the front.

"Kerensky is very popular. In fact, the most popular man with the men at the front. The men will do anything for him," I replied.

Rodzianko then related an incident which made us all laugh. There was an old porter in the Government Offices who had served many Ministers of the Tsar. Kerensky, it appeared, made it a habit to shake hands with everybody. So that whenever he entered his office, he shook hands with the old porter, thus quickly becoming the laughing-stock of the servants.

"Now, what kind of a Minister is it," the old porter was overheard complaining to a fellow-servant," who shakes hands with me?"

After dinner, Rodzianko took me to the Tauride Palace, where he introduced me to a gathering of soldiers' delegates, then in session. I was warmly welcomed and even a prominent seat. The speakers gave descriptions of conditions at various sections of the front that tallied exactly with my own observations. Discipline was gone, fraternization was on the increase, the agitation to leave the trenches was gaining strength. Something must be done quickly, they argued. How could the men be kept up to the mark till the moment when an offensive should is ordered? That was the problem.

Rodzianko arose and proposed that I should be asked to suggest a solution. He told them that I was a peasant who had volunteered early in the war and fought and suffered with the men. Therefore, he thought, I ought to know what was the right thing to do. Naturally, I was very much embarrassed. I was totally unprepared to make any suggestions and, therefore, begged to be excused until I had thought the matter over.

The session continued, while I sank deep into thought. For half an hour I racked my brain in vain. Then suddenly an idea dawned upon me. It was the idea of a Women's Battalion of Death.

"You have heard of what I have done and endured as a soldier," I said, rising to my feet and turning to the audience. "Now, how would it do to organize three hundred women like myself to serve as an example to the army and lead the men into battle?"

Rodzianko approved of my idea. "Provided," he added, "we could find hundreds more like Maria Bochkareva, which I greatly doubt."

To this objection I replied that numbers were immaterial, that what was important was to shame the men, and that a few women at one place could serve as an example to the entire front. "It would be necessary that the women's organization should have no committees and be run on the regular army basis in order to enable it to help towards the restoration of discipline," I further explained.

To this objection I replied that numbers were immaterial, that what was important was to shame the men, and that a few women at one place could serve as an example to the entire front.

Rodzianko thought my suggestion splendid and dwelt upon the enthusiasm that would inevitably be kindled among the men if women should occupy some of the trenches and take the lead in an offensive.

There were objections, however, from the audience. One delegate got up and said, "None of us can take exception to a soldier like Bochkareva. The men at the front know her and have heard of her deeds. But who will guarantee that the other women will be as decent as she and will not dishonor the army?"

Another delegate remarked, "Who will guarantee that the presence of women soldiers at the front will not lead to the birth there of little soldiers?"

There was a general uproar at this criticism. I replied, "If I take up the organization of a women's battalion, I will hold myself responsible for every member of it. I will introduce rigid discipline and will allow no speechmaking and no loitering in the streets. When Mother Russia is drowning, it is not a time to run an army by committees. I am a common peasant myself, and I know that only discipline can save the Russian Army. In the proposed battalion I should exercise absolute authority and insist upon obedience. Otherwise, there would be no use in organizing it."

The Provisional Committee. Seated on the right at the desk is Mikhail Rodzianko, seated next to him is Alexander Guchkov, standing in the back row, r. to l. are General Nikolai Ruszki, Alexandr Kerensky, Georgy Lvov, and Pavel N. Milyukov.

There were no objections to the conditions which I outlined as preliminary to the establishment of such a unit. Still, I never expected that the Government would consider the matter seriously and permit me to carry out the idea, although I was informed that it would be submitted to Kerensky upon his return from the front.

President Rodzianko took a deep interest in the project. He introduced me to Captain Dementiev, Commandant of the Home for Invalids, asking him to place a room or two at my disposal and generally take care of me. I went home with the Captain, who presented me to his wife, a dear and patriotic woman who soon became very much attached to me.

The following morning Rodzianko telephoned, suggesting that before the matter was broached to the War Minister, Kerensky, it would be wise to take it up with the Commander-in-Chief, General Brusilov, who could judge it from the point of view of the army. If he approved of it, it would be easier to obtain Kerensky's permission.

General Headquarters were then at Mogilev and there we went, Captain Dementiev and I, to obtain an audience with the Commander-in-Chief. We were received by his Adjutant on the 14th of May. He announced our arrival and purpose to General Brusilov, who ordered that we should be shown in.

Hardly a week had elapsed since I left the front, and here I was again, this time not in the trenches, however, but in the presence of the Commander-in-Chief. It was a very sudden metamorphosis, and I could not help wondering, deep in my soul, over the strange ways of fortune. Brusilov shook hands with us cordially. He was interested in the idea, he said. Wouldn't we sit down? We did. Wouldn't I tell him about myself and my ideas concerning the scheme?

I told him about my soldiering and my leaving the front because I could not reconcile myself to the prevailing conditions. I explained that the purpose of the plan would be to shame the men in the trenches by letting them see the women go over the top first. The Commander-in-Chief then discussed the matter from various points of view with Captain Dementiev and approved of my idea. He bade us *adieu*, expressing his hope for the success of my enterprise, and, in a happy frame of mine, I left for Petrograd.

Kerensky had returned from the front. We called on Rodzianko and told him of the result of our mission. He informed us that he had already asked for an audience with Kerensky and that the latter wanted to see him at seven o'clock the following morning, when he would broach the subject to him. After his call on Kerensky, Rodzianko telephoned to tell us that he had arranged for an audience for me with Kerensky at the Winter Palace at noon the next day.

Captain Dementiev drove me to the Winter Palace, and a few minutes before twelve I was in the antechamber of the War Minister. I was surprised to find General Brusilov there, and he asked me if I had come to see Kerensky about the scheme I had discussed with him. I replied that I had. He offered to support my idea with the War Minister, and introduced me to General Polovtsov,[30] Commander of the Petrograd Military District, who was with him.

Suddenly the door swung open and a young face, with eyes inflamed from sleeplessness, beckoned to me to come in. It was Kerensky, at that moment the idol of the masses. One of his arms was in a sling. With the other he shook my hand. He walked about nervously and talked briefly and dryly. He told me that he had heard about me and was interested in my idea. I then outlined to him the purpose of the project, saying that there would be no committees, but regular discipline in the battalion of women.

Kerensky listened impatiently. He had evidently made up his mind on the subject. There was only one point of which he was not sure. Would I be able to maintain a high standard of morality in the organization? He would allow

---

30. Pyotr Alexandrovich Polovtsov (1874-1964) was a military leader who served in Siberia, India, China and commanded a Tatar cavalry unit in World War I. He replaced Kornilov as head of the Petrograd Military District in 1917, and fled Russia in 1918.

me to recruit it immediately if I made myself answerable for the conduct and reputation of the women. I pledged myself to do so. And it was all settled. I was granted the authority there and then to form a unit under the name of The First Russian Women's Battalion of Death.

It seemed unbelievable. A few days ago it had dawned upon me as a mere fancy. Now the dream was adopted as a practical policy by the highest in authority. I was in ecstasy. As Kerensky showed me out, his eyes fell on General Polovtsov. He asked him to give me all necessary help. I was overwhelmed with happiness.

A brief consultation took place immediately between Captain Dementiev and General Polovtsov, who made the following suggestion:

"Why not start at the meeting to be held tomorrow night in the Mariinsky Theatre for the benefit of the Home for Invalids? Kerensky, Rodzianko, Chkheidze,[31] and others will speak there. Let us put Bochkareva between Rodzianko and Kerensky on the programme."

I was seized with nervousness and objected strenuously that I could never appear in public and that I should not know what to talk about.

"You will tell them just what you told Rodzianko, Brusilov and Kerensky. Just tell them how you feel about the front and the country," they said, making light of my objections.

Before I had time to realize it, I was already in a photographer's studio, and there had my portrait taken. The following day this picture appeared at the head of big posters pasted all over the city, announcing my appearance at the Mariinsky Theatre for the purpose of organizing a Women's Battalion of Death.

I did not close an eye during the entire night preceding the evening fixed for the meeting. It all seemed a fantastic dream. How could I take my place between two such great men as Rodzianko and Kerensky? How could I ever face an assembly of educated people, I, an illiterate peasant woman? And what could I say? My tongue had never been trained to elegant speech. My eyes had never beheld a place like the Mariinsky Theatre, formerly frequented by the Tsar and the Imperial family. I tossed in bed in a state of fever.

"Holy Father," I prayed, my eyes streaming with tears, "show Thy humble servant the path to truth. I am afraid; instil courage into my heart. I can feel my knees give way; steady them with Thy strength. My mind is groping in the dark; illumine it with Thy light. My speech is but the common talk of an ignorant baba; make it flow with Thy wisdom and penetrate the hearts of my hearers.

---

31. Nikolay Chkheidze, a Georgian Social Democrat and Menshevik. Served as chairman of the Petrograd Soviet. He failed to thwart the efforts of the Bolsheviks to assume power and was against continuation of the war.

Do all this, not for the sake of Thy humble Maria, but for the sake of Mother Russia, my unhappy country."

My eyes were red with inflammation when I arose in the morning. I was nervous all day. Captain Dementiev suggested that I should commit my speech to memory. I refused his suggestion with the remark, "I have placed my trust in God and rely on Him to put the right words into my mouth."

It was the evening of May 21, 1917. I was driven to the Mariinsky Theatre and escorted by Captain Dementiev and his wife into the former Imperial box. The house was packed, the receipts of the ticket office amounting to thirty thousand rubles. Everybody seemed to be pointing at me, and it was with great difficulty that I controlled my nerves.

Kerensky appeared and was given a tremendous reception. He spoke only about ten minutes. Next on the programme was Madame Kerensky, and I was to follow her. Madame Kerensky, however, broke down as soon as she found herself confronted by the audience. That did not add to my courage. I was led forward as if in a trance.

"Men and women citizens!" I heard my voice say. "Our mother is perishing. Our mother is Russia. I want to help to save her. I want women whose hearts are loyal, whose souls are pure, whose aims are high. With such women setting an example of self-sacrifice, you men will realize your duty in this grave hour!"

Then I stopped and could not proceed. Sobs choked the words in me, tremors shook me, my legs grew weak. I was caught under the arm and led away amid a thunderous outburst of applause.

Registration of volunteers for the Battalion from among those present took place the same evening, there and then. So great was the enthusiasm, that fifteen hundred women applied for enlistment. It was necessary to put quarters at my immediate disposal and it was decided to let me have the building and grounds of the Kolomensk Women's Institute, and I directed the women to come there on the morrow, when they would be examined and officially enlisted.

The newspapers contained accounts of the meeting and the publicity which it gained helped to swell the number of women who volunteered to join the Battalion of Death to two thousand. They were gathered in the garden of the Institute, all in a state of jubilation. I arrived with Staff Captain Kuzmin, assistant to General Polovtsov, Captain Dementiev, and General Anosov,[32] who was introduced to me as a man very interested in my idea. He looked about fifty years of age and was of impressive appearance. He wanted to help me, he

---

32. Nikolai Stepanovich Anosov (1866-1920) for a time after the February Revolution was in charge of all troops in the Petrograd Military District. Shot in 1920 by the Bolsheviks.

explained. In addition, there was about a score of journalists. I mounted a table in the center of the garden and addressed the women in the following manner :

"Women do you know what I have called you here for? Do you realize clearly the task lying ahead of you? Do you know what war is? War! Look into your hearts, examine your souls and see if you can stand the great test.

"At a time when our country is perishing, it is the duty of all of us to rise to its succour. The morale of our men has fallen low, and it is for us women to serve as an inspiration to them. But only such women as have entirely sacrificed their own personal interests and affairs can do this.

"Woman is naturally light-hearted. But if she can purge herself for sacrifice, then through a kindly word, a loving heart and an example of heroism she can save the Motherland. We are physically weak, but if we be strong morally and spiritually, we shall accomplish more than a large force.

"I will have no committees in the Battalion. There will be strict discipline, and any offense will be severely punished. There will be punishment for even slight acts of disobedience. No flirtations will be allowed, and any attempts at them will be punished by expulsion and sending home under arrest. It is the purpose of this Battalion to restore discipline in the army. It must, therefore, be irreproachable in character. Now, are you willing to enlist under such conditions?"

"Yes, we are! we are! we are!" the women responded in a chorus.

"I will now ask those of you who accept my terms to sign a pledge, binding you to obey any order of Bochkareva. I warn you that I am stern by nature, that I shall personally punish any misdemeanor, that I shall demand absolute obedience. Those of you who hesitate had better not sign the pledge. There will now be a medical examination."

There were nearly two thousand signed pledges. They included names of members of some of the most illustrious families in the country, as well as those of common peasant girls and domestic servants. The physical examination, conducted by ten doctors, some of whom were women, was not ruled by the same standard as that in the case of the men. There were, naturally, very few perfect specimens of health among the women. But we rejected only those suffering from serious ailments.

Altogether there were about thirty rejections. Those accepted were allowed to go home with instructions to return on the following day when they would be quartered permanently in the Institute and begin training.

It was necessary to obtain outfits, and I applied for these to General Polovtsov, Commander of the Military District of Petrograd. The same evening two thousand complete outfits were delivered at my headquarters.

I also asked General Polovtsov for twenty-five men instructors, who should be well disciplined, able to maintain good order, and acquainted with every detail of military training, so as to be able to complete the course of instruction in two weeks. He sent me twenty-five officers of all grades from the Volynsky Regiment.

Then there was the question of supplies. Were we to have our own kitchen? It was found more expedient not to establish one of our own but to make use of the kitchen of a guard regiment stationed not far from our quarters. The ration was that of regular troops, consisting of two pounds of bread, cabbage soup, *kasha* (gruel), sugar and tea. I would send a company at a time, provided with pails, to fetch their meals.

On the morning of May 26 all the recruits gathered in the grounds of the Institute. I had them placed in rows, so as to arrange them according to their height, and divided the whole body into two battalions of approximately one thousand each. Each battalion was divided into four companies, and each company subdivided into four platoons. There was a man instructor in command of every platoon, and in addition there was an officer in command of every company, so that altogether I had to increase the number of men instructors to forty.

I addressed the women again, informing them that from the moment that they entered upon their duties they were no longer women, but soldiers. I told them that they would not be allowed to leave the grounds, and that only between six and eight in the evening would they be permitted to receive relatives and friends. From among the more intelligent recruits – and there were many university graduates in the ranks – I selected a number for promotion to platoon and company officers, their duties being limited to the domestic supervision of the troop, since the men commanders were purely instructors, returning to their barracks at the end of the day's work.

Next I marched the recruits to four barbers' shops, where from five in the morning to twelve at noon a number of barbers cut short the hair of one woman after another. Crowds outside the shops watched this unaccustomed proceeding, greeting with jeers each woman as she emerged, with hair close cropped and perhaps with an aching heart, from the barber's saloon.

The same afternoon my soldiers received their first lessons in the large garden. A recruit was detailed to stand guard at the gate and not to admit anybody without the permission of the officer in charge. The watch was changed every two hours. A high fence surrounded the grounds, and the drilling went on without interference. Giggling was strictly forbidden, and I kept a sharp watch over the women. I had about thirty of them dismissed without ceremony the first day. Some were expelled for too much laughing, others for frivolities. Several of them threw themselves at my feet, begging for mercy. However, I made up my mind that without severity I might just as well give up my project at the beginning. If my word was to carry weight, it must be final and unalterable, I decided. How could one otherwise expect to manage two thousand women? As soon as one of them disobeyed an order I quickly removed her uniform and sent her away. In this work it was quality and not quantity that counted, and I determined if necessary to dismiss without scruple several hundreds of the recruits.

We received five hundred rifles for training purposes, sufficient only for a quarter of the force. This necessitated the elaboration of a method whereby the supply of rifles could be made use of by the entire body. It was thought well that the members of the Battalion of Death should be distinguished by special insignia. We, therefore, devised new epaulets: white, with a red and black stripe. A red and black arrowhead was to be attached to the right arm. I ordered two thousand such insignia.

When evening came and the hour for going to bed arrived, the women ignored the order to turn in for the night at ten o'clock and continued chatting and laughing. I reproved the officer in charge, threatening to place her at attention for six hours in the event of the soldiers keeping awake after ten. Fifty of the women I punished forthwith by ordering them to remain at attention for two hours. To the rest I said, "Every one of you to bed this instant! I want you to be so quiet that I could hear a fly buzz. Tomorrow you will be up at five o'clock."

I spent a sleepless night. There were many things to think about and many difficulties to overcome.

At five only the officer in charge was up. Not a soul stirred in the barrack. The officer reported to me that she had twice ordered the women to get up, but none of them moved. I came out and in a voice of thunder ordered :

"*Vstavai!*"[33]

Frightened and sleepy, my recruits left their beds. As soon as they had finished dressing and washing, there was a summons to prayer. I made praying a daily duty. Breakfast followed, consisting of tea and bread.

At eight I had issued an order that the companies should all be formed into ranks ready for review in fifteen minutes. I came out, passed each company, greeting it. The company would answer in a chorus, "Good health to you, Commander."

33. Get up!

Training was resumed, and I continued the combing out process. As soon as I observed a girl making eyes at an instructor, behaving frivolously, and generally neglecting her work, I quickly ordered her to take off her uniform and go home. In this manner I weeded out about fifty on the second day. I could not insist too strongly on the burden of reponsibility I carried. I constantly appealed to the women for the utmost seriousness in facing the task that lay before us. The Battalion must either be a success or I must become the laughing-stock of the country, at the same time bringing disgrace upon those who had supported my idea. I admitted no new applicants, because rapid completion of the course of training so as to be able to dispatch the Battalion to the front was of the greatest importance.

For several days the drilling went on, and the women mastered the rudiments of a soldier's training. On several occasions I resorted to slapping as punishment for misbehavior.

One day the sentry reported to the officer in charge that two women, one a famous Englishwoman, wanted to see me. I ordered the Battalion to remain at attention while I received the two callers, who were Emmeline Pankhurst and Princess Kikuatova, the latter of whom I knew.

Mrs. Pankhurst was introduced to me, and I ordered the Battalion to salute the eminent visitor who had done much for women and her country." Mrs. Pankhurst became a frequent visitor of the Battalion, watching it with deep interest as it grew into a well-disciplined military unit. We became very much attached to each other. Mrs. Pankhurst invited me to a dinner at the Astoria, the leading hotel in Petrograd, at which Kerensky and the various Allied representatives in the capital were to be present.

Meanwhile, the Battalion was making rapid progress. At first we suffered little annoyance. The Bolshevik agitators did not take the project seriously, expecting it to come to a speedy end. At the beginning I received only about thirty threatening letters. Gradually, however, it became known that I maintained the strictest discipline, commanding without a committee ; and the propagandists began to regard me as a danger, and sought a means for the frustration of my scheme.

On the evening appointed for the dinner I went to the Astoria. There Kerensky was very cordial to me. He told me that the Bolsheviks were preparing a demonstration against the Provisional Government and that at first the Petrograd garrison had consented to organize a demonstration in favor of the Government. Later, however, the garrison had decided not to march. The War Minister then asked me if I would march with the Battalion in support of the Provisional Government.

I gladly accepted the invitation. Kerensky told nic that the Women's Battalion had already exerted a beneficial influence, that several bodies of troops had expressed a willingness to leave for the front, that man\ of the wounded had organized themselves for the purpos(of going to the fighting line, declaring that if women could fight, then they – the cripples – would do so, too. Finally he expressed his belief that the announcement of the marching of the Battalion of Death would stimulate the garrison to follow suit.

It was a pleasant evening that I spent at the Astoria.

Upon leaving, an acquaintance who was going in the same direction offered to drive me to the Institute. I accepted the invitation, alighting, however, at a little distance from headquarters, as I did not wish him to drive out of his way. It was about eleven o'clock when I approached the temporary barrack. There was a small crowd at the gate, about thirty-five men, of all descriptions, soldiers, roughs, vagrants, and even some decent looking fellows.

"Who are you? What are you doing here?" I questioned sharply.

"Commander," cried the sentry," they are waiting for you. They have been here more

Members of the Battalion.

than an hour; they broke through the gate and have been searching the grounds and the house for you. When they became convinced that you were away they decided to wait here for your return."

"Well, what do you want?" I demanded of the group as they surrounded me.

"What do we want, eh? We want you to disband the Battalion. We have had enough of this discipline. Enough blood has been shed. We don't want any more armies and militarism. You are only creating new trubles for the common people. Disband your Battalion and we will leave you alone."

"I will not disband!" was my answer.

Several of them pulled out revolvers and threatened to kill me. The sentry raised an alarm and all the women appeared at the windows, many of them with their rifles ready.

Maria Bochkareva and Emmeline Pankhurst

"Listen," a couple of them argued again,"you are of the people and we only want the weal of the common man. We want peace, not war. And you are inciting to war again. We have had enough war, too much war. We now understand the uselessness of war. Surely you don't like to see the poor people slaughtered for the sake of the few rich. Come, join our side, and let us all work for peace."

"You are scoundrels!" I shouted with all my strength." You are idiots! I myself am for peace, but we shall never have peace till we have driven the Germans out of Russia. They will make slaves of us and ruin our country and our freedom. You are traitors!"

Suddenly I was kicked violently in the back. Some one dealt me a second blow from the side.

"Fire!" I shouted to my girls at the windows as I was knocked down, mindful that I had instructed them always to shoot in the air first as a warning.

Several hundred rifles rang out in a volley. My assailants quickly dispersed, and I was safe. However, they returned during the night and stoned the windows, breaking every pane of glass fronting the street.

CHAPTER XII
MY FIGHT AGAINST COMMITTEE RULE

It was after midnight when I entered the barracks. The officer in charge reported to me the events of the evening. It appeared that at first one of the group, a Bolshevik agitator, had made his way inside by telling the sentry that he had been sent by me for something. As soon as he was admitted, he got the women together and began a speech, appealing to them to form a committee and govern themselves, in accordance with the new spirit. He scoffed at them for submitting to the system of discipline which I had established, calling it Tsaristic, and expressing his compassion for the poor girls whom I had punished. Declaiming against the war, appealing for peace at any price, he urged my recruits to act as free citizens, depose their reactionary chief and elect a new one in democratic fashion.

The result of the address was a split in the ranks of my Battalion. More than half of them approved of the speaker, crying: "We are free. This is not the old regime. We want to be independent. We want to exercise our own rights." And they seceded from the troop, and finding themselves in the majority after taking votes, elected a committee.

I was deeply agitated, and in spite of the late hour ordered the girls to form into ranks. As soon as this was accomplished I addressed the following command to the body:

"Those who want a committee move over to the right. Those who are against it go to the left."

The majority went to the right. Only about three hundred stood at the left.

"Now those of you who are willing to be treated by me as you have been treated hitherto, to receive punishment when necessary, to maintain the severest possible discipline in the Battalion and to be ruled without a committee, say yes," I exclaimed.

The group of three hundred on the left shouted in a chorus : "Yes, we consent! We are willing, Commander."

Turning to the silent crowd on the right I said:

"Why did you join? I told you beforehand that it would be hard. Did you not sign pledges to obey? I want action, not phrases. Committees paralyse action by a flood of words."

"We are not slaves; we are free women," many of the mutineers shouted." This is not the old regime. We want more courteous treatment, more liberty. We want to govern our own affairs like the rest of the army."

"Ah, you foolish women!" I answered with a sorrowing heart. "I did not organize this Battalion to be like the rest of the army. We were to serve as an example, and not merely to add a few *babas* to the ineffectual millions of soldiers now swarming over Russia. We were to strike out a new path and not imitate the demoralized army. Had I known what stuff you were made of, I would not have had anything to do with you. Consider, we were to lead in a general attack. Now, suppose we had a committee and the moment for the offensive arrived. Then the committee suddenly decides not to advance and our whole scheme is brought to nothing."

"Certainly," the rebels shouted. "We should want to decide for ourselves whether to attack or not."

"Well," I said, turning to them in disgust, "you are not worthy of the uniforms you are wearing. This uniform stands for noble sacrifice, for unselfish patriotism, for purity and honor and loyalty. Every one of you is a disgrace to the uniform. Take it off and leave this place."

My order was met by an outburst of scoffing and defiance.

"We are in the majority. We refuse to obey your orders. We no longer recognize your authority. We will elect a new chief!"

I was deeply hurt, but I controlled myself so as not to act rashly. I resolved to make another appeal to them, and said:

"You will elect no new chief. But if you want to go, go quietly. Make no scandal, for the sake of womanhood. If all this becomes public it will injure and humiliate all of us. Men will say that women are unfit for serious work, that they do not know how to carry through an enterprise and that they cannot help quarrelling. We shall become a byword all over the world and your act will be an eternal blot on our sex."

"But why are you so cruel and harsh to us?" the rebels began to argue again. "Why do you treat us as if we were in a prison, allowing us no holidays, giving us no opportunity to go for walks, always shouting and ordering us about? You want to make us slaves."

"I told you at the beginning that I should be strict, that I should shout and punish. As to not letting you out of the grounds, you know that I do it because I cannot be sure of your conduct outside. I wanted this house to be a holy place. I prayed to God to hallow us all with His chastity. I wished you to go to the front as saintly women, hoping that the enemy's bullets would not touch you."

All night an argument raged between the three hundred loyal women and the mutineers. I retired, leaving instructions with the officers to let the rebels do as they pleased, even to leave in their uniforms. I was filled with despair as I reflected on the outcome of my enterprise. My soul ached for all women as I thought of the disgraceful conduct of the girls who had pledged their honor on behalf of an idea and then deserted the banner they had themselves raised.

In the morning I was informed that the rebels had elected a deputation to go to General Polovtsov, Commander of the Military District, to make complaint against me, and that they had all departed in uniform. The same day I was called to report to General Polovtsov on the whole matter. The General advised me to meet some of the demands of the rebels and come to terms.

"The whole army is now being run by committees of soldiers. You alone cannot preserve the old system. Let your girls form a committee so that a scandal will be averted and your great work thereby saved," General Polovtsov tried to persuade me. But I would not be persuaded.

He then went on to tell me that the soldiers of the First and Tenth Armies, having heard of my work, had bought for me two icons, one of the Holy Mother and the other of Saint George, both of silver, framed in gold. They had telegraphed instructions to embroider two standards with appropriate inscriptions. Kerensky, the General told me, had thought of making the presentation a solemn occasion and had had my record in the army fully investigated, after which he had decided to buy a gold cross to present to me at the same time.

"Now what will become of this ceremony if you do not pacify your women?" the General asked.

I was, naturally, flattered by what Polovtsov told me, but I considered that duty came first and that I must not give in for the sake of the honors promised to me, in spite of the assurances he gave me that he would order the women to ask my pardon if I consented to form a committee.

"I would not keep the rebels in the Battalion for anything," I said. "Once having been insulted by them, I shall always consider them prejudicial to the organization. They would sap my strength here and would disgrace me at the front. The purpose of the Battalion was to set an example to the demoralized men. Give them a committee, and all is lost. I shall have the same state of things as in the army. The disintegration there is a sufficient reason for my determination not to introduce the new system."

"Yes, I agree with you that the committees are a curse," confided the General." But what is to be done?"

"I know this much, that I, for one, will have nothing to do with committees," I declared emphatically.

The General jumped to his feet, struck the table with his fist and thundered: "And I order you to form a committee!"

I jumped up as well, I also struck the table and declared loudly:

"I will not! I started this work on condition that I should be allowed to run the Battalion as I saw fit and without any committees."

"Then there is nothing left but to disband your Battalion!" proclaimed General Polovtsov.

"This very minute if you wish!" I replied.

I drove to the Institute. Knowing that the women had been ordered to return, I placed ten sentries armed with rifles at the gates with instructions not to allow any one to enter, and to shoot in case of truble. Many of the rebels came but on being threatened with the rifles they retired. They went back to Polovtsov who, for the moment at least, could do nothing for them. He reported the matter to Kerensky with a recommendation that some action should be taken to control me.

I proceeded to reorganize my Battalion. There was only a remnant of three hundred left of it, but it was a loyal remnant, and I was not upset by the diminution in numbers. Most of the remaining women were peasants like myself, illiterate but very devoted to Mother Russia. All of them but one were under thirty-five years of age. The exception was Orlova, who was forty, but of an unusually powerful constitution. We resumed the drilling with greater zeal than ever.

A day or two later Kerensky's adjutant telephoned. He wanted me to come to the Winter Palace to see the War Minister. The antechamber was again crowded with many people and I was greeted by several acquaintances. At the appointed time I was shown into Kerensky's study.

Kerensky was pacing the room vigorously as I entered. His forehead was knit in a heavy frown.

"Good morning, Minister," I greeted him.

"Good morning," he answered coldly, without extending his hand.

"Are you a soldier?" he asked abruptly.

"Yes," I replied.

"Then why don't you obey your superiors?"

"Because I am in the right in this case. The orders are against the interests of my country and in violation of my charter."

"You must obey!" Kerensky raised his voice to a high pitch, and his face was flushed with anger. "I order you to form a committee tomorrow, to treat the women courteously, and to cease punishing them! Otherwise I will get rid of you!" The War Minister banged his fist on the table to give emphasis to his words.

But I felt that I was right, so this fit of temper did not frighten me, but, on the contrary, strengthened my determination.

"No!" I shouted, bringing down my fist, too, "no, I am not going to form any committees. I started out with the understanding that there would be the strictest discipline in the Battalion. You can disband it now. A soldier I was and a soldier I shall remain. I shall go home, retire to a village and settle there in peace." And I ran out, slamming the door angrily in the face of the astonished Minister.

In high agitation I returned to the Institute, and having assembled the women, I addressed them as follows :

"I am going home tomorrow. The Battalion will be disbanded, because I would not consent to form a committee. You all know that I had warned all the applicants previously that I should be a severe disciplinarian. I wanted to make this Battalion an example that would shine for ever in the history of our country. I hoped to show that where men failed women could succeed. I dared to dream that women would inspire men to great deeds and save our unhappy land. But my hopes are now shattered. The majority of the women who responded to my appeal proved themselves weak and cowardly, and they have wrecked my scheme for the salvation of suffering Russia. I have just come back from Kerensky. He told me that I must form a committee, but I refused. Have you any idea what a committee would mean?"

"No, no, Commander," the women answered.

"A committee," I explained, "means nothing but talk, talk, talk. The committees have destroyed the army and the country. This is war, and in war there should be not talk, but action. I can't submit to the order to introduce in this Battalion the very system that has shattered our glorious army. So I am going home. . . . Yes, I leave tomorrow..."

The women threw themselves at my feet in tears. They wept and begged me to remain with them. "We love you. We will stand by you to the last," they cried. "You can punish us, beat us if you will. We know and appreciate your motives. You want to help Russia and we want you to make use of us. You can treat us as you please, you can kill us, but don't leave us. We will go anywhere for you. We will go to General Polovtsov and tear him to pieces!"

They embraced my feet, hugged me, kissed me, professed their affection and loyalty. I was profoundly stirred. My heart was filled with gratitude and love for these brave friends. They seemed like children to me, like my children, and I felt like a tender mother. If I had offended fifteen hundred unworthy members, I had won the deep devotion of these three hundred noble souls. They had tasted the rigors of military life but did not flinch. The others were cowards, masquerading their worthlessness under the cover of "democracy." These sought no excuses. The prospect of complete self-sacrifice did not daunt them. The thought of three hundred Russian women, courageous of heart, pure of soul, ready for self-sacrifice, was one to comfort my aching heart.

"I wish that I could, but it is impossible for me to remain," I replied to the pleadings of my women. "The orders from those in authority are to form a committee or to disband the Battalion. Since I flatly refused to do the former, there remains nothing for me but to go home. Goodbye for the present: I am going to the Duchess of Lichtenberg for the afternoon."

The Duchess was one of the circle of society women who had taken a deep interest in my work. She was a very simple and lovable soul, and I needed someone to whom I could pour out my heart. I was always sure that the Duchess would understand and be helpful.

"What ails you, Maria?" were the words with which she greeted me as soon as I appeared on the threshold of her house.

I could not restrain my sobs, and told her haltingly of the mutiny and the consequent collapse of the Battalion. It weighed heavily on me and I felt myself crushed by the disaster. She was shocked at the news and cried with me. The beautiful dream we had cherished was shattered. It was indeed a melancholy evening. I stayed with her for dinner.

About eight o'clock, one of my women called and asked to see me and she was shown in. She had been sent from the barracks as a messenger to report to me the results of a visit they had paid to General Polovtsov. It appeared that my three hundred loyalists had armed themselves with their rifles and had gone to the Commander of the Military District, demanding that he should come out to see them. They were not in a mood for trifling and meant business. The General came out.

"What have you done to our Commander?" they demanded sternly.

"I haven't done anything to her," Polovtsov answered, amazed at this threatening demonstration.

"We want back our Commander!" my women shouted. "We want her back immediately. She is a saintly woman, her heart is bleeding for unhappy Russia. We will have nothing to do with those bad, unruly women, and we will not disband the Battalion. We are the Battalion. We want our Commander. We want strict discipline in accordance with our pledges to her, and we will not form any committees."

It was reported to me that General Polovtsov was actually frightened, surrounded by the throng of angry and threatening women. He sent them back to the Institute, promising that he would not disband them and that he would come to the barracks at nine o'clock the following morning. I went with the messenger to the quarters and found everything in splendid order. The girls seemed anxious to comfort their leader and so kept calm and moved about noiselessly.

In the morning everything went as usual, the rising hour, prayers, breakfast and drilling. At nine I was informed that General Polovtsov, the adjutant of Kerensky, Captain Dementiev, and several of the women who took an interest in the Battalion, were at the gate. I quickly formed the Battalion. The General greeted us and we saluted. He then shook hands with me and gave orders that the women should be sent into the garden, for he wanted to talk things over with me.

I asked myself, as I led the group of distinguished visitors into the house, what it all meant. "If it means that they have come to persuade me to form a committee," I thought, "then it will be very hard for me, but I shall resist all persuasion."

My anticipation proved correct. The General had brought all these patronesses of mine to help him overcome my obstinacy. He immediately launched into an exposition of the necessity for complying with general regulations and introducing the committee system in the Battalion. He argued along the already familiar lines, but I would not yield. He gradually became angry.

"Are you a soldier?" he repeated the question put to me by Kerensky.

"Yes, General!"

"Then why don't you obey orders?"

"Because they are against the interests of the country. The committees are a plague. They have destroyed our army," I answered. "But it is the law of the country," he declared.

"Yes, and it is a ruinous law, designed to break up the front in time of war."

"Now I ask you to do it as a matter of form," he argued in a different tone altogether, perhaps himself realizing the truth of my words. "All the army committees are beginning to make inquiries about you. 'Who is this Bochkareva?' they ask, 'and why is she allowed to command without a committee?' Do it only for the sake of form. Your girls are so devoted to you that a committee elected by them would never seriously bother you. At the same time it would save trouble."

Then my lady-visitors surrounded me and begged and coaxed me to give way. Some of them wept, others embraced me, all of them exasperated my nerves. Nothing was more calculated to enrage me than this wheedling. I grew impatient and completely lost self-control, abandoning myself to hysteria.

"You are rascals, all of you! You want to destroy the country. Get out of here!" I shrieked wildly.

"Be silent! How dare you shout like that? I am a General. I will kill you!" Polovtsov thundered at me, trembling with rage.

"All right, you can kill me! Kill me!" I cried out, tearing my coat open and pointing to my chest. "Kill me!" The General then threw up his hands, muttering angrily under his breath. "What the devil! This is a demon, not a woman! There is nothing to be done with her," and with his mixed following he withdrew.

The following morning a telegram came from General Polovtsov, informing me that I should be allowed to continue my work without a committee!

Thus ended the dispute caused by the mutiny in the Battalion, which had nearly wrecked the entire undertaking. It was a hard fight that I had made but, convinced of my right, there was no question of retreating for me.

Events have completely justified my conviction. The Russian Army, once the most colossal military machine in the world, was wrecked in a few months by the committee system. Coming from the trenches, where I had learned at first hand what a curse the committees were proving, I realized early their fatal significance. To me it has always been clear that a committee meant ceaseless speech-making. That was the oustanding factor about it to me. I considered no other aspect of it. I knew that the Germans worked all day while our men talked, and in war, I always realized that it was action that counted and conquered.

CHAPTER XIII
THE BATTALION AT THE FRONT

The same morning on which the telegram came from General Polovtsov there also arrived a banner, with an inscription that read something like this:

"Long live the Provisional Government! Let Those Who Can, Advance! Forward, Brave Women! To the Defense of the Bleeding Motherland!"

We were to march with this banner in the demonstration that had been organized in opposition to the Bolshevik demonstration, fixed for the same day. The invalids were to march in the same procession. I talked matters over with their chief when we met at Morskaya.

The air was charged with alarming rumors. The Captain of the invalids placed fifty revolvers at my disposal. I distributed them among the instructors and my other officers, reserving a pair for myself.

The band of the Volynsky regiment headed the Battalion of Death, as half the soldiers of that regiment had refused to march against the Bolsheviks, having already been contaminated with Bolshevik ideas, although it was only June.

Mars Field, our destination, was about five *versts* from our barracks.[34] The whole route was lined with enormous crowds that cheered us and the invalids, of whom there were about five hundred. Many women on the pavements wept, grieving for the girls whom I was leading into what seemed a conflict with the Bolsheviks, Everybody said, "Something is going to happen today."

As we approached the Mars Field, where the opposing demonstration was held, I ordered my soldiers to sit down and rest for fifteen minutes.

"Form ranks!" I ordered at the end of that time. We were all more or less nervous, as if on the eve of an offensive. I addressed a few words to the Battalion, instructing them to support me to the end, not to insult anybody, not to run away at the least provocation, in order to avoid a panic. They all pledged themselves to fulfil my instructions.

Before resuming the march, the Captain of the invalids, several of his subordinate officers, and all my instructors came forward and asked to march

---

34. A *verst* is roughly equivalent to a kilometer.

in the front row with me. I objected, but they insisted, and I finally had to give way, in spite of my desire to show the Bolsheviks that I was not afraid.

The crowds on the Mars Field were indeed enormous. A long procession, with Bolshevik banners, flowed into the great square. We stopped within fifty feet of a Bolshevik cart and were met promptly by a hail of jokes and curses. There were jeers at the expense of the Provisional Government and shouts of: "Long live the revolutionary democracy! Down with the war!"

Some of the women could not suppress their indignation and began to answer back, provoking heated argument.

"When you cry, 'Down with the war!' you are helping to destroy Free Russia," I declared, stepping forward and addressing my turbulent neighbors. "We must beat the Germans first and then there will be no war."

"Kill her! Kill her!" several voices threatened.

Greatly excited, I rushed a few steps nearer to the crowd. My fingers gripped the two pistols, but in all the tumult that followed, the idea was fixed in my mind that I must not shoot at my own people, common workers and peasants.

"Wake up, you deluded sons of Russia! Think what you are doing! You are destroying the Motherland! Scoundrels!" I concluded as their jeers continued.

My instructors tried to hold me back as the throng swarmed round me, but I tore myself out of their arms and plunged into the thick of it. I worked myself up to such a state of frenzy that I did not cease talking even when a volley of shots was sent into our midst. Then my officers ordered the Battalion to fire. There followed a terrible scuffle.

Two of my instructors were killed, one while defending me. Two others were wounded. Ten of my women were also wounded. Many bullets grazed me, but I escaped until struck unconscious by a blow on the head with an iron bar, from behind! Many of the onlookers were drawn into the scrimmage and the result was a panic.

I recovered consciousness in the evening. I was in my own bed with a physician beside it. He told me that although I had lost a good deal of blood, my wound was not serious, and that I should be able to resume my duties soon.

Late in the evening the officer in charge reported that Michael Rodzianko had come to see me. The physician went out to meet him and I heard the two conversing in the room next to mine. Rodzianko's first question was whether I had been killed. It appeared that rumors were being spread in the town that I had been struck dead on the Mars Field. The doctor's account of my condition apparently came as a joyful relief to the President of the Duma.

He then came in and smilingly approached my bed and kissed me.

"My little heroine, I am very glad that you escaped serious injury. There were many alarming reports about you. It was a brave act to march straight into the midst of the Bolsheviks. Nevertheless, it was foolish of you and the wounded men to oppose such tremendous odds. I have heard of your victory in the fight against the introduction of the committee system in the Battalion. Well done! I wanted to call and congratulate you earlier, but I have been very busy."

I sat up in bed to show my visitor that I was quite well. He told me of the appointment of General Kornilov[35] to the command of the southwestern front, and of a luncheon to be given the following day at the Winter Palace, at which Kornilov would be present. Rodzianko inquired if I should be strong enough to attend it, and the physician thought that I probably should. Rodzianko then took his leave, assuring me of his readiness to help me at all times and wishing me a speedy recovery.

Lavr Kornilov, 1916.

The following morning I spent at the window, with my head bandaged, watching my women drill. I felt strong enough to go with Rodzianko to the luncheon. He called before noon and drove me to the Winter Palace. In the reception room there I was introduced by the President of the Duma to General Kornilov.

Middle-aged, with a spare, manly, vigorous frame, a keen face, grey moustache, Mongol eyes, semi-Mongol cheekbones – this was Kornilov. He spoke little, but every word he uttered rang out clearly. One felt instinctively that here was a man of powerful character and of dogged perseverance.

"I am very glad to meet you," he said, shaking my hand. "I congratulate you on your determined fight against the committees."

"General," I replied, "I was determined because my heart told me that I was in the right."

---

35. Lavr Kornilov (1870-1918) was a decorated officer in the Russo-Japanese War and led troops in Galicia and the Carpathians during the First World War. Captured by the Austrians, he escaped and was made General of the Petrograd Military District in March 1917 and commander in chief of the army in July. He is best known to history, however, for "The Kornilov Affair," an event that some saw as a coup, while others saw it as a regrettable miscommunication between Kerensky and the General when both sought to bring the pre-revolutionary situation under control. Kornilov assaulted the Petrograd Soviet so as to disband it. But the effort failed because Kerensky had armed the Soviet's army of workers and soldiers. Kornilov was arrested.

"Always follow the advice of your heart," he said, "and you will do right."

At this moment Kerensky appeared. We rose to greet him. He shook hands with Kornilov, Rodzianko and me. The War Minister was in a good humor and smiled benignly at me.

"Here is an obstinate little person. I never saw her like," Kerensky said, pointing at me. "She took it into her head not to form a committee, and nothing could break her will. One must do her justice. She is a diehard, holding out all alone against us all. She foolishly persisted in maintaining that no such law existed."

"Well," said Rodzianko in my defense, "she isn't such a fool. She is perhaps wiser than you and me together."

We were then asked into the dining room. Kerensky was seated at the head of the table, I at its opposite end. Rodzianko was on Kerensky's right, Kornilov was on my right. There were also three Allied Generals present. One was on my left, and the other two were between Kerensky and Kornilov.

The conversation was carried on mostly in a foreign tongue and I understood nothing. Besides, I had my troubles with the dishes and table etiquette. I did not know how to deal with the unfamiliar dishes, and blushed deeply several times, while I watched my neighbors from the corners of my eyes.

Now and then I engaged in conversation with Kornilov. He approved my decided views about the necessity of discipline in the army, and declared that if discipline were not restored, then Russia was lost. The burden of Kerensky's conversation at the table was that, in spite of the considerable disintegration that was thinning the ranks of the army, it was not too late as yet. He was contemplating a trip to the front, feeling certain that it would lead to our troops taking the offensive.[36]

Finally Kerensky got up, and the luncheon was over. He told me before leaving that there would be a solemn presentation to me of the two standards and icons sent by the soldiers from the front. I replied that I did not deserve such honors, but hoped to be able to justify his trust in me.

Kornilov parted from me cordially, inviting me to call on him at his headquarters when I arrived at the front. Rodzianko then escorted me home and asked me to come to see him before leaving for the front.

The time remaining before the date fixed by Kerensky for the dedication of the Battalion's battle flag was spent in intensive training and rifle practice.

---

36. The ill-fated Kerensky Offensive across the western front began on June 17, 1917 (by the old calendar in use at the time), or July 7, new style. Maria's dates in the text are new style.

The women were almost ready to go to the front and awaited June 25 with impatience.

Finally that day arrived. The women were in high spirits. My heart was filled with expectation. The Battalion arose early. Every soldier had a new uniform. The rifles were spic and span. There was a holiday feeling in the air. We were all cheerful, though nervous under the weight of responsibility which the day was to bring.

At nine in the morning two bands arrived at our gates. They were followed by Captain Kuzmin, assistant Commander of the Petrograd Military District, with instructions for the Battalion to be at the St. Isaac's Cathedral at ten o'clock in full military array. We started out almost immediately, led by the two military bands.

The throng of people moving in the direction of the Cathedral was enormous. The entire neighborhood was lined up with units of the garrison. There were troops of all kinds. There was even a body of Cossacks, with flags on the points of their spears. A group of distinguished citizens and officers stood on the steps leading to the entrance of the church. It included Kerensky, Rodzianko, Milyukov, Kornilov, Polovtsov and others. The Battalion saluted as we marched into the huge building.

The officiating clergy were two bishops and twelve priests. The church was filled to overflowing. A hush fell on the vast gathering as I was asked to step forward and give my name. I was seized with fear, as if in the presence of God Himself. The standard that was to be consecrated was placed in my hand and two old battle flags were crossed over it, hiding me almost completely in their folds. The officiating bishops then addressed me, dwelling upon the unprecedented honor implied in the dedication of an army standard for a woman.

It was not customary to inscribe the name of a Commander on the flag of a military unit, he explained, but the name of Maria Bochkareva was emblazoned on this standard, which, in case of my death, would be returned to the Cathedral and never used by another Commander. As he spoke and said the prayers, in the course of which he sprinkled me three times with holy water, I prayed to the Lord with all my heart and might. The ceremony lasted about an hour, after which two soldiers, delegates from the First and Third armies, presented to me two icons, given by fellow soldiers, with inscriptions on the cases, expressing their trust in me as the woman who would lead Russia to honor and renown.

I was humbled. I did not consider myself worthy of such honors. When asked to receive the two icons I fell on my knees before them and prayed for God's guidance. How could I, an ignorant woman, justify the hope and trust of so many brave and enlightened sons of my country?

General Kornilov, representing the army, then presented me with a revolver and sword with handles of gold.

"You have deserved these gallant weapons, and you will not disgrace them," he said, and kissed me on the cheek.

I kissed the sword, and pledged myself never to disgrace the weapons and to use them in the defense of my country.

Kerensky then pinned the epaulets of a Lieutenant on my shoulders, promoting me to the rank of an officer. He, also, kissed me, and was followed by some of the distinguished guests, who congratulated me warmly.

The high officials departed and General Polovtsov took charge for the rest of the day. I was too overcome to regain my self-possession quickly. I was raised up by the hands of General Polovtsov and General Anosov first. Then some officers of junior rank carried me. Next I was raised above the crowd by some enthusiastic soldiers, and dragged out of their hands by even more jubilant sailors. All the time I was very uncomfortable, but the ovation continued and the cheers would not subside. Women in the throng forced their way to me, kissing my feet and blessing me. It was a patriotic throng, and love for Russia was the dominant note. Orators mounted improvised platforms and talked of the coming offensive and the Battalion of Death, finishing with a "Long live Bochkareva!" The emotion of the soldiers at the moment was such that they cried: "We will go with Bochkareva to the front." Speakers pointed to the women as heroes, calling upon every able-bodied man to rise to the defense of Russia.

It was a wonderful day: a dream, not a day. Had my fancy come true? Had this group of women already accomplished the object for which it was organized? It seemed so that day. I felt that Russia's manhood was ready to follow the Battalion and strike the final blow for the salvation of the country.

It was an illusion, and my disenchantment was not very long delayed. But it was such a beautiful illusion that I gained enough strength from it to work patiently for its renewal and realization. What those thousands of Russian soldiers, assembled in the neighborhood of the St. Isaac's Cathedral, felt on June 25, 1917, was the thrill that comes from self-sacrifice for the truth, from unselfish devotion to the Motherland, from lofty idealism. It convinced me that the millions of Russian soldiers, scattered over their vast country, were amenable to the word of truth, and instilled into me faith in the ultimate restoration of my country.

After the consecration of the Battalion's standard, there remained less than two days before leaving for the front. These were spent in preparations. We had to organize a supply unit of our own, as we could not take with us the kitchen of the Guard Regiment that we had used. Also, every member of the Battalion received complete war equipment.

On June 29 we left the grounds of the Institute and marched to the Kazan Cathedral, on the way to the railway station. The bishops addressed us, dwelling upon the significance of the moment and blessing us. Again large crowds followed us into the Cathedral and to the station. When we started out from the church a group of Bolsheviks blocked our way. The women immediately began to load their rifles. I ordered them to stop this, put my sword in the scabbard, and marched forward to the Bolsheviks.

"Why do you block the way? You scoff at us women, claiming that we can't do anything. Then, why did you come here to interfere with our going? It is a sign that you are afraid of us," I said to them. They dispersed, jeering.

Accompanied by the hearty cheers of the people who lined the streets, we marched to the station. Our train consisted of twelve vans and one second-class passenger coach. We boarded the train under orders to proceed to Molodechno, the headquarters of the First Siberian Corps, to which the Battalion was to be attached.

The journey was a triumphal procession. At every station we were hailed by crowds of soldiers and civilians. There were cheers, demonstrations and speeches. My women had strict orders not to leave the cars without permission. Our meals were provided for us at certain stations, through telegraphic orders, and we alighted for our meals at those places. At one stopping-place, while I was resting, a demonstration took place in our honor, and I was suddenly taken out of bed and carried out in view of the crowd.

Thus we moved to the front, arriving at Molodechno. I was met there by a group of about twenty officers and taken to dine with the Staff. The Battalion was quartered in two barracks upon our arrival at Corps Headquarters.

There were about a score of barracks in Molodechno. Almost half of these were filled with deserters from the front, former police and gendarmes who had been impressed into the army at the outbreak of the Revolution, and had soon escaped from the ranks. There were also some criminals and a number of Bolshevik agitators. In a word, they were the riff-raff of that sector of the front.

They soon got word of the arrival of the Battalion, and while I was being driven to dinner they crowded round my women and began to curse and molest them. The officer in charge perceived with alarm the growing insolence of these ruffians, and hurried to the Commandant of the station to beg protection.

"But what can I do?" answered the Commandant helplessly. "I am powerless. There are fifteen hundred of them, and there is nothing to be done but to submit patiently to their derision and win their goodwill by kindness."

The death penalty had already been abolished in the army.

The officer in charge returned with empty hands. She found a few of the rioters in the barracks, behaving offensively towards the women. Having tried vainly to get rid of them by persuasion, she telephoned to me. I had barely seated myself at the dinner table when her summons reached me. I hastened into a motor and drove to the barracks.

"What are you doing here?" I asked sharply, as I jumped from the car and ran inside. "What do you want? Go out of here! I will talk to you outside if you want anything."

"Ha, ha, ha!" the men jeered. "Who are you? What sort of a *baba* is this?"

"I am the Commander."

"The Commander, eh? Ha, ha, ha! Look at this Commander!" they scoffed.

"Now," I spoke slowly and firmly, "you have no business here whatever. You have got to go away. I will be at your service outside. If you want anything you can tell me there. But you must get out of here!"

The men, there were only a score of them, went towards the door, still jeering and muttering curses. I followed them. Immediately outside a large crowd had collected, attracted by the noise. As I faced these depraved men in soldiers' uniforms my heart was pained at the sight of them. A more ragged, tattered, demoralized lot of soldiers I had never seen. Most of them had the faces of murderers. Others were mere boys, corrupted by the Bolshevik propaganda.

A little while ago, in the old days of January, 1917, it would have been sufficient to execute a couple of them to transform the fifteen hundred into respectable and obedient human beings. Now, the mighty Russian military organization, while engaged in a mortal combat with an enemy of stupendous strength, had been rendered incapable of coping with even such a small group of recalcitrants! This was my first experience of the front after an interval of two months. But what a great stage the disintegrating influences had advanced in this short period of time! It was four months since the Revolution, and the front was already seriously infected by the blight of disobedience.

"Why did you come here? What devil brought you here? You want to fight? We want peace! We have had enough fighting!" was shouted at me from every side.

"Yes, I want to fight. How can we have peace save by fighting the Germans? I have had more experience of war than you, and I want peace as much as any one here. If you want me to talk more to you and answer any questions you care to ask me, come tomorrow. It is getting late now. I shall be at your disposal tomorrow."

The gang drifted away in groups, some still scoffing, others arguing. I transferred the women from the second barrack into the first for greater safety, and posted sentinels at every entrance. This cheered up the women somewhat, but they were even more encouraged when they heard me refuse an invitation to spend the night at Staff Headquarters. How could I leave my women alone with these fifteen hundred ruffians in the neighborhood? So I resolved to sleep with them, under the same roof.

Night came and my soldiers went to bed. Many of us must have wondered that evening whether the deserters would heed my words or return during the night and attack the barrack. It was not yet midnight when a party of them came knocking at the windows and the thin wooden walls. They cursed us all, and particularly me. They tried to enter through the doors, but were met by fixed bayonets. When their scoffing proved ineffective, they stoned the barrack, breaking every pane of glass and bruising about fifteen of my women.

Still we made no complaint. If the Commandant confessed his powerlessness to control them, what could we do? Besides, we were going to the front to fight the Germans, not to engage in a battle with three times our number of desperadoes.

The more patience we exercised, the bolder grew the attacks of the men. Some of them would suddenly thrust their hands through the shattered window panes and seize some of the women by their hair, causing them to cry out with pain. Nobody slept. All were excited and on edge. The crashing of the stones against the wooden walls would every now and then shake the whole building. It required a lot of patience to endure it all, but my orders were not to provoke a fight.

However, as the night wore on and the noises and jeering did not cease, my blood began to boil, and I finally lost control of myself. Hastily putting on my overcoat I ran out of the barrack. The day was just breaking, an early July day. The band of scoundrels, about fifty in all, stood still for an instant.

"You villains, you rogues! What are you doing?" I shouted with all my strength. "Didn't you want a rest on the way to the trenches? Can't you let us alone, have you no sense of shame? Perhaps some of the girls here are your sisters. And I see that some of you are old men. If you want anything, come to see me. I am always ready to talk and argue and answer questions. But leave the women alone, you shameless ruffians!"

My tirade was met by an outburst of laughter and jeers that incensed me even more.

"You will go away this instant or kill me here!" I shrieked, flinging myself forward. "You hear? Kill me!" I was trembling with rage. The roughs were impressed by my tone and words. They left one by one, and we settled down for a couple of hours of sleep.

In the morning, General Valuyev, now Commander of the Tenth Army, reviewed the Battalion. He was greatly pleased and expressed his gratification to me at the perfect discipline and bearing of the unit. Our own two kitchens then prepared dinner, after they had received a supply of food and provender. There were twelve horses attached to the Battalion, six drivers, eight cooks, two shoemakers. In addition to these sixteen men, there were two military instructors accompanying us. The men were always kept separate from the women.

After dinner the deserters began to assemble around our barracks. I had promised to debate with them on the preceding day, and they now took me at my word.

"Where are you taking your soldiers? To fight for the bourgeoisie? What for? You claim to be a peasant woman, then why do you want to shed the peoples' blood for the rich exploiters?"

These and many similar questions were fired at from many directions.

I stood up, folded my arms and eyed the crowd sternly. I must confess that a tremor ran over me as my eyes passed from one rascal to another. They were a desperate lot, looking more like beasts than human beings. The dregs of the army, truly.

"Look at yourselves," I began, "and think what has become of you! You, who once advanced like heroes against the enemy's devastating fire and suffered like faithful sons of the Motherland in the defense of Russia, lying for weeks in the muddy, vermin-infested trenches, and crawling through No Man's Land. Consider for a moment what you are now and what you were a little while ago. Only last winter you were the pride of the country and the world. Now you are the execration of the army and nation. Surely there are some among you who belonged to the Fifth Siberian Corps, aren't there?"

"Yes, yes."

"Then you ought to remember me – Yashka – or have heard of me."

"Yes, we do! We know you!" came from several parts of the crowd.

"Well, if you know me, you ought also to know that I waded in the mud of the trenches together with you; that I slept on the same wet ground as you or your brother; that I faced the same dangers, suffered the same hunger, shared the same cabbage soup that you had. Why then do you attack me? Why do you jeer at me? How and when have I earned your contempt and derision?"

"When you were a common soldier," answered a couple of voices, "you were like one of us. But now, being an officer, you are under the influence of the bourgeoisie."

"Who made me an officer if not you? Didn't your comrades, the common soldiers of the First and Tenth Armies, send special delegates to honor me and present icons and standards to me, thus raising me to the grade of officer? I am of the people, blood of your blood, a toiling peasant girl."

"But we are tired of war. We want peace," they complained, unable to find fault with me personally.

"I want peace, too. But how can you have peace? Show me how?" I insisted vigorously, observing that my words were soothing the temper of the crowd considerably.

"Why, simply by leaving the front and going home. That's how we can have peace."

"Leave the front!" I shouted, with all the force at my command."What will happen then? Tell me! Will you have peace? Never! The Germans will just walk over our defenses and crush the people and their freedom. This is war. You are soldiers and you know what war is. You know that all is fair in war. To leave the trenches! Why not hand Russia over to the Kaiser! It's the same thing, and you know it as well as I. No, there is no other way to peace than through an offensive and the defeat of the enemy. Conquer the Germans and there will be peace! Shoot them, kill them, stab them, but do not fraternize with the foes of our beloved Russia!"

"But they fraternize with us. They are tired of the war, too. They want peace as much as we," said a few men.

"They are deceiving you. They fraternize here and send soldiers to fight our Allies."

"What are the Allies to us if they do not want peace?" some argued.

"They do not want peace now because they know that the Germans are treacherous. You and I know it, too. Haven't the Germans asphyxiated thousands of our brethren with their deadly gases? Haven't we all suffered, from their base tricks? Aren't they now occupying a large part of our country? Let's drive them out and have peace!"

There was silence. Nobody had anything to say. Greatly encouraged, I resumed, just as a happy idea dawned upon me.

"Yes, let us drive them out of Russia. Suppose I were to take you along to the front, to feed you well, to equip you with new uniforms and boots, would you go with me to attack the treacherous enemy?"

"Yes, yes! We will go! You are our comrade. You are not a bourgeois vampire! With you, we will go!" many voices rang from all sides.

"But if you go with me," I said, "I shall keep you under the severest discipline. There can be no army without discipline. I am a peasant like you, and I would take your word of honor to remain faithful. But should any one of you attempt to escape, I would have him shot promptly."

"We agree! We are willing to follow you! You are one of us! Hurrah for Yashka! Hurrah for Bochkareva!" the crowd roared almost unanimously.

It was a soul-stirring scene. But an hour ago these tattered men acted as if their hearts were deadened. Now they were beating warmly. A short time ago they looked like the most degraded ruffians; now their faces were lit with the fire of humanity. It seemed a miracle. But it was not. Such is the soul of the Russian; at one moment it is hardened and brutal, at another it is full of devotion and love.

I spoke to General Valuyev and begged permission to take the body of deserters to the front, asking for equipment for them. The General refused. He was afraid that they would demoralize the rest of the men. I offered to be responsible for their conduct, but I could not bring over the General to my point of view.

So I had to return with empty hands, but I did not disclose the truth to the men. I told them that there was no equipment available and that as soon as it arrived they would be dispatched to the Battalion's sector. Meanwhile, I invited them to escort us out of Molodechno in the morning.

We started out, in full array, at ten the following day. Each of the girls carried her full equipment, a burden of about sixty-five pounds. There were twenty miles ahead of us to Corps Headquarters. The road was open, fields alternating with woods stretching on both sides of it.

I had telegraphed to Headquarters ordering supper, expecting to arrive there early in the evening. But clouds gathered overhead and showers impeded our progress to such an extent that the women could scarcely keep up their strength. Whenever we passed a village, it was a great temptation to let them take a rest in it, but I knew that I should never be able to rally them again that day if I once allowed them to break the ranks. So I was compelled to keep the Battalion on the march and to press on regardless of the condition of the road or the weather.

It was eleven at night when we arrived at Corps Headquarters and were met by General Kostyayev, Chief of Staff, who invited us to go to eat the meal prepared for us. The General in command would review us tomorrow, he said.

The girls were too tired to eat. They fell like logs in the barn assigned to the Battalion and slept all night in their clothes.

The Corps Headquarters were situated at Redki. We breakfasted in the barracks, after which we proceeded to prepare for review by the general in command. I had been invited to lunch at Staff Headquarters after review.

It was then that I found that several of my girls were suffering from the effects of the arduous march on the preceding day. Two of them, Skridlova, my adjutant, the daughter of an Admiral who had commanded the Black Sea Fleet, and Dubrovskaya, the daughter of a General, were too ill to remain in the ranks and were sent to a hospital. I appointed Princess Tatuyeva, who belonged to a famous Georgian family in Tiflis, to be my adjutant. She was a brave and loyal girl, of high education and spoke fluently three foreign languages.

At twelve I formed the Battalion for review. Knowing how much the women had gone through the previous day, I relaxed my sternness for the moment and joked with my soldiers, coaxing them to make an effort to make a good impression on the General. The girls did their best to pull themselves together and were ready to show the General what the Battalion was worth. The Corps Commander arrived soon. He reviewed my soldiers, gave them a thorough examination, resorting even to some catch tests.

"Magnificent!" he said enthusiastically at the conclusion of the test, congratulating me and shaking my hand. "I would not have believed it possible for men, let alone women, to master the training in four weeks so well. Why, we have had recruits here who had undergone three months' drilling, and they could not compare with your girls."

He then spoke a few words of praise to the women themselves, and my soldiers were immensely pleased. I proceeded with the General and his suite to Headquarters, where luncheon was awaiting us. He nearly kissed me when he learned that there were no committees in my Battalion, so genuine was his delight.

"Since the committees were instituted in the army, everything has changed," he said. "I love the soldiers and they always loved me. But now all is changed. There is endless trouble. Every day, almost every hour, there come some impossible demands from the ranks. The front has lost almost all of its former strength. It is a farce, not war."

We had not had time to begin the luncheon when a telegram arrived from Molodechno, notifying the Staff of Kerensky's arrival there for luncheon and requesting the General's and my attendance. Losing no time, the General ordered his car and we drove to Molodechno at top speed.

There were about twenty persons present at the luncheon at Army Headquarters. Kerensky sat at the head of the table. The Commander of my Corps was on my right and another General on the left. During the meal the conversation was about conditions at the front and the state of preparedness for a general offensive. I took practically no part in the discussion. At the end of the meal, when all arose, Kerensky walked up to the Commander of my Corps and delivered himself unexpectedly of the following peremptory speech:

"Since the committees were instituted in the army, everything has changed," he said. *"I love the soldiers and they always loved me. But now all is changed. There is endless trouble. Every day, almost every hour, there come some impossible demands from the ranks. The front has lost almost all of its former strength. It is a farce, not war."*

"You must see to it that a committee is formed immediately in the Battalion of Death, and that she," pointing at me, "ceases to punish the women!"

I was thunderstruck. All the officers in the room strained their ears. There was a tense moment. I felt my blood rush to my head like a flame. I was furious.

With two violent jerks I tore off my epaulets and threw them into the face of the War Minister.

"I refuse to serve under you!" I exclaimed. "Today you are one way, tomorrow, the opposite. You allowed me once to run the Battalion without a committee. I shall not form any committees! I am going home."

I flung these words at Kerensky, who had turned very red, before any one in the room had recovered from the shock, ran out of the house, threw myself into the Corps Commander's motor and ordered his chauffeur to drive to Redki instantly.

A friend of the Chief of Staff, Kostyayev, told me later that there was a great commotion as soon as I left the room. Kerensky was furious at first.

"Shoot her!" he ordered in a fury.

"Minister," said General Valuyev, the Commander of the Tenth Army, in my defense, "I have known Bochkareva for three years. She first tasted war as a member of my Corps. She suffered more than any other soldier at the front, because she suffered both as a woman and as a soldier. She was always the first to volunteer for any enterprise, thus serving as an example. She is a plain soldier and a word is a pledge to her. If she had been promised the command of the Battalion without the aid of a committee, she would never understand a violation of the pledge."

The Commander of my Corps and other officers also spoke up for me. Finally some remembered that Kerensky had abolished capital punishment.

"Capital punishment has been abolished, Minister," they said." If Bochkareva is to be shot, then why not let us shoot some of those fifteen hundred deserters who are raising the devil here?"

Kerensky then abandoned the thought of shooting me, but insisted before departing from Molodechno that I should be tried and punished. The trial never took place.

The Corps Commander was very agitated when he discovered that I had disappeared with his car. He had to borrow one to get to Redki, and although pleased in his heart with my outburst he decided to give me a scolding and remind me of discipline. I was too excited and nervous to do anything when I returned from Molodechno, and so lay down in my barrack, trying to picture what would now become of the Battalion. I knew I had committed a serious breach of discipline and reproached myself for it.

I was called before the Commander late in the afternoon, and he reprimanded me for my unmilitary conduct. The General's rebuff was severe. I acknowledged every point of it without argument, recognizing that my behavior was unpardonable.

The hour for dinner came, and I went to Headquarters. The scene at the table was one of suppressed merriment. Everybody knew of what had happened at Molodechno. The officers winked knowingly and exchanged smiles. I was the hero of the secret rejoicing. Nobody dared to laugh out loud, for the General at the head of the table had assumed a grave expression, as if struggling not to sanction by an incautious smile the clandestine mirth of the Staff over my treatment of Kerensky. Finally the General could not preserve his gravity any longer and joined in the laughter. The restraint was removed.

"Bravo, Bochkareva!" one of the men exclaimed.

"That's the way to treat him," said another.

"As if there weren't enough committees in the army, he wants still more!" spoke a third.

"He himself abolished capital punishment, and now he orders her to be shot!" laughed a fourth.

The officers were plainly hostile toward Kerensky. Why? Because they saw that Kerensky did not understand the temper of the Russian soldier. His flying excursions to the front perhaps left Kerensky and the world with the impression that the army was a living, powerful, intelligent organism. The officers who were with the soldiers day and night knew that the same crowd which had given an enthusiastic welcome to Kerensky an hour before would accord a similar reception to a Bolshevik or Anarchist agitator. Above all, it was Kerensky's development of the committee system in the army that had undermined his reputation with officers.

After dinner I applied to the General for seven officers and twelve men instructors to accompany the Battalion to the trenches. One of the officers, a young Lieutenant named Leonid Grigorevich Filippov, was recommended to me for the post of adjutant in battle. Filippov was known as a brave fellow, as he had escaped from a German prison camp. I addressed to the group of instructors a warning to the effect that if any of them were unable to consider my soldiers as men, it would be better for them not to join the Battalion, and thus avoid unpleasantness in the future.

The Battalion was assigned to the 172nd Division, situated within four miles of Redki, in the village of Beloye. We were met by the units in reserve, who were drawn up to welcome us, with great enthusiasm.

It was a sunny day in midsummer. We spent little time at Division Headquarters. After lunching we resumed our march, having been further assigned to the 525th Kuryag-Daryusky Regiment, about a mile from Beloye and a little over a mile from the fighting line. We arrived at Senki, the Regimental Headquarters, after sunset and were met by a "shock battalion," formed of volunteer soldiers for offensive warfare. There were many such battalions scattered throughout the army, comprising in their ranks the best elements of the Russian forces.

Two barns were placed at the disposal of the Battalion and one dug-out for the officers. Another dug-out was occupied by the instructors and members of the supply detachment. However, as the men in the place began to manifest a certain amount of curiosity in regard to my women, I decided to sleep in one barn and let Tatuyeva take charge of the second. At night a crowd of soldiers surrounded the barns and would not let us sleep. They were inoffensive. They made no threats. They were simply curious, intensely curious.

"We merely want to see. It is something new," they replied to the remonstrances of the sentinels, "babas in breeches! And soldiers, as well! Isn't it extraordinary enough to attract attention?"

In the end I had to go out and talk with the soldiers. I sat down and argued it out. Didn't they think it right for the women to want a rest after a day of marching? Yes, they did. Wouldn't they admit that rest was necessary before taking the offensive? Yes, they would. Then why not suppress their curiosity and give the exhausted women a chance to gather new strength? The men agreed and dispersed.

The girls were in high spirits the following day. The Russian artillery had got to work early and poured a stream of fire into the enemy positions. Of course, that meant an offensive. The Commander of the Regiment came out to review us and made a cordial speech to the Battalion, calling me their mother and expressing his hope that the girls would love me as such. The firing increased in violence as the 6th of July, 1917, was drawing to a close. The German artillery did not remain silent long. Shells began to fall round about us.

The night was passed in the same barns at Senki. How many of the girls slept, I do not know. Certainly most of them must have been awed in the actual presence of war. The guns were booming incessantly, but my brave little soldiers, whatever they felt in their hearts, behaved with fortitude. Were not they going to lead in a general attack against the foe that would set the entire Russian front ablaze? Were not they sacrificing their lives for beloved Russia, who would surely remember with pride this gallant group of three hundred women? Death was dreadful. But a hundred times more dreadful was the ruin of Mother Russia. Besides, their Commander would lead them over the top, and with her they would go anywhere.

And what was the Commander thinking about? I had a vision. I saw millions of Russian soldiers rise in an invincible advance after I and my three hundred women had disappeared in No Man's Land on the way to the German trenches. Surely, the men would be shamed at the sight of their sisters going into battle. Surely, the front would awake and rush forward like one man, to be followed by the powerful armies of the rear. No force on earth could withstand the irresistible onrush of fourteen million Russian soldiers. Then there would be peace...

CHAPTER XIV
AN ERRAND FROM KERENSKY TO KORNILOV

In the dusk of July the 7th we made our last preparations before going into the trenches. The Battalion was provided with a detachment of eight machine guns and a crew to man them. I was also furnished with a wagonload of small ammunition.

I addressed my girls, telling them that the whole regiment would take part in an offensive the coming night.

"Don't be cowards! Don't be traitors! Remember that you volunteered to set an example, to the laggards of the army. I know that you are of the stuff to win glory. The country is watching for you to set an example for the entire front. Place your trust in God, and He will help us save the Motherland."

To the men who were standing by I spoke of the necessity of cooperation. As Kerensky had just completed a tour of this section, the soldiers were still under the influence of his passionate appeals to defend the country and freedom. The men responded to my call, promising to join us in the coming attack.

Darkness settled over the earth, broken now and then by the flare of explosions. This was to be the night of nights. The artillery roared louder than ever as we stealthily entered a communication trench and filed singly into the front line. The rest of the regiment was pouring in the same direction through other communication trenches. There were casualties during the operation. Some soldiers were killed, and many were wounded, among the latter being several of my girls.

The order from General Valuyev, Commander of the Tenth Army, was for our whole corps to go over the top at 3 a.m., July 8th. The Battalion occupied a section of the front trench, flanked on both sides by other companies. I was at the extreme right of the line held by the Battalion. At the extreme left was Captain Petrov, one of the instructors. My adjutant, Lieutenant Filippov, was in the center of the line. Between him and myself two officers were stationed among the girls at equal distances. Between him and Captain Petrov another two officers occupied similar positions. We waited for the signal to advance.

The night was passed in great tension. As the hour fixed for the beginning of the attack approached, strange reports reached me. The officers were uneasy. They noted a certain restlessness among the men and began to wonder if they would advance after all.

The hour struck three. The Colonel gave the signal. But the men on my right and to the left of Captain Petrov would not move. They replied to the Colonel's order with questions and expressions of doubt as to the wisdom of advancing. The cowards!

"Why should we die?" asked some.

"What's the use of advancing?" remarked others.

"Perhaps it would be better not to attack," expressed the hesitation of many more.

"Yes, let us see first if an offensive is necessary," debated the remaining companies.

The Colonel, the Company Commanders and some of the braver soldiers tried to persuade the regiment to go over the top. Meanwhile, day was breaking. Time did not wait. The other regiments of the corps were also hesitating. The men, raised to a high pitch of courage by Kerensky's oratory, lost heart when the advance became imminent. My Battalion was kept in the trench by the cowardly behavior of the men on both flanks. It was an intolerable situation, unthinkable, grotesque.

The sun crept out in the East, only to shine down upon the extraordinary spectacle of an entire corps debating upon their Commander's order to advance. It was four o'clock. The debate still continued heatedly. The sun rose higher. The morning mist had almost vanished. The artillery fire was slackening. Still the debate continued. It was five o'clock. The Germans were wondering what in the world had become of the expected Russian offensive. All the spirit accumulated in the Battalion during the night was waning, giving way under the physical strain which we were enduring. And the soldiers were still discussing the advisability of attacking!

Every second was precious. "If they would only decide in the affirmative, even now it might not be too late to strike," I thought. But minutes grew into hours, and there was no sign of a decision. It struck six, and then seven. The day was lost. Perhaps all was lost. One's blood boiled with indignation at the absurdity, the futility of the whole thing. The weak-kneed hypocrites! They feigned concern as to the advisability on general principles of starting an offensive, as if they hadn't talked for weeks about it to their hearts' content. They were nothing but cowards, concealing their fear in floods of idle talk.

Orders were given to the artillery to continue the bombardment. All day the cannon boomed while the men argued. The shame, the humiliation of it! These very men had given their words of honor to attack! Now fear for the safety of their skins had taken possession of their minds and souls. The hour of noon still found them in the midst of the debate! There were meetings and speeches in the immediate rear. Nothing more stupid, more empty of meaning could be imagined than the arguments of the men. They were repeating in stumbling speech those old, vague phrases that had been proved false again and again, to the complete satisfaction of their own minds. And yet they lingered, drawn by their faint souls towards doubt and vacillation.

The day declined. The men had arrived at no final resolution. Then, about seventy-five officers, led by Lieutenant Colonel Ivanov, came to me to ask permission to enter the ranks of the Battalion for a joint advance. They were followed by about three hundred of the most intelligent and gallant soldiers in the regiment. Altogether, the Battalion's ranks had swollen to about a thousand. I offered the command to Lieutenant-Colonel Ivanov as to a superior, but he declined.

Every officer was provided with a rifle. The line was so arranged that men and women alternated, a girl being flanked by two men. The officers, now numbering about a hundred, were stationed at equal distances throughout the line.

We decided to advance in order to shame the men, having arrived at the conclusion that they would not let us perish in No Man's Land. We all felt the gravity of the decision. We had nothing to justify our belief that the men would not abandon us to our fate, except feeling that such a monstrosity could not happen. Besides, something had to be done. An offensive had to be launched soon. The front was rapidly deteriorating to a state of impotence.

Colonel Ivanov communicated to the Commander by telephone the decision of the Battalion. It was a desperate gamble, and every one of us realized the grimness of the moment. The men on our flanks were joking and deriding us.

"Ha, ha! The women and officers will fight!" they jeered.

"They are pretending. Who ever saw officers go over the top like soldiers, with rifles in hand?"

"Just watch those women run!" joked a fellow, amid a chorus of merriment.

We clenched our teeth in fury but did not reply. Our hope was still in these men. We clung to the belief that they would follow us over the top and, therefore, avoided giving them cause for offense.

At last the signal was given. We crossed ourselves and, hugging our rifles, leaped out of the trenches, every one of our lives dedicated to "the country and freedom." We moved forward under a devastating fire from machine guns and artillery, my brave girls, encouraged by the presence of men at their sides, marching steadily against the hail of bullets.

Every moment brought death with it. There was but one thought in every mind: "Will they follow?" Each fleeting instant seemed like an age that lurid morning. Already several of us were struck down, and yet no one came after us. We turned our heads every now and then, piercing the darkness in vain for support. Many heads were raised above the trenches in our rear. The laggards were wondering if we were in earnest. No, they decided that it was all a trick. How could a bare thousand women and officers attack after a two days' bombardment on a front of several miles? It seemed incredible, impossible.

But, dauntless of heart and firm of step, we moved forward. Our losses were increasing, but our line was unbroken. As we advanced further and further into No Man's Land, the shadows finally swallowing us completely, with only the fire of explosions revealing our figures at times to the eyes of our men in the rear, their hearts were touched.

Through the din and crash of the bombardment we suddenly caught the sound of a great commotion in the rear. Was it a feeling of shame that stirred them from their lethargy? Or was it the sight of this handful of intrepid souls that aroused their spirit? Anyhow, they were roused at last. Numbers had already climbed over the top and were running forward with shouts, and in a few moments the front to the right and left of us became a swaying mass of soldiers. First our regiment poured out and then, on both sides, the contagion spread and unit after unit joined in the advance, so that the entire corps Was on the move.

We swept forward and overwhelmed the first German line, and then the second. Our regiment alone captured two thousand prisoners. But there was poison awaiting us in that second line of trenches. Vodka and beer were in abundance. Half of our force got drunk forthwith, throwing themselves ravenously on the alcohol. My girls did splendid work here, destroying the stores of liquor at my orders. But for that, the whole regiment would have been drunk. I rushed about appealing to the men to stop drinking.

"Are you mad?" I pleaded. "We must take the third line yet, and then the Ninth Corps will come to relieve us and keep up the push."

I realized that the opportunity was too precious to be lost. "We must take the third line and make a breach in their defenses," I thought, "so as to turn this blow into a general offensive."

But the men were succumbing one by one to the terrible curse. And there were the wounded to be taken care of. Some of my girls were killed outright, many were wounded. The latter almost all behaved like Stoics. I can see, even now, the face of Klipatskaya, one of my soldiers, lying in a pool of blood. I ran up to her and tried to help her, but it was too late. She had twelve wounds, from bullets and shrapnel. Smiling faintly her last smile, she said, "My dear, it's no matter."

The Germans organized a counter-attack at this moment. It was a critical time, but we met the shock of the attack with our bayonets. As usual in such cases, the enemy turned and fled. We pursued them and swept them out of their third line, driving them into the woods ahead of us.

We had hardly occupied the enemy's third line when orders came by field telephone from the Commander to keep up the pursuit so as not to allow the Germans to entrench themselves, with a promise that the supporting corps would start out immediately. We cautiously sent some patrols into the woods to find out the strength of the enemy. I led one such scouting party, and was able to detect that the German force was being slowly but steadily augmented. It was then decided that we should immediately advance into the forest and occupy positions there till reinforcements arrived enabling us to resume the advance.

It was early dawn. The Germans being in the thick of the woods had the advantage of observing every movement we made, while we could not see them at all. We were met by such a violent and effective fire that our soldiers lost heart and took to their heels by the hundred, reducing our force to about eight hundred, two hundred and fifty of whom were those of my girls who had escaped death or injury.

Our situation rapidly became critical. The line running through the forest was long. Our numerical strength was wholly inadequate for it. Our flanks were unprotected. Our ammunition was running low. Fortunately, we turned on the enemy several of his own abandoned machine guns. We stripped the dead of rifles and bullets. And we reported to the Commander that we had been deserted under fire by the men and were in imminent danger of capture. The Commander begged us to hold out till three o'clock, when the Ninth Corps would come up to our succour.

Had the Germans had any idea of the size of our force, we should not have remained there more than a few minutes. We dreaded every moment that we should be outflanked and surrounded. Our line was stretched out so that each soldier held a considerable number of feet, our force altogether covering a distance of two miles. The Germans organized an attack on the left flank. Aid was despatched from the right flank, which was left almost without machine guns, and the attack was repulsed. In this engagement Lieutenant Colonel Ivanov was wounded. There were many other wounded officers and men lying about. We could not spare the hands necessary to carry them to the first-aid dressing stations far away in our rear.

Three o'clock came, and the expected reinforcements were not yet in sight. The Germans made an attack on the right flank. My adjutant, Lieutenant Filippov, was now commanding there. As our line was curved, he ordered the machine guns on the left flank to direct a slanting fire at the advancing enemy. At the same time, our artillery was instructed to let down a barrage in the same section, and the attack was repulsed.

At my request, the Commander sent out about a hundred stretcher-bearers to collect the dead and wounded scattered between our former line and the captured German third line. About fifty of my girls were dead and more than a hundred wounded.

Meanwhile the sun had risen and time was passing. Our condition grew desperate. We sent an urgent appeal for help to Headquarters. From the other end of the wire came the appalling answer: "The Ninth Corps has been holding a meeting. It arrived from the reserve billets and went forward till it came to the trenches we had held before the attack. There it stopped, wavered, and began to debate whether to advance or not."

We were struck by the news as if by some terrific blow. It was crushing, unimaginable, unbelievable.

Here we were, a few hundred women, officers, men – all on the brink of a precipice, in imminent danger of being surrounded and wiped out of existence. And there, within a mile or two, were they, thousands of them, with the fate of our lives, the fate of this whole movement, nay, the fate, perhaps, of all Russia, in their hands. And they were debating!

Where was justice? Where was brotherhood? Where was manhood and decency?

"How can you leave your comrades and those brave women to certain destruction?" the Commander appealed to them. "Where is your sense of honor and justice and comradeship?"

The officers begged and implored their men to go forward as our calls for help grew more and more insistent. There was no response. The men said they would defend their positions in case of a German attack, but would not take part in any offensive.

It was in these desperate circumstances, as I was rushing about from position to position, exposing myself to bullets in the hope that I might be struck dead rather than see the collapse of the whole enterprise, that I came across a couple hiding behind a trunk of a tree. One of the pair was a girl belonging to the Battalion, the other a soldier. They were making love!

This was even more overpowering than the deliberations of the Ninth Corps, which were sentencing us to annihilation. I was almost out of my senses. My mind failed to grasp that such a thing could be really happening at a moment when we were trapped like rats at the enemy's mercy. My heart turned into a raging cauldron. In an instant I flung myself upon the couple,

I ran my bayonet through the girl. The man took to his heels before I could strike him, and escaped.

There being no immediate prospect of a conclusion of the debate in the Ninth Corps, the Commander ordered us to save ourselves by retreat. The difficulty was to extricate ourselves without being detected by the Germans. I ordered first one group to go back some distance and stop, and then another and then a third group to do the same till we reached almost the fringe of the forest. It was a slow and perilous undertaking, full of anxious moments during the shiftings of the line, but everything went smoothly and our hopes were raised.

Our line was drawn in, and we were preparing for the final retreat when terrific shouts of "Hurrah!" suddenly rang out, almost simultaneously, on both flanks. We were half surrounded! Another quarter of an hour and the net would have completely surrounded us. There was no time to lose. I ordered a helterskelter retreat.

The German artillery increased in violence, and the enemy's rifles played havoc with us from both sides. I ran for all I was worth several hundred feet, till knocked unconscious by the terrific concussion of a shell that landed near me. My adjutant, Lieutenant Filippov, saw me fall, picked me up and dashed through the devastating fire, the German trench system, the open space that was No Man's Land before the offensive, and into the Russian trenches.

There the Ninth Corps was still debating. But it was already too late. As the breathless survivors of the Battalion, bespattered with mud and blood, made their way one by one into our trenches, it became obvious that there was no use in any further deliberations. The offensive had been all to no purpose. The Germans re-occupied, without opposition, all the ground and trenches we had won at such terrible cost. There were only two hundred women left in the ranks of my Battalion.

I regained consciousness at a hospital in the rear. I was suffering from shell-shock. My hearing was affected and, while I could understand what was said to me, I was unable to talk. I was sent to Petrograd and was met at the station by a distinguished gathering, including many of my patronesses and some distinguished army officers. Kerensky sent his adjutant. General Vasilkovsky,[37] successor to Polovtsov as Commander of the Petrograd Military District, was also present. I was deluged with flowers and kisses. But to all the congratulations I could make not a sound in reply, lying motionless on the stretcher.

I was taken to a hospital and given a large, beautiful room. Kerensky came to see me, kissed me on the forehead, and presented me with a handsome bouquet. He made a little speech, apologizing for the trouble he had given me in the controversy about introducing the committee system in the Battalion, praising me for my bravery, and declaring that I had set a wonderful example to the men all over the front. He invited me to call on him as soon as I got well.

President Rodzianko visited me the following day. He was very depressed and pessimistic over the condition of the country.

"Russia is perishing," he said, "and there is no salvation in prospect for her. Kerensky relies too much on his own power, and is blind to what is going on around him. General Kornilov requested that Kerensky should grant him the necessary authority to restore discipline in the army, but Kerensky refused, saying that he was able to accomplish it himself in his own fashion."

While I was in the hospital a delegate from the front brought me a testimonial from my Corps Committee! It appeared that two days after I was wounded the Committee, which usually comprised the more intelligent soldiers, met in session and discussed all night how they could best reward my conduct. A resolution was passed in which praise and thanks were expressed to me for brave leadership in an attack which resulted in the capture of two thousand prisoners. The testimonial was a record of the resolution, signed by the members of the Corps Committee. Later, the men would have done anything to revoke their signatures, as they deeply regretted this tribute to me, an implacable enemy of the Germans, from the entire corps, which was infected even then with the Bolshevik spirit.

> "Russia is perishing," he said, "and there is no salvation in prospect for her. Kerensky relies too much on his own power, and is blind to what is going on around him.

---

37. Oleg Petrovich Vasilkovsky (1879-1944) was elevated to this post in July 1917, but was sent into retirement after the Kornilov Affair. He later took part in anti-Bolshevik actions and then escaped to Estonia, where he represented the short-lived People's Republic of Belarus (which nonetheless still retains a government in exile). When the Soviets annexed the Baltic states in 1941, under the Molotov-Ribbentrop Pact, he was arrested and sentenced to ten years in the Gulag, and is believed to have died in prison in Tomsk.

I learned that Lieutenant Filippov had taken charge of the Battalion, gathering the survivors from all the units with which they identified themselves during and after the retreat. However, he did not remain with the Battalion, resigning in order to join an aviation detachment in the South, after he had organized the remnant of my unit. It was also reported to me that the Commander of the Corps had recommended me for a cross.

Another week passed before I recovered my speech and my normal condition, although the effects of the shock did not disappear completely for some weeks. A woman friend of mine told me that Kornilov was expected to arrive in Petrograd the next day, and that his relations with Kerensky were strained, on account of their different views as to the restoration of discipline at the front. I telephoned to the Winter Palace for an appointment, and the War Minister's adjutant reported my request to Kerensky, who said that he could receive me immediately, even sending his car for me.

Kerensky welcomed me heartily, expressing his gladness at my recovery. He asked me what was the reason why the soldiers would not fight. In reply I told him in detail the story of my fruitless offensive, how the men had called meetings and debated for hours and days whether to advance or not. I told only the facts, as narrated above, and Kerensky was deeply impressed.

In conclusion I said, "You can see for yourself that the committees stand for talk, endless talk. An army that talks is not a fighting army. In order to save the front it is necessary to abolish the committees and introduce strict discipline. General Kornilov seems to be the man to accomplish this. I believe he can do it. All is not yet lost. With an iron hand the Russian Army can be restored. Kornilov has such a hand. Why not give him the right to use it?"

Kerensky agreed with me generally. "But," he said, "Kornilov wants to restore the old regime. He may take the power into his own hands and put back the Tsar on the throne."

This I could not believe, and I said so to Kerensky. He replied that he had grounds for believing that Kornilov wanted the monarchy re-established.

"If you are not convinced," Kerensky continued, "go over to General Headquarters, have a talk with Kornilov, find out all you can about his intentions, and come back to report to me."

I realized immediately that Kerensky was asking me to act for him in the role of a secret agent, but I was interested. The thought occurred to me again and again, "What if Kerensky is right, and Kornilov really wants the Tsar back?"

My country was in a bad state, but I dreaded to think of a return of Tsarism. If Kornilov was for the old regime, then he was an enemy of the people, and

Kerensky was right in hesitating to invest the General with supreme authority. I therefore accepted his proposal.

I was, however, uneasy at the thought of the errand I had undertaken and resolved to go to Rodzianko, whom I look upon as my best friend, and make a clean breast of it. When I told him of my conversation with Kerensky he said, "This is Kerensky's old game – suspecting everybody of being for the old regime. I don't believe it of Kornilov. He is an honest, straightforward man. Still, if you feel in doubt about it yourself, come, let us go over together to Headquarters. Do not go as a spy, but tell Kornilov the truth to his face."

We took a train for General Headquarters and were admitted to Kornilov soon after our arrival. I told him frankly what had passed between Kerensky and myself a couple of days before. Kornilov reddened. He jumped up and began to pace the room in a rage.

"The scoundrel! The upstart! I swear by the honor of an old soldier that I do not want Tsarism restored. I love the Russian *muzhik* as much as any man in the country. We have fought together and understand one another. If I were only given authority, I would soon restore discipline by punishing, if necessary, a few regiments. I could organize an offensive in a few weeks, beat the Germans and have peace this year, even now. He is driving the country to perdition, the rascal!"

Kornilov's words were like sword-thrusts. There was no question but that the man spoke from the depth of his soul. His agitation was real beyond a doubt. He continued to walk the room fiercely, talking of the certain collapse of the front if measures were not taken without delay. "The idiot! He cannot see that his days are numbered. Bolshevism is spreading rapidly in the army, and it will not be long before the tide swamps him. Today he allows Lenin to carry on his propaganda in the army without hindrance. Tomorrow Lenin will have got the upper hand, and everything will be wrecked."

We left Komilov, and I had to decide whether to make a report to Kerensky or not. I must confess to a feeling of shame when I thought of how I had carried out the errand. I therefore asked Rodzianko to tell Kerensky of Kornilov's attitude toward Tsarism and I boarded a train for Moscow, where I had been invited to review the local Women's Battalion, organized in imitation of mine. There were many such battalions formed all over Russia.

When I arrived at the barracks and was taken before the fifteen hundred girls who had enlisted in the Moscow unit, I nearly fainted at the sight of them. They were nearly all rouged, they were wearing slippers and fancy stockings, they were wantonly dressed and very casual in their bearing. There were a good many soldiers about, and their behavior with the girls was revolting.

"What is this, a house of shame?" I cried out in my grief. "You are a disgrace to the army! I would have you disbanded at once, and I shall do my best to see that you are not sent to the front!"

A storm of protest broke loose.

"What is all this, the old regime or what?" shouted some indignant, voices.

"What's that? Discipline? How dare she talk in that fashion?" cried others.

In a moment I was surrounded by a mob of indignant men who drew closer and closer, threatening to kill me. The officer who accompanied me apparently knew the temper of the crowd and realized the danger I had brought upon myself. He sent an urgent call to General Verkhovsky,[38] Commander of the Moscow Military District, who was very popular with all the troops.

Meanwhile my escort was doing his best to calm the raging throng which soon grew to about one thousand. Closer and closer the circle drew in about me, and I was ready to say my last prayers. One man tripped me by the foot, and I fell. Another brought down the heel of his boot on my back. Only another minute and I should have been lynched. But God was with me. Verkhovsky arrived not an instant too soon and dashed into the crowd, which separated to make way for him. He addressed a few words to the men. They had a magic effect. I was saved.

From Moscow I went to the front, and when my girls saw me arrive there was general jubilation. "The Commander has come back!" they shouted, as they danced about. They had had a hard time in my absence, but unfortunately I did not remain long. In the evening of the day of my arrival a telegram came from General Kornilov, requesting my immediate presence. I left without delay for Army Headquarters, and there met the Commander-in-Chief and Rodzianko. The three of us went to Petrograd to see Kerensky. It was on the eve of the great Moscow Assembly, which met on the 28th of July.

During this journey Kornilov talked of his childhood. He was born in Mongolia, the son of a Russian father and a Mongolian mother. The conditions of life some fifty years ago in the Far East were such as to innure one to any

38. Alexander Ivanovich Verkhovsky (1886-1938) had been appointed to the post in May and was a strong supporter of the February Revolution. He was, however, opposed to Kornilov and in August sought to convince him not to act. In late August he was promoted to Major General and became the last Defense Minister of the Provisional Government. A week prior to the Bolshevik Revolution, Verkhovsky came out in support of peace with Germany but garnered no support in the government, and was relieved of duty for two weeks, and thus happened to be on Valaam Island during the coup. He led efforts to fight against the Bolsheviks but was soon arrested. In 1918, he was released and allowed in the Red Army, continuing to have brushes with the law while serving in the rear as instructor and commander. Arrested in 1931, he was sentenced to ten years. While imprisoned, he did research and wrote on military history. He was released early, in 1934, after Kliment Voroshilov forwarded to Stalin Verkhovsky's assessment of lessons of the 1905 war with Japan and how they related to the present day. He returned to teaching, but in 1938 was arrested on trumped up charges and shot.

hardships. Thence it was that Komilov derived his contempt for danger and his spirit of adventure. He was given a good education by his father, who, I believe, was a frontier trader of peasant stock, but rose to his high position by sheer ability and doggedness. He learned to speak a dozen languages and dialects, more from mixing with all kinds of people than from books. In short, Kornilov was not of an aristocratic family or brought up in select surroundings. His knowledge of men and affairs was gained at first hand. He had enjoyed close contact with the Russian *muzhik* and workman. Himself of reckless valor, he came to love the Russian peasant-soldier for his contempt of death.

Upon our arrival at Petrograd, we all went together to the Winter Palace. Kornilov entered Kerensky's study first, leaving us to wait in the antechamber. It was a long wait for Rodzianko and myself. Kornilov remained locked up with Kerensky for two whole hours, and our ears bore witness to the stormy nature of the interview inside. When the Commander-in-Chief finally emerged from the office his face was flushed.

Rodzianko and I were admitted next. Kerensky was visibly agitated. He said that he had not expected me to carry out his errand in such a manner. I had not acted rightly, he declared.

"Perhaps I am guilty towards you. Minister," I replied. "But I acted according to my conscience, and did what I felt was my duty to the country."

Rodzianko then addressed Kerensky in some such manner as the following, "Bochkareva reports from the front that you are rapidly losing favor with both men and officers; the officers because of the decay of discipline, the men because of their desire to go home. Now, consider what is happening to the army. It is going to pieces. The fact that the soldiers could allow a group of women and officers to perish is proof that the situation is critical. Something must be done immediately. Give absolute authority in the army to Kornilov, and he will save the front. And you remain at the head of the Government, to save us from Bolshevism."

I joined Rodzianko in his plea. "We are rapidly nearing an abyss," I urged, "and it will soon be too late. Kornilov is an honorable man, I am convinced of it. Let him save the army now, so that people shall not say afterwards that Kerensky destroyed the country!"

"That will never happen!" he cried, banging his fist on the table. "I know what I am doing!"

"You are destroying Russia!" exclaimed Rodzianko, angered by Kerensky's arrogance. "The blood of the country will be on your head."

Kerensky turned red, then white as a corpse. His appearance frightened me. I thought he would fall down dead.

"Go!" he shrieked, beside himself, pointing toward the door. "Leave this room!"

Rodzianko and I moved to the exit. At the door Rodzianko stopped for a moment, turned his head and flung a few biting words at the Minister.

Kornilov was waiting for us in the anteroom. We drove to Rodzianko's house for luncheon. There, Kornilov related to us the substance of his conference with Kerensky. He had told him that the soldiers were deserting the front in droves and that those who remained were useless, as they visited the German trenches every night and came back drunk in the morning. The fraternization had extended to the entire front. A whole Austrian regiment, well provided with liquor, came over to our trenches at one point and a debauch followed. Kornilov described the experience of my Battalion as related in official reports that had reached him and declared that numerous messages from officers asking for instructions were coming to him daily. But what instructions could he give? He had to seek instructions himself from Kerensky.

At this point the Minister asked him what was to be done, and he replied that capital punishment must be reestablished, that the committees must be abolished, that the Commander-in-Chief must be given full authority to disband units and execute agitators and rebels, if the front was to be saved from collapse and the country from an immense disaster.

Kerensky replied that Komilov's suggestions were impracticable, that all that could be done was for the officers to submit the various complications arising at the front to the Regimental, Corps and Army Committees for solution. Kornilov retorted that the committees had already, again and again, been confronted with such problems, had them investigated and confirmed, passed resolutions of censure and obtained pledges from the men that they would not repeat the offenses, but, like weak children, the soldiers would immediately resume drinking and fraternizing. Only rigid discipline, he insisted, could make the Russian Army a force to be reckoned with.

However, Kerensky was obstinate. He would not consent to put Kornilov's recommendation into practice.

A deadlock was reached which aroused Kornilov's temper. He blurted out, "You are driving the country to destruction. You know that the Allies already regard us with contempt. Should our front collapse, they would consider Russia a traitor. You are under the delusion that the rank and file still believe in you. But almost all of them are Bolsheviks now. Only a little while, and you will find yourself overthrown, and your name will go down in history as the destroyer of the country. All your life you fought Tsarism. Now you are even worse than the Tsar was. Here you sit in the Winter Palace, unwilling to leave, too jealous to hand over the power to some one else. Although I knew the Tsar well, your distrust of me and belief that I am in favor of Tsarism now is utterly unfounded. How can I be in favor of a Tsar when I love my country and the *muzhik*? My whole aspiration is to build up a strong democratic nation, by means of a Constituent Assembly and a chosen leader. I want Russia to be powerful and progressive. Give me a free hand in the army and our Motherland will be saved."

Kerensky heatedly rejected Kornilov's request.

"You will have to resign," he exclaimed, "and I will appoint Alexeyev[39] in your place, and use force against you in the event of your failure to obey me!"

"Scoundrel!" exclaimed Kornilov, and he left Kerensky's study.

During lunch Kornilov told Rodzianko that if Kerensky carried out his threat he would lead the Savage Division, consisting of tribesmen loyal to him, against Kerensky. Rodzianko pleaded against such action, begging Kornilov not to war against the Government, as that would divide the country into several factions and lead to civil war. After a long, private conversation Kornilov was induced by the President of the Duma to stick to his post as Commander-in-Chief for the sake of the peace of the nation.

At the table I also learned that General Alexeyev had more than once been offered the Chief Command, but had declined to take it unless he had authority to exercise a free hand. It also appeared that Kerensky was growing more and more autocratic and irritable, and was reluctant to see people and accept advice.

I parted from Rodzianko and Kornilov. The latter kissed me and pledged his friendship to me for my efforts to maintain discipline. I returned to the front, while they went to Moscow to attend the Assembly.

My heart was heavy with sorrow. It was five months since freedom was born, only five months. But what a nightmare it had become! We were at war, but playing with the enemy. We were free, but disorder was on the increase. Our best men were happy and united five months ago. Now, they were divided and quarrelling among themselves. The people were divided, too. When the revolution first broke, all had rejoiced together, the soldier, the townsman, the peasant, the workman, the merchant. All were glad. All hoped for good and

---

39. Mikhail Vasilyevich Alexeyev (1857-1918) was an old school general who served as Tsar Nicholas' Chief of Staff from August 1915 to March 1917. After the 1916 Battle of Naroch (where Maria pulled wounded to safety from under fire), he held little confidence in the offensive capabilities of the Russian Army and his attitudes contributed to the general apathy in the senior command. In February 1917, he wrote a decisive telegram urging Nicholas to abdicate, and he served as Commander-in-Chief under the Provisional Government from April through May of 1917. He agreed to again take the top post in August 1917, in order to be the one to arrest Kornilov and stave off civil war. He intentionally had Kornilov and his aides sent to a prison in Belarus from which they could escape. He resigned from the army a week later. After the Bolshevik revolution he played a part in the organization of anti-Bolshevik forces in the South, but died early in late 1918 of pneumonia.

happiness. Now, there had sprung up a number of parties that were setting one group of the people against the other. Each of them claimed to have the truth. All of them promised a blissful era, but what was good to one was evil to the other. They talked, argued, fought among themselves. And the minds of the people grew confused and their hearts divided. In the face of such a terrible foe as the Germans, how long could a disunited country endure? I prayed to God for Russia.

CHAPTER XV
THE ARMY BECOMES A SAVAGE MOB

My women were enthusiastic over the return of their Commander. I reported to the Commander of the Corps and was invited to luncheon with the Staff. The officers were interested to know what was going on in the rear. I did not tell them the details of the quarrel between the Prime Minister and the Commander-in-Chief, but I did indicate in general terms that a difference had arisen.

Toward the end of the meal it was reported that the Chairman of the Corps Committee had come to see the Commander on important business. It appeared that the corps in the trenches was to be relieved at seven in the evening and orders had been issued to the corps in reserve, some miles behind, to move toward the trenches at five in the morning. However, they had not moved. The Chairman now came to explain the cause of the delay. He was himself a patriotic and intelligent soldier and was asked to sit down by the General while he told the story.

"The rascals!" he said of the men who had elected him as their leader, "they wouldn't move. They have been holding meetings all the morning and refuse to go to relieve their comrades."

We were all shocked. The General became excited.

"What the devil!" he exclaimed angrily." That passes all bounds! If the soldiers refuse to relieve the very men who had relieved them a couple of weeks ago, then there is no use in continuing at the front, making a pretence of war. It's a farce! It's no use staying here, let them lay down their arms and go home and save the Government the truble of keeping up the semblance of an army. The villains! Just shoot a few of them, and they will learn to do their duty! At seven o'clock the trenches will be empty. Go and tell them that I command them to move immediately!"

The Chairman returned to the billets and told his soldiers that the General ordered them into the trenches under penalty of death. This incensed the men.

"Aha, he is threatening to shoot!" cried one. "He's of the old regime," exclaimed another. "He wants to practise on us the Tsar's methods!" shouted several voices.

"He is a blackguard!" suggested another. "He ought to be killed! He wants to rule us with an iron hand!" the men roared, working themselves up to a fever.

Meanwhile the news came from the trenches that the men were holding meetings there, proclaiming their determination not to remain in their position after seven o'clock. The General was in great difficulty. He was faced with the probability of his section of the front being left entirely open to the enemy. He telephoned to the reserve billets and asked the Chairman of the Committee what was going on there.

Suddenly the General grew pale, dropped the receiver and said :

"They want to kill me."

Chief of Staff Kostayev took up the receiver and in a trembling voice inquired what the trouble was. I listened to the answer.

"They are in an ugly mood. They have mutinied and threaten to mob the General. The excitement is spreading, and some of them have already started out for Headquarters."

The voice of the Chairman at the other end of the wire was clearly expressive of his alarm. In reply to questions what the General could do to calm the mob he said that the committee admired and respected the General, that its members were doing their best to allay the passions that had been aroused, but seemed helpless.

A few minutes later several officers and men ran into the house, greatly agitated.

"General, you are lost if you don't get away in time!" one of them said.

Shortly afterwards Colonel Belonogov, a man of sterling heart, beloved by his soldiers even before the revolution, rushed in. He brought the same tidings, asking the General to hide. I joined in, imploring the Commander to conceal himself till the storm had passed. But he refused.

"Why should I hide?" he exclaimed. "What wrong have I done? Let them come and kill me! I have only done my duty."

He went into his study and locked himself in.

The mob was moving nearer and nearer. There was a deathly pallor on the faces of all those present. Every minute or so some one would dash in breathlessly, with eyes full of horror, to herald the approaching tempest.

The tide of tumultuous humanity reached the house. There were cries and howls. For a second we were all in suspense. Then Colonel Belonogov said he would go out and talk to them and try to make them see reason. The Colonel had a gentle voice and a gentle heart. He never addressed even his own orderly in the ordinary fashion. When a little time before he had asked to be transferred to another position, his own soldiers persuaded him into staying where he was.

In a word, the Colonel was an exceptional man. Without question there was no other officer in the Corps as fit as he to undertake the task of mollifying an excited mob. He went out on the porch and calmly faced the steadily increasing multitude.

"Where is the General? Where is he? We want to kill him!" the savage chorus bawled.

"What are you thinking of?" the Colonel began. "Come to your senses and consider the order. It was an order to relieve your own comrades, soldiers like yourselves. Now, you know that this was no more than fair. The General simply wanted you to take the places of your comrades."

"But he threatened to shoot us!" interrupted the men.

"You did not quite understand. He only said generally that to get obedience one must shoot..."

"Shoot!" a hundred voices went up from every side, catching the word but not the meaning.

"Shoot! Aha, he wants to shoot! He's for the old regime himself!" a thousand voices roared, without even giving the ashen-faced Colonel a chance to explain.

"Kill him! Show him what shooting is!" raged the vast throng, while the speaker tried vainly to raise his voice and get a hearing.

Suddenly some one jerked the stool from under his feet. In an instant a hundred heavy heels had trampled the life out of that noble body. It was a horrible, terrifying scene. Several thousand men had turned into beasts. The lust of blood was in their eyes. They swayed backwards and forwards as if intoxicated, crushing the last signs of life out of their victim, stamping on the corpse in a frenzy.

The mob's thirst for blood became inflamed. The officers realized that every moment was precious, Kostayev thought that the only way to save ourselves was to escape through the rear of the house.

"I will go out to them," I declared.

The remaining officers thought me mad and tried to dissuade me.

"Belonogov was the idol of his regiment, and see what's become of him. If you go it is certain death," they said. Colonel Kostayev disappeared and several of the Staff followed him.

I could not see how the situation would be saved by escaping. It might save a couple of lives, although even that was unlikely, but the mutiny would extend and might grow beyond control. "I will go out," I resolved, crossed myself and dashed into the infuriated mob.

"What is the matter?" I shouted at the top of my voice. "What has happened to you? Let me pass!"

The crowd separated and made a way for me to the stool.

"Look at her!" jeered some voices.

"Eh, eh, look at this bird!" echoed others.

"Your Excellency!" scoffed one man.

"Now," I began sharply, as soon as I had jumped on the stool. "I am no 'Your Excellency!' but plain Yashka! You can kill me right away, or you can kill me a little later, five, ten minutes later. But Yashka will not be afraid.

"I will have my say. Before you slay me, I must speak my mind. Do you know me? Do you know that I am one of you, a plain, peasant soldier?"

"Yes, we do," the men answered.

"Well," I resumed, " why did you kill this man?" and I pointed at the disfigured body at my feet." He was the kindest officer in the Corps. He never beat, never punished a soldier. He was always courteous, to privates and officers alike. He never spoke contemptuously to any one. Only a month ago he wanted to be transferred and you insisted on keeping him. That was four weeks ago. Had he changed, could he have changed, in such a short time?

"He was like a father to his men. Weren't you always proud of him? Didn't you always boast that in his regiment the food was good, the soldiers were well shod, the baths were regular? Didn't you, of your own accord, reward him with a Soldiers' Cross, the highest honor that the free Russian army has to offer?

"And now you have killed, with your own hards, this noble soul, this rare example of human kindness. Why?

"Why did you do it?" I turned fiercely on the men.

"Because he was of the exploiting class," came one answer.

"They all suck our blood!" shouted some others.

"Why let her talk? Who is she that she should question us?" somebody cried out.

"Kill her! Kill her, too! Kill them all! We have shed enough of our blood! The bourgeois! The murderers! Kill her!" was shouted from many throats.

"Scoundrels!" I screamed. "You will kill me yet, I am at your mercy, and I came out to be killed. You ask why I should be allowed to talk. You ask who I am. As if you didn't know me! Who is Yashka Bochkareva?

"Who sent delegates to present icons to me, if not you? Who had me promoted to the rank of an officer, if not you? Who sent me this testimonial to Petrograd only a couple of weeks ago, if not you?"

Here I drew out from my breast pocket the resolution passed and signed by the Corps Committee and despatched to me while I was in the Petrograd

Hospital. I had brought it with me. Pointing to the signatures, I cried, "You see this? Who signed it, if not you yourselves? It is signed by the Corps Committee, your own representatives, whom you, yourselves, elected!"

The men were silent.

"Who suffered, fought with you, if not I? Who saved your lives under fire, if not Yashka? Don't you remember what I did for your comrades at Narach,[40] when, up to my armpits in mud, I dragged dozens of you to safety and life?"

Here, I turned abruptly on a gaping fellow, looked directly at him and asked, "Suppose the rank and file were to elect their own officers. Now, what would you do in the Commander's place, if you were chosen? You are a plain soldier, of the people. Tell me what you would do!" I thundered.

The man looked foolish, making an effort to laugh.

"Ha, I would see," he said, "once I got there."

"That is no answer. Tell me what you would do if our Corps were in the trenches and another one refused to relieve it. What would you do? What?" I demanded of the whole crowd.

"Would you hold the trenches indefinitely or leave? Answer me that!"

"Well, we would leave, anyhow," replied a number of men.

"But what are you here for," I shouted fiercely, "to hold the trenches or not?"

"Yes, to hold," they answered.

"Then how could you leave them?" I fired back.

There was silence.

"That would be treason to Free Russia!" I continued.

The men bowed their heads in shame. Nobody spoke.

"Then why did you kill him?" I cried out bitterly. "What did he want you to do but hold the trenches?"

"He wanted to shoot us!" several sullen voices replied.

"He never said anything of the sort. What he wanted to say was to explain that the General did not threaten you either, but remarked that in other circumstances your action would be punished by shooting. No sooner did Colonel Belonogov mention the word 'shoot' than you threw yourself upon him without even giving the man a chance to finish what he was saying."

"That was not what we understood. We thought he threatened to shoot us," the men weakly defended themselves.

At this point the orderlies and friends of the murdered Colonel rushed up. They raised such a cry of grief when they saw the mutilated corpse that all

40. See note 19, page 99.

speech was silenced. They cursed and wept and threatened the mob, although they were few and the crowd numbered thousands.

"Murderers! Bloodthirsty ruffians! Whom have you killed? Our little father! Did ever soldiers have a better friend than he was? Was there ever a commander who took greater care of his men? You are worse than the Tsar and his hangmen. You are given freedom, and you act like cutthroats. You devils!"

And the mourners broke out in even louder lamentations. The wailing rent the air. It gripped everybody's throat. Many in the mob wept. As the dead man's friends began to relate the various favors they had received from him, I could not choke down my tears and stepped down from the stool, convulsed with sobs.

Meanwhile, in response to calls for help, a division from a neighboring corps arrived to quell the mutiny. The Committee of the Division came forward and demanded the surrender of the ringleaders of the movement that had resulted in the soldiers' refusal to return to the trenches and in the murder of Colonel Belonogov. There were negotiations between the two committees, which finally ended in the surrender by the mob of twenty agitators, who were placed under arrest.

The officers who had fled and the General now reappeared, although the latter was still afraid to order the soldiers to relieve the corps in the trenches. He asked me to broach the subject.

I first addressed the men about the funeral.

"We must have a coffin made. Who will do it?" I asked.

Several volunteered to get some timber and make one.

"How about a grave? We must bury him with full military honors," I went on. Some soldiers offered their services as gravediggers.

An officer went to look for a priest. I sent a soldier to the woods to make a wreath. Then I turned and asked, "Now, will you go to the trenches to relieve your comrades?"

"Yes," the men answered meekly.

It was an unforgettable scene. These five thousand men, all so docile and humble, some with tears still fresh on their cheeks, were like a forlorn flock of sheep that had lost its shepherd. It seemed impossible to believe that these men were capable of murder. You could curse them now, you could even strike them, and they would bear it without protest. They were conscious, deeply conscious of a great crime. Quietly they stood, from time to time, uttering a word of regret, engrossed in mourning. And yet these same lambs were ferocious beasts two hours ago. All the gentleness now mirrored in their faces was then extinguished by a hurricane of savage passion. These obedient children had actually been inhuman a short time ago. It was incredible, and still it was the truth.

Such is the character of the Russian people.

The coffin, an oblong box of unshaven boards, draped inside and out with a white sheet, was brought at four o'clock. The body had been washed, but it was impossible to restore the face to its normal appearance. It was disfigured beyond recognition. With the help of some of the men, I wrapped the body in canvas and placed it in the coffin. Instead of one there were four green wreaths made. The priest began to read the service but could not control himself and burst into sobs. The General, the Staff, and I, with candles in our hands, were sobbing too. Immediately behind the coffin, as the procession started, the dead officer's orderly wailed in heartrending tones, recalling aloud the virtues of his master. Behind us marched almost the whole Corps, including the Regiment commanded by the dead man. The weeping was so general and so increased with every step that by the time the procession reached the grave the wailing could be heard for miles around. As the body was laid to rest everybody dropped a handful of sand into the grave. The lips of all were moving in prayer.

"Did ever soldiers have a better friend than he was? Was there ever a commander who took greater care of his men? You are worse than the Tsar and his hangmen. You are given freedom, and you act like cutthroats. You devils!"

The order was given that by seven o'clock the Corps should be moved to relieve the soldiers at the fighting line. I went to my girls and gave the word for them to be ready too. They had heard of the disturbance and had passed some anxious moments, and therefore they gave me a hearty welcome. The General had telephoned to the front line that the Corps was a few hours late and asked the soldiers there to remain in the trenches for the night. The distance that we had to cover was about ten miles, and we arrived at the front before dawn. The Battalion, now consisting of only some two hundred women, occupied a small sector to itself, opposite the town of Kreva. There was no sign of actual warfare at the fighting line. Neither the Germans nor the Russians used their arms. Fraternization was general. There was a virtual, if not formal, truce. The men met every day, indulged in long arguments and drank beer brought by the Germans.

I could not tolerate such war and ordered my women to conduct themselves as if everything were as usual. The men became very irritated by our militant attitude toward the enemy. A group of them, with the Chairman of the Regimental Committee, came over to our trench to discuss the matter.

"Who are our enemies?" began the Chairman. "Surely, not the Germans who want peace. It's the bourgeoisie, the ruling class, that is the real enemy of the people. It's against them that we ought to wage war, for they would not listen to the German peace proposals. Why does not Kerensky obtain peace for us? Because the Allies will not let him. Well, we will very soon drive Kerensky out of his office!"

"But I am not of the ruling class. I am a plain peasant woman," I objected. "I have been a soldier since the beginning of the war and have fought in many battles. Don't agitate here against officers."

"Oh, I don't mean you," he replied, trying to win me over to the pacificist idea. Several German soldiers joined the Russian group. The discussion became heated. They repeated the old argument that the Germans had asked for peace and that the Allies had not accepted it. I replied that the Germans could have peace with Russia if they withdrew from the invaded parts of our country. So long as they kept our land, it was the duty of every Russian to fight and drive them out.

Thus life dragged on. Nights and days passed in discussions. Kerensky had almost entirely lost his hold on the men, who were drifting more and more toward Bolshevism. Finally, the feud between Kerensky and Kornilov reached a crisis. Kerensky asked the Commander-in-Chief by telephone to send some loyal troops to Petrograd, apparently realizing that his days were numbered. Kornilov replied with a message through Alexeyev, requesting a written certificate from Kerensky, investing the Commander-in-Chief with full authority to restore discipline in the army. It would seem that Kornilov was willing to save Kerensky, provided the latter allowed him to save the front.

But Kerensky evidently saw in this an opportunity of restoring his fallen prestige and securing his position. He therefore turned against Kornilov, publicly declaring that the latter was aiming at supreme power and he appealed to the workmen and soldiers to rise against the Commander of the army. The result was the brief encounter between the revolutionary masses and Kornilov's Savage Division. Kornilov was defeated. Kerensky triumphed, and for the moment it looked as if he had attained his object. All the radical forces were united and Kerensky, as the savior of the revolution from an attempt at a counter-revolution, again became the idol of the soldiers and the working class.

The larger part of the army sided with Kerensky when he appealed for support against Kornilov. But this did hot last long. Kerensky little by little lost the confidence of the masses which he had suddenly acquired, because he did not bring them the much desired peace.

Those of the soldiers and officers who sided with Kornilov were nicknamed Kornilovets.[41] To call a man by this name was equivalent to calling him a counterrevolutionary, an advocate of the old regime, or an enemy of the people.

The inactivity of life in the trenches became wearisome. One rainy day I sent out a listening party into No Man's Land, with instructions to shoot at the enemy in case of his approach. I watched the party go forward. Suddenly, a group of Germans, numbering about ten, came in the direction of our trenches. They walked along at their ease with their hands in their pockets, some whistling, others singing. I aimed my rifle at the leg of one of the troup and wounded him.

The whole front was in an uproar in a second. It was scandalous! Who dared do such a thing! The Germans and the Russians were seething with rage. Several of my women came running up to me greatly alarmed.

"Commander, why did you do that?" they asked, seeing me with a smoking rifle in hand.

A number of soldiers who were friends of mine next hastened into our trench to warn me of the men's ugly temper and threats. I told them that I saw the Germans approach my girls and make an effort at flirtation. But this defense did not appease the soldiers. They placed machine guns in the first trench and were preparing to slaughter us all. Fortunately, we were informed in time and were hidden in a side trench. The machine guns raked our position, without causing any casualties. The firing was finally interrupted by the sharp orders of the Chairman of the Regimental Committee. I was called before him to give an explanation. I bade farewell to my girls, telling them that there would probably be a repetition of the episode of Colonel Belonogov's lynching.

I was received by the men with threats and ugly words.

"Kill her!"

"She's a *Kornilovka!*"

"Make an end of her!"

I was surrounded by the members of the committee, who held back the mob. Several speakers rose in my defense, but hardly succeeded in appeasing the crowd. Then an officer got up to talk on my behalf. He was a popular speaker. But this time his popularity did not avail him. He said that I was right. He would have done the same thing had he been in my place. That was as far as he got.

"Aha, so you are a *Kornilovets* too!" shouted the crowd." Kill him! Kill him!"

---

41. Or, as we shall see, *Kornilovka* if a woman, *Kornilovki* in plural.

In an instant the man was thrown off the chair and struck on the head. In another instant he was crushed to death under a thousand heels.

Then the mob swayed in my direction. But the committee seized me and carried me off to the rear, hiding me in a dugout. One of my girls, Medvedevskaya, was placed at the entrance to guard it.

Meanwhile, my girls heard what had happened and hurried to my aid. The mob dispersed to look for me and some of the men came to the dugout in which I was concealed.

"Where is Bochkareva? Let us in to see if she is there!" they shouted. The girl sentry said she had orders to shoot if they approached near her. They did. She fired, wounding one in the side.

The poor girl was bayoneted by the brutes.

The committee and my friends, numbering about one hundred, insisted that I should be given a trial and not lynched. My girls were ready to die for me to the last one. I was taken out from the dugout by my defenders, who made an effort to lead me to safety for an open trial.

The mob, which had now increased, pressed closer and closer. The two sides were fighting for me. It was agreed that no weapons were to be used in the scramble. The mass of humanity swayed back and forth, my girls fighting with the strength of infuriated wild beasts to stave off the mob. Now and then a man would get close enough to strike a blow at me. As the struggle developed, these blows increased in number till I was knocked senseless. In that state my friends dragged me away from the scene of the struggle.

My life was saved, although I was badly knocked about. It cost the lives of a loyal girl and an innocent friend. I was sent to Molodechno, a couple of my girls going with me to look after me. The Battalion was taken from the front to the reserve billets. But even there their lives were not safe. They were insulted, annoyed, and dubbed Kornilovki. There were daily tumults. The windows of their dugouts were broken. The officers were powerless and seldom showed their faces. My instructors did their best to defend me and the Battalion, explaining that we were non-party.

One morning a car came for me from Headquarters at Molodechno. There I met the Commanding General of my Corps, who described the unbearable conditions in which my girls were placed. They were waiting for me, refusing to go home, unless I disbanded them. He had sent them to dig reserve trenches in order to keep them away from the men. They did splendid work, he said, but as soon as they returned the men began to molest them. Only the previous night a gang of soldiers made an assault on the dugouts in which my girls were billeted. They beat the sentry and broke in with the intention of attacking the women.

There was a panic. Some of the girls seized their rifles and fired in the air. The noise attracted the attention of my instructors and several other soldiers, among whom there were numerous decent men. The situation was saved by the latter.

But what was to be done? Life for the Battalion was becoming absolutely unbearable, at least at this part of the front. It was difficult to understand the change which had come over the men in a few months. How long ago was it that they almost worshipped me, and I loved them? Now they seemed to have lost their senses.

The General advised me to disband the Battalion. But that would be to admit failure and despair as to my country's condition. I was not ready to make such admissions. No, I would not disband my unit. I would fight to the end. The General could not understand my point of view. Was not the case hopeless, since the soldiers had turned machine guns on the Battalion? Wouldn't I have been lynched but for the desperate struggle of my girls and the soldiers who were my friends? So I resolved to go to Petrograd and ask Kerensky to transfer me to a fighting sector.

I went to see my girls before leaving for the capital. It was a pathetic meeting. They were glad to learn of my intended journey. They could not stand it much longer where they were. They were prepared to fight the Germans, to be tortured by them, to die at their hands or in prison camps. But they were not prepared for the torments and humiliation that they were made to suffer by our own men. That had never entered into our calculations at the time the Battalion was formed.

I took my documents with me and left the same evening, telling my soldiers that I would not stay away longer than a week, which was the limit that they set on their endurance. Upon my arrival in Petrograd I went to the quarters occupied by the Battalion while in training.[42] It was evident at a glance that an atmosphere of depression weighed heavily on the Russian capital. The smiles and rejoicings were gone from the streets. There was gloom in the air and in everybody's eyes. Food was very scarce. Red Guards were plentiful. Bolshevism walked the streets openly and defiantly, as if its day had already come.

My friends, who had taken an interest in the Battalion, were horrified to learn of conditions at the front. Their accounts of the state of affairs in the capital depressed me greatly. Kerensky, after his dispute with Kornilov, had cut himself off completely from his friends and acquaintances of the upper classes. I went to General Anosov, telling him of my mission. But he would

---

42. It would seem to be early September – after Kornilov was arrested, but before the October 25 revolution. Verkhovsky was appointed on September 1 (all dates Old Style).

not accompany me anywhere, although he placed his motorcar at my disposal. I drove to the Commander of the Military District, General Vasilkovsky, a Cossack, who looked impressive and strong, but was actually a weakling. He received me cordially and asked the purpose of my visit to the city. He had heard of the rough handling I had endured and expressed his sympathy.

"But," he added," no one is safe in these days. I, myself, expect to be thrown out at any time. It is a matter of days, of hours, for the Government. Another revolution is ripening and is close upon us. Bolshevism is everywhere, in the factories and in the barracks. And how are things at the front?"

"The same or even worse," I answered, and I told him of all my trials and troubles, and the help I expected to obtain from him and the War Minister.

"Nothing can help you now," he said." The authorities are powerless. Orders are not worth the paper on which they are issued. I am going now to Verkhovsky, the new War Minister. Would you like to come with me?"

On the way we discussed Verkhovsky's appointment. He was the same man who, as Commander of the Moscow Military District, had rescued me from the mob at Moscow some weeks before. He was a very popular leader and had considerable influence with the soldiers.

"Perhaps if he had been appointed some months ago he might have saved the army. But it is too late now," said Vasilkovsky.

When we arrived at the War Ministry, we found that Kerensky was in Verkhovsky's study. We were announced, and I was asked to come in first. As I opened the door I saw immediately that all was lost. The Prime Minister and the War Minister were both standing. They presented a pathetic, heartbreaking sight. Kerensky looked like a corpse. There was not a vestige of color in his face. His eyes were red, as if he had not slept for nights. Verkhovsky seemed to me like a man who is drowning, reaching for help. My heart sank. War had made me callous, and I was seldom shocked. But this time I was nearly overcome by the sight of these two agonized figures. I saw the agony of Russia reflected in their despairing faces.

They made an effort to smile, but it was a failure. The War Minister then inquired how things were at the front." We heard you were roughly treated," he said.

I gave a detailed account of everything that I had myself witnessed and experienced. I told them in detail about the lynching of Colonel Belonogov, of the officer who tried to defend me, of the bayoneting of my girl, of the machine guns that were turned on me because I wounded one of the enemy.

Kerensky seized his head in his hands and cried out, "Oh, horror! horror! We are perishing! We are drowning!"

There was a tense, painful pause.

I ended my story with the suggestion that action was urgently needed or all would be wrecked.

"Yes, action is needed, but what action? What is to be done now? What would you do if you were to be given authority over the army? You are a common soldier, tell me what you would do?"

"It is too late now," I answered after thinking a little time. "Two months ago I could have accomplished a great deal. Then they still respected me. Now they hate me."

"Ah!" exclaimed the War Minister. "Two months ago I might have saved the situation myself, if I had only been here then!"

We then discussed the purpose of my journey. I asked for a transfer to a more active part of the front and for a certificate that the Battalion was to be run without committees.

War had made me callous, and I was seldom shocked. But this time I was nearly overcome by the sight of these two agonized figures. I saw the agony of Russia reflected in their despairing faces.

This certificate I obtained from the War Minister without delay, and I still have it in my possession. He also agreed to my first request and promised to look into the matter and issue orders for my transfer.

Kerensky was silent during the conversation. He stood like a ghost, the symbol of once mighty Russia. Four months before he was the idol of the nation. Now almost all had turned against him. As I looked at him I felt I was in the presence of that immense tragedy which was rending my country into fragments. Something seemed to clutch my throat and shake me. I wanted to cry, to sob. My heart dripped blood for Mother Russia. What would I not have done to avert that impending catastrophe? How many deaths would I not have died at that moment?

Here was my country drifting towards an abyss. I could see it sliding down, down, down... And here were the heads of the Government powerless, helpless, clinging hopelessly to the doomed ship, despairing of salvation, abandoned, forlorn, stricken...

"God only knows the future – shall we ever meet again?" I asked the two men in a stifled voice, as I bade them farewell.

Kerensky, livid, motionless, answered in a hoarse whisper, "Hardly."

PART FOUR

TERROR

A May 1917 demonstration in Palace Square.

CHAPTER XVI
THE TRIUMPH OF BOLSHEVISM

I returned to the front. The trains were frightfully crowded, but fortunately I found accommodation in a first-class compartment. At Molodechno I reported to General Valuyev, Commander of the Tenth Army, and lunched with the staff. The General was painfully surprised to learn of the punishment I had received at the hands of the soldiers.

"Did they really strike you?" he asked incredulously, as if he found it hard to imagine the soldiers maltreating Yashka.

"Yes, General, they did," I answered.

"But why?"

I told him of the German I had wounded as he came over with several comrades.

"God, what has become of my once glorious army!" he cried out.

As I related to him the remaining phases of the episode, he punctuated my story with exclamations of surprise.

At the end of the meal General Valuyev informed me that I had been promoted to the rank of Captain. He pinned an extra star on my epaulets and congratulated me.

I was provided with a car and driven to Corps Headquarters, where I reported to my Commanding General. He and the officers of the Corps Staff were anxious to know of the latest developments in the rear. I told them the impression made upon me by Kerensky and Verkhovsky two days before.

"Their appearance bears witness to the fact that all is lost," I said.

"And how about the transfer?" the General asked. "The Battalion is waiting for you to come and take it to a more sympathetic sector."

I answered that orders would soon arrive for the transfer, and showed the certificate authorizing me to command without a committee. The General was glad for my sake.

Meanwhile, my girls learned of my arrival. They formed ranks, desiring to give me a cheerful welcome. My presence seemed to put heart into them. After

Maria Bochkareva

thanking them for their welcome, I went with them to mess. It was my custom to eat the same food as the girls. Only I seldom ate with them. Before eating, I usually supervised the mess, satisfying myself that there was plenty of food and that all was in good order. I knew from experience that there is nothing like food for keeping up a soldier's heart.

Was it my promotion that was the cause of a happy mood, or my return to the girls, to whom I had grown deeply attached? I don't know. But after dinner it occurred to me that it would be the right thing to let the girls have some fun. So I suggested a game, and my soldiers took up the idea with delight. As the game proceeded, many men gathered round the circle in which it was going on. They watched longingly, clearly desirous to play too, but not daring to join in for fear lest I should order the girls away. It gave me pleasure to observe how these grown-up children longed to take part in the sports. But I pretended not to notice it.

Finally they sent several delegates to express their desire to me.

"Captain," the men said bashfully, "we want to speak to you."

"All right, speak out," I answered, "only don't address me as an officer. Call me plain Yashka or Bochkareva."

"May we be allowed to take part in the game?" they asked, encouraged by my words.

"Yes, but only on condition that you do not molest my girls and consider them as fellow-soldiers only," I declared.

The men swore that they would behave, and the girls were not at all displeased at the new arrangement. They played for two or three hours, and the men kept their pledge. When the game ended they left with quite a different feeling towards me. It was a feeling of respect and even love, instead of their former one of hostility.

The Battalion remained in the reserve billets for several days. There developed, as a result of that game, a new attitude on the part of many soldiers toward us women. Companies of them would come over and join the Battalion in sports or singing and various entertainments.

The expected order for a transfer did not come promptly. Meanwhile, the time arrived to relieve the Corps in the trenches. I decided that we had had enough rest, and upon our arrival at the fighting line I put my Battalion on a regular war footing. I sent out scouting parties, established observation posts, and swept No Man's Land with my machine guns and rifles. The Germans were very much agitated. Our own soldiers became excited too, but because of the friendly relations we had established in the rear, they contented themselves with sending delegates and committees to argue the matter with me.

"We have freedom now, you say," I argued. "You insist that you do not want to fight. Very well. I will not ask you to fight the Germans. But you have no right to ask me to act against my convictions. We came here not to fraternize but to fight, to kill and get killed. I claim my freedom to get killed if I want to. Then let me fight the Germans at my sector. Let the Germans fight only against the Battalion. We will leave you alone, and you leave us alone."

The soldiers admitted that this was no more than fair and consented to such an arrangement. When they asked me why I was so anxious to kill Germans I told them that I wanted to avenge my husband who was slain early in the war. For this invention I had only a slight foundation – a rumor that had reached me of the death in battle of Afanasy Bochkarev. Of course, it was an absurd excuse. But I had used it before and I used it afterwards on a number of occasions, and it finally became widely known and believed.

It was exhilarating to be able to do some real fighting again. It is true, we were a mere handful, scarcely two hundred women. But we raised quite a storm. Our machine guns rattled and No Man's Land was turned from a promenade for agitators and drunkards into a real No Man's Land. The news spread rapidly along the front of the activity of the Women's Battalion, and I believe that for hundreds of miles our little sector was the only fighting part of the line. I was naturally very proud of this distinction.

For several days this state of affairs continued. Finally the Germans became so annoyed that they ordered their artillery to bombard my position. There had not been any artillery fire at our sector for some time, and the opening of the big guns caused tremendous excitement. Many of the men were caught in the bombardment and were killed or wounded. The Battalion's casualties were four dead and fifteen wounded.

The whole Corps was roused to a high state of agitation, and a stormy meeting took place immediately. The men demanded my instant execution.

"She wants war," they cried, "and we want peace. Kill her and make an end of it!"

But the members of the committee and my friends insisted that I acted in accordance with an agreement. "She only engages her own Battalion in fighting," my defenders argued, "and leaves us alone. It is not her fault that the German artillery could not find the range quickly and killed some of our comrades."

When word reached me of the indignation and threats of the men I decided to organize an offensive of my own and die fighting. I requested our artillery to answer in kind the enemy's fire. The engagement developed into a regular little battle. We were firing furiously.

While this was going on and the soldiers in the rear were holding the meeting the news arrived of the overthrow of Kerensky and the Bolsheviks' victory in Petrograd. It was announced to the men by the Chairman and was hailed with such an outburst of enthusiasm that the shouts almost drowned the rattling of the machine guns.

"Peace! Peace!!" thundered through the air.

"We will leave the front now! We are going home! Hurrah for Lenin! Hurrah for Trotsky! Hurrah for Kollontai!"

"Land and freedom! Bread! Down with the bourgeoisie!"

As the rejoicing was at its height, the ears of the multitude suddenly caught the sound of the shooting at my sector. The men were roused to fury.

"Kill her! Kill them all! We have peace now!" they roared as they stampeded in our direction.

Several girls dashed up to me to tell me of the approach of the bloodthirsty mob. Almost simultaneously the Commanding General rang up on the field telephone.

"Run!" was his first word. "We are all lost. I am escaping myself. Go to Krasnoye Selo!"

I ordered my girls to seize their rifles and whatever belongings they could and run without stopping. To one of the men instructors I gave the direction in which we were to go, asking him to transmit the information to our supply detachment.

Meanwhile the mob was advancing. It encountered in the immediate rear about twenty of my girls, who were engaged in the supporting line.

These twenty girls were lynched by the maddened mob.

Four of the instructors, who made an attempt to defend these innocent women, were crushed under the heels of the savage crowd.

I and my remaining soldiers ran for ten miles. Although we could see no sign of pursuers, we ran no risks. We stopped in the woods beside the road to Molodechno. It was dark. We drank tea for supper and prepared sleeping quarters under the trees. Our supply train came up during the night and was intercepted by one of the sentries.

We were up at four in the morning. I had a connection made with the telephone wire running to Army Headquarters at Molodechno and talked to the officer in charge, telling him of our approach and asking for dugouts. The officer replied that Molodechno was overflowing with deserters and that it was as dangerous a place for the Battalion as the front itself.

But what could I do? I had to go somewhere. I could not very well continue living in the forest. It was an awful situation. We had escaped from one mob, leaving twenty victims in its hands, and were running straight into the arms of another, perhaps even more bloodthirsty. So we resumed our march. Within two miles of Molodechno I led the Battalion far into the woods and left it there with the supply detachment, comprising twenty-five men. I went to Molodechno alone, having decided to make preliminary investigations and see what was to be done.

Groups of soldiers here and there, in the streets of Molodechno, stopped me with jeering remarks, "Ha, there goes the Commander of the Women's Battalion. She demands iron discipline. Ha, ha!" they would laugh, turning to me, "What now?"

With smiles and conciliatory answers I managed to get to Headquarters. I made a report to the Commandant and was assigned some dugouts for the Battalion. There were crowds of soldiers everywhere as I walked to the billets. They began to harangue me.

"You were late with your Battalion," they said. "It's peace now."

"I am always with you, I am myself a common peasant soldier," I answered. "If you make peace now I will abide by your decision. I am not going to fight against the people."

"Yes, you are for the people now, but where were you before?" they inquired. "You maintained the discipline of the old regime in your Battalion."

"If I had had no discipline," I answered, "my Battalion would have become a shameful thing. You would have sneered at it yourselves. Women are not like men. It is not customary for women to fight. Imagine what would have become of three hundred girls among thousands of men let loose without supervision and restraint, and you will agree with me that I was right."

The men appreciated my argument.

"We think you are right about that," they assented, and became more sympathetic.

I requested their help in cleaning out the dugouts for my girls, and they gave it cheerfully. I dispatched an instructor for the Battalion, and by night my soldiers were comfortably quartered. Under the protection of sentinels picked from the men attached to my unit we passed a restful night. But our presence offered too good an opportunity for the agitators to let it pass. So in the morning, after breakfast, as I started on my way to Headquarters, a small group of insolent soldiers, not more than ten in number, blocked my path, heaping insults upon me.

In a few minutes the ten ruffians were increased to twenty, thirty, fifty, a hundred. I tried to parry their jeers and threats, but without success. In ten minutes I was almost surrounded by several hundreds of these ruffians in uniform.

"What do you want with me?" I cried out, losing patience.

"We want to disband your Battalion. We want you to surrender all the rifles to us."

Now there can hardly be a greater dishonor for a soldier than to surrender his arms without a fight. However, my girls knew that I hated the idea of perishing at the hands of a mob. When they heard of the demand of the crowd they all came out, with rifles in hand.

I made a couple of attempts to argue, but it was apparent that the men came with the purpose fixed in their minds by propagandists. They would not give way and finally cut me short by giving me three minutes to decide. One of the ringleaders stood there, watch in hand, counting the time. Those were moments of indescribable agony.

"I would rather advance against an entire German army than surrender arms to these Bolshevik scoundrels," I thought. "But it is not my life only that is at stake. Everything is lost, anyhow. They say that peace has been declared already. Have I a right to play with the lives of my girls? But, Holy Mother, how can I, a soldier true to my oath and loyal to my country, order the surrender of my Battalion's arms without a fight?"

The three minutes were up. I had arrived at no decision. Still, I mounted the speaker's bench. There was complete silence. The crowd of course expected my capitulation. My girls waited in great tension for their Commander's orders. My heart throbbed violently as my mind still groped for a solution.

"Shoot!" I suddenly shouted at the top of my voice to the girls.

The men were so surprised that for a moment they remained petrified. They were unarmed.

A volley from two hundred rifles went up into the air.

The crowd dispersed in all directions. My order almost drove the men out of their senses with rage. They ran to their barracks for weapons, threatening to return and do for us all.

The real crisis now arose. There was no question that the mob would return, several times stronger, and tear us to pieces. A decision had to be arrived at and carried out instantly. It would take not more than ten minutes for the men to come back. If we did not escape it was certain death.

"In five minutes the Battalion must be ready to march!" I thundered. I sent one of my instructors to the barracks, to mix with the crowd, and later report to me in the woods on the mob's activity. Simultaneously I directed the supply detachment to follow the road in the direction of Krasnoye Selo. Then I called for a volunteer from among the instructors to take care of our battle flag under oath that he would defend it to his death. Accompanied by three other instructors he was sent ahead with the flag.

All this was done in less than five minutes. It was no ordinary feat for a military unit to form in full marching formation in that space of time. But my girls did it. I sent one squad after another into tho woods, leaving with the last squad myself.

I had fixed as our destination a certain clearing in the woods, five miles distant. This distance we covered at break-neck speed. I knew that the infuriated men would follow the road in pursuing us, and I ordered the Battalion to go into the heart of the woods. There were few of us who did not trip on the way several times. Our uniforms were torn by thorns and brambles, and many of us had cuts in our legs and arms. There was little time for dressing the wounds.

A couple of hours later, after reaching the clearing, we heard a distant' whistle, the signal of the instructor I had left behind. He was in high glee over his own experience, and in spite of our precarious position we heartily enjoyed his story.

The mob, it appeared, had returned to our billets, as we had anticipated, fully armed. The men were in a ferocious mood and rushed into the dugouts. They were thunderstruck upon discovering that the dugouts were deserted! They ran about like madmen, scouring the neighborhood, but there was no sign of us. They could not realize that in such a brief space of time the Battalion had been marched away with all the equipment.

"The witch!" they shouted. "She must have spirited them away."

But this did not seem a plausible explanation to the cooler heads. They telephoned to Headquarters, but received an answer of complete astonishment. Nobody there knew of my sudden withdrawal. The mob started along the road to Krasnoye Selo and soon overtook my supply wagons, which were in charge of old soldiers. These said that they had received orders to leave for Krasnoye, and that they knew nothing of the movements of the Battalion. The mob decided that we were on the same road and sent a couple of horsemen to overtake us. The horsemen, of course, returned empty-handed.

"She is a witch!" many soldiers shook their heads with superstitious awe.

"A witch, undoubtedly!" was repeated in tones of uneasiness by others.

The four men with our flag lost their way in the woods, and seeing that they did not arrive, I sent out about twenty girls and instructors to look for them. They were finally discovered. Next we had to get in touch with the supply wagons, and managed to bring them to our camp. Once this was accomplished, we were fairly well established behind the protection of the thickets. There was only one question confronting us: How to get away in safety.

Molodechno was not to be thought of. Krasnoye Selo was also a dangerous place, as our pursuers had warned the garrison there of our approach and had requested that we should be dealt with summarily. The prospects were far from cheerful. I decided to get into secret communication with the Commandant through the instructors.

We camped in the forest for a couple of days, till the Commandant found an opportunity to slip out and come to see us. We held a conference for the purpose of finding a way out of the dilemma.

It was agreed that the career of the Battalion was ended and that nothing remained but to disband it. The problem was, how? The Commandant suggested that he should procure women's garments for the girls and let them return home.

The tide was too strong. It had swamped all that was good and noble in Russia, Russia herself seemed wrecked for ever in that maelstrom of unbridled passions... Everything seemed upside down. There was no friendship, only hatred.

The plan did not strike me as practical. It was hardly possible to obtain nearly two hundred outfits for us in a day or two. It might, therefore, take a couple of weeks to disband the Battalion, which would not be advisable. I proposed a different scheme, namely, to discharge the girls singly and dispatch them to a score of scattered stations and villages. This plan was adopted, as it did not seem difficult for individual members of the Battalion to board trains or obtain vehicles in the neighboring villages and get away.

It took a day or so for the Commandant to ready the necessary documents and funds for all the girls. Then the disbanding began. Every ten or fifteen minutes a girl was sent away, now in one direction, now in the opposite. It was a pitiful finale to an heroic chapter in the history of Russian womanhood. The Battalion had struggled gallantly to stem the tide of destruction and ignorance. But the tide was too strong. It had swamped all that was good and noble in Russia, Russia herself seemed wrecked for ever in that maelstrom of unbridled passions. One did not want to live. There remained only the glory and satisfaction of sharing the overthrow of all that had been honorable in the country. Everything seemed upside down. There was no friendship, only hatred. The unselfishness of the days when Tsarism was overthrown, now, after the fall of Kerensky, had given place to a wave of greed and revenge. Every soldier, every peasant and workman, saw red. They all hunted phantom bourgeoisie, bloodsuckers, exploiters. When freedom was first born, there was universal brotherhood and joy. Now intolerance and petty covetousness reigned supreme.

As I kissed my girls goodbye and we exchanged blessings, my heart quivered with emotion. What had I not hoped for from this Battalion! But as I searched my soul I could find little to regret. I had done my duty by my country. Perhaps I had been too rash when I had imagined that this handful of women could save the army from ruin. And yet I was not alone in that expectation. There was a time when even Rodzianko believed as I did, and Brusilov and Kerensky had thought that the self-sacrifice of the women would shame the men. But the men knew no shame.

My girls had departed. Of the whole Battalion there remained only myself and a few of the instructors. In the evening I made my way to the road where a motorcar was waiting to smuggle me away. The Commandant had arranged for me to go to Petrograd under the personal escort of two members of the Army Committee. They were to join me at the train. The peril lay in the journey to the station. Hidden at the bottom of the car, I was driven to the railway, where the two men took me under their protection. I had decided to go home, to the village of Tutalsk, near Tomsk, where my people had moved during the war.

CHAPTER XVII
FACING LENIN AND TROTSKY

Petrograd seemed populated by Red Guards. One could not make a step without encountering one. They kept a strict watch over the station and the incoming and outgoing trains. My escorts left me on the station platform, as they were to return to the front immediately.

I had hardly emerged from the station, intending to look for a cabman, when a Red Guard Commissar, accompanied by a private with a naked sword, stopped me with the polite query, "Madame Bochkareva?"

"Yes."

"Will you come with me, please?" he suggested.

"Where?" I asked.

"To the Smolny Institute."

"But why?"

"Because I have orders to detain all officers returning from the front," he replied.

"But I am only going home!" I tried to argue.

"Yes, I understand. But as an officer you will also understand that I must obey orders. They will probably release you."

He hailed a cabman and we drove to the Smolny Institute, the seat of the Bolshevik Government. It impressed me as a strongly garrisoned fortress. There were armed sentries everywhere. Accompanied by Red Guards I was led inside. There were Guards at every desk. I was taken before a sailor. He was very rough and brusque.

"Where are you going?" he demanded curtly. "I am going home, to a village near Tomsk," I replied.

"Then why are you armed?" he sneered.

"Because I am an officer, and this is my uniform," I answered.

He blazed up.

"An officer, eh? You will be an officer no more. Give me that pistol and sword!" he ordered.

Troops on Liteyny Prospekt, Petrograd, during the revolution.

The arms were those given to me at the consecration of the flag of the Battalion. I prized them too much to hand them over to this rogue of a sailor, and I refused to comply with his demand. He grew furious. It would have been useless to resist as the room was full of Red Guards. I declared that if he wanted my arms he could take them, but I would never surrender them myself.

He violently tore the pistol and sword from me and pronounced me under arrest. There was a dark cellar in the Institute which was used as a place of detention, and I was sent down there and locked up. I was hungry, but received no answer to all my calls, and remained in the hole till the following morning. As soon as I was brought upstairs I began to demand my arms. The various officials, however, remained deaf to my pleas.

I was informed that I should be taken before Lenin and Trotsky, and was soon led into a large, light room where two men of contrasting appearance were seated, apparently expecting my entrance. One had a typical Russian face. The other looked Jewish. The first was Nikolai Lenin,[43] the second Leon Trotsky. Both arose as I stepped in and walked toward me a few steps, stretching out their hands and greeting me courteously.

---

43. A common error, because Lenin's *nom de guerre*, and that with which he signed some works, was "N. Lenin." But the N was never written out as Nikolai, instead it was a common misconception made chiefly by western sources. This points to the biases of Maria's "translator," Levine. Lenin's birth name was Vladimir Ilyich Ulyanov.

Lenin apologized for my arrest, explaining that he had learned of it only that morning. Inviting me to a seat, the two Bolshevik chiefs complimented me upon my record of service and courage, and began to sketch to me the era of happiness that they intended to procure for Russia. They talked simply, smoothly and very beautifully. It was for the common people, the toiling masses, the disinherited that they were fighting. They wanted justice for all. Wasn't I of the working class myself? Yes, I was. Wouldn't I join them and cooperate with their party in bringing happiness to the oppressed peasant and workman? They wanted peasant women like myself; they had the highest esteem for them.

"You will bring Russia not to happiness but to ruin," I said.

"Why?" they asked. "We seek only what is good and right. The people are with us. You saw for yourself that the army is behind us."

"I will tell you why," I replied. "I have no objection to your beautiful plans for the future of Russia. But as for the immediate situation, if you take the soldiers away from the front, you are destroying the country."

"But we do not want any more war. We are going to conclude peace," the two leaders replied.

"How can you conclude peace without soldiers at the front? You are demobilizing the army already. You have got to make peace first and then let the men go home. I myself want peace, but if I were in the trenches I would never leave before peace had been signed. What you are doing will ruin Russia."

"We are sending the soldiers away because the Germans will not advance against us, anyhow. They do not want to fight either," was the reply.

It irritated me, this view of the Germans held by the men who now controlled the Government of my country.

"You don't know the Germans!" I cried out. "We have lost so many lives in this war, and now you would give everything away without a struggle! You don't know war! Take the soldiers away from the front and the Germans will come and seize upon everything they can lay hands on. This is war. I am a soldier and I know. But you don't. Why did you take it upon yourselves to rule the country? You will ruin it!" I exclaimed in anguish.

Lenin and Trotsky laughed. I could see the irony in their eyes. They were learned and worldly. They had written books and traveled in foreign lands. And who was I? An illiterate Russian peasant woman. My lecture undoubtedly afforded them amusement. They smiled condescendingly at my suggestion that they did not know what war was in reality.

I rejected their proposal to co-operate with them and asked if I were free to leave. One of them rang a bell and a Red Guard entered. He was requested to accompany me out of the room and to provide me with a passport and a free ticket to Tomsk. Before leaving I asked for my arms, but was refused. I explained that they were partly of gold and given to me on an occasion that rendered them almost priceless to me. They answered that I would receive them back as soon as order was restored. Of course, I never got them back.

I left the room without saying goodbye. In the next room I was given a passport, and proceeded by tramcar to the station. I decided not to linger in Petrograd and to depart without even seeing any of my friends. On the way I was recognized everywhere, but was allowed to proceed unmolested. The same evening I boarded one of the three cars attached to a train that went to Irkutsk by way of Vologda and Chelyabinsk. I was going home. With me I had some two thousand rubles, saved during my command of the Battalion, when I had received a salary of four hundred rubles a month.

The train was overcrowded with returning soldiers, almost all ardent Bolsheviks. I remained in the compartment for eight days, leaving it only occasionally at night. I sent out a companion passenger to buy food for me at the stations. As we neared Chelyabinsk, at the end of the eight days, the crowd had diminished in number, and I thought I might safely go out on to the gangway and get off at the great station for a little walk. No sooner did I appear on the gangway than I was recognized by some soldiers.

"Oh, look who is here!" one exclaimed.

"It's Bochkareva! The harlot!" a couple of others echoed.

"She ought to be killed!" shouted somebody.

"Why?" I turned on them." What harm have I done to you? Oh, you fools, fools!"

The train slowed down, approaching the station. I had scarcely turned my head away from the insolent fellows, when I was suddenly lifted by two pairs of arms, swung to and fro once, twice, three times, and thrown off the moving train.

Fortunately the momentum of the swinging was so great that I was thrown across the parallel tracks and landed in a bank of snow piled along the railway. It was the end of November, 1917. It was all so sudden that the laughter of the brutes behind me still rang in my ears as I became conscious of pain in my right knee.

The train was halted before pulling into the station. In a few moments a big crowd collected round me, composed of passengers, railway officials and others.

All were indignant at the brutality of the soldiers. The Commandant of the station and members of the local committee hurried to the spot. I was placed on a stretcher and taken to the hospital. It was found that I had a dislocated knee, and my leg was bandaged. I then declared that I desired to continue the journey, and I was given a berth in a hospital coach attached to a train going east. There were attendants and a medical assistant on the car.

My injured leg grew more and more painful as I proceeded homeward. It began to swell, and the medical assistant telegraphed to the stationmaster of Tutalsk, the village in which my family now lived, to provide a stretcher for me.

My sister, Arina, was employed at the station as attendant at the tea-urn, which is always kept boiling at Russian railway stations. It was this employment of hers that had caused the family to move to Tutalsk from Tomsk, where they had no means of livehhood whatever. When the message from the doctor in charge of the car reached my sister and through her my parents, there was an outburst of grief. It was three years since they had seen their Marusia and now she was apparently being brought to them on her death bed!

On the fourth day of the journey from Chelyabinsk the train stopped at Tutalsk. My leg was badly swollen and was as heavy as a log. The pains were agonizing. My face was deadly pale.

A stretcher was prepared for me at the station. My sisters, my mother and father and the stationmaster were at the door of the coach when I was carried out. My mother shrieked in heartrending tones, "My Marusia! My Manka!" stretched her hands toward heaven and threw herself full length on me, mourning over me as if I were ready for burial.

Her prodigal daughter had returned, my mother sobbed, but in what a condition! She thought that I must have been wounded and had asked to be sent home to die. I could not speak, I could only grasp her bony arms, as my throat was choked with a tempest of tears and sobs. Everybody was crying, my sisters calling me by caressing names, my father standing over me bent and white, and even the strange stationmaster...

I became hysterical and the doctor was sent for. He had me removed home immediately, promising in response to my mother's entreaties to do everything in his power for me. I was ill for a month, passing Christmas and meeting the New Year, 1918, in bed.

The two thousand rubles I had saved I gave to my parents. But this sum, which would have been reckoned a fortune before the war, was barely sufficient to keep us for a few months. It cost nearly a hundred rubles to buy a pair of shoes for my youngest sister, Nadia, who was going about barefoot! It cost almost twice as much to buy her a second-hand jacket at the Tomsk market. Manufactured goods sold at a premium when they were to be had, but it was much more difficult to find what one needed than to pay an exorbitant price for it. There was plenty of flour in the country. But the peasants would not sell it cheaply because they could get nothing in town for less than fifty or a hundred times its former price. The result was that flour sold at sixty rubles a *pud!*[44] It may be imagined how far two thousand rubles would carry one in Russia.

Tutalsk had also been swept by the hurricane of Bolshevism. There were many soldiers who had returned from the front imbued with Bolshevik teachings. Just before my arrival, the newly-fledged heretics even burned the village church, to the great horror of the older inhabitants. It was not an unusual case; it was typical of the time. Hundreds of thousands of deluded young men had returned from the trenches with the passion to destroy, to tear down everything that had existed before: the old system of Government, the church, nay, God Himself – all in preparation for the new order of life they were going to establish.

But one institution – the scourge of the nation – they failed to wipe out. Nay more, they restored it. The Tsar had abolished vodka.[45] The prohibition was continued in force by the new regime, but only on paper. Nearly every returned soldier took to distilling vodka at home, and the old plague of the country recovered its power and took its part in the building of the Bolsheviks' new world.

Every town and village had its committee or Soviet. They were supposed to carry out orders from the Central Government. An order was issued to confiscate all articles of gold and silver. Committees searched every house for such belongings. There was, also, or was supposed to be, an order taxing furniture and clothes. When the taxes arbitrarily demanded were not paid, the furniture and clothes were taken away.

In the towns it was the townsmen who suffered, in the villages the peasants, all under the pretext of confiscating the riches of the bourgeoisie. It was sufficient for a peasant to buy a new overcoat, perhaps with his last savings, for him to be branded as an exploiter and lose his precious garment. The peculiar thing about such cases was the fact that the confiscated article would almost invariably appear on the back of one of the Bolshevik ringleaders. It was merely looting, and the methods were pure terrorism, practiced mostly by the returned soldiers.

I received some letters at Tutalsk. One was from my adjutant, Princess Tatuyeva,[46] who had arrived safely in Tbilisi, her native town.

---

44. 32 pounds.

45. The Tsarist government put in place a "dry law" in 1914, outlawing sale of vodka except in restaurants. Of course, *samogon* (homebrew) production continued, and it picked up pace after the end of the war, despite the Bolsheviks' declaring there would be "no trade in rotgut." But by 1925 *samogon* was allowed (as long as it was not sold), and by 1930, Stalin ramped up state-owned production and sale of vodka.

46. Apparently her Georgian last name was Tatishvili.

One morning I went to the post office to ask for letters.

"There goes Bochkareva!" I heard a man cry out.

"Ah, Bochkareva! She is for the old regime!" another fellow replied, apparently one of the Bolshevik soldiers.

There were several of them and they shouted threats and insults at me. I did not reply but returned home with a heavy heart. Even in my own home I was not safe.

"My God," I prayed, "what has come over the Russian people? Is this my reward for the sacrifices I have made for my country?"

I resolved not to leave the house again. Surely this madness would not last long, I thought. I spent most of the day reading the Bible and praying to Heaven for the awakening and enlightenment of my people.

On the 7th of January 1918, I received a telegram from Petrograd, signed by General X. It read: "Come. You are needed."[47]

The same day I bought a ticket for the capital, bade farewell to my family, and set out. I removed the epaulets from my uniform, thus appearing in the garb of a private.

About this time the Germans, to the profound shock of the revolutionary masses, began their sudden advance into Russia. It had an almost miraculous effect on the Bolshevik sympathizers. The train was as usual packed with soldiers, but there was a noticeable difference in their expression and conversation. All the braggadocio had been knocked out of them by the enemy's action. They had been lulled into the sweet belief that peace had come and that a golden age was about to open for them. They could not reconcile that with the swift advance of the Kaiser's soldiers toward Petrograd and Moscow.

It was refreshing, exhilarating to listen to some of the men.

"We have been sold!" one heard here and there.

"We were told that the German soldiers would not advance if we left the front," was another frequent expression.

"It is not the common people, it is the German bourgeoisie that is fighting us now," was an argument ordinarily given in answer to the first opinions, "and there is nothing to be afraid of. There will soon be a revolution in Germany."

"Who knows," some would doubtfully remark, "that Lenin and Trotsky have not delivered us into the hands of the accursed Germans?"

There were always delegates from local committees going somewhere, and they talked to the soldiers, answering questions and explaining things. They could not very well explain away the German treachery, but they held out the

---

47. This is believed by one source to have been General Nikolai Anosov (see note, page 134).

promise of a revolution in Germany almost any day. The men listened but were not greatly impressed by the assurances of the agitators. One felt that they were still groping in the dark, although the fight was dawning on their minds. The awakening could not be long postponed.

I had a safe and comfortable journey to Petrograd. Nobody molested me, nobody threatened my life. I arrived at the capital on the 18th of January. The station was not as strongly guarded as two months before. Red Guards were not in such evidence in the streets, which appeared more normal. I went to one of my former patronesses and learned of the terror in which the capital lived.

The following day I called on General X, who greeted me cordially. Kiev, he told me, had just been captured by the Germans. They were threatening Petrograd, and the opposition of the Red Guards would not prevent or even postpone its capture by one day if the Germans were bent upon taking the city.

Red Terror was rampant in Petrograd. The river was full of corpses of officers who had been slain and lynched. Those who were alive were leading a wretched existence fearing to show themselves in public because of the temper of the mob, and therefore on the verge of death from starvation. Even more harrowing was the situation of the country. It was falling into the hands of the enemy so rapidly that immediate action of some sort was imperative.

A secret meeting of officers and sympathizers had been held at which it was decided to get in touch with General Kornilov, who was reported as operating in the Don region. There were so many conflicting reports concerning Kornilov that it had been suggested that a courier should be sent to him to find out definitely his plans and his resources. After an exhaustive discussion General X suggested that I, as a woman, was the only person who could possibly get through the Bolshevik lines and reach Kornilov. Would I go?

"I would not join the officers here or Kornilov in the South for the purpose of waging war against my own people," I replied. "I can't do it because every Russian is dear to my heart, whether he be a Bolshevik, a Menshevik, or a Red Guard. But I will undertake to go to Kornilov, in order to satisfy your, as well as my own, desire for information."

It was agreed that I should dress as a Sister of Mercy. A costume was obtained for me, and I put it on over my uniform. My soldier's cap I tucked away in a pocket and donned the ordinary headgear of a Sister of Mercy, which left visible only my eyes, nose, mouth and cheeks, and made me look like a matron of about forty-five.

A passport was furnished to me, bearing the name of Alexandra Leontievna Smirnova, which was to be my name on the journey. As I wore army boots there was no danger of my trousers showing under the skirt. I took with me a letter from Princess Tatuyeva, in which she invited me to visit her in her home in the Caucasus. A ticket from Petrograd to Kislovodsk, a Caucasian health resort within several hundred miles of the place where Kornilov was stationed, was given me, to be used only in an emergency. It was agreed that in case of danger I should discard my garb of a Sister of Mercy, and disclose my identity, supported by the evidence of the emergency ticket to Kislovodsk and the letter from Princess Tatuyeva, declare that I was on my way to take a cure at that place. In addition, I was, of course, provided with money for expenses.

It was very amusing to lose one's identity and appear as a complete stranger. I was no longer Maria Bochkareva, but Alexandra Smirnova. And as I glanced at myself in the mirror it seemed even to my own eyes that I had been reincarnated from a soldier into a Sister of Mercy.

When I started from Petrograd my destination was Nikitino, a station which one would ordinarily pass on the way to Kislovodsk. Nobody recognized me on the train. Sometimes a soldier asked :

"Where are you going, little sister?"

"Home, to Kislovodsk," was my usual answer.

The next question would be about the service I had seen at the front, and the sectors at which I worked. I would reply with facts from my actual experience as a soldier. There was nothing strange about a Sister of Mercy returning home, and as I preferred silence and solitude to conversation, I reached Nikitino, at the end of several days, without any truble.

From Nikitino all trains were by order of the authorities switched off to other lines and sent to their destination by roundabout routes. The road running directly south from Nikitino was used for military purposes exclusively by the Bolshevik forces engaged in fighting Kornilov. Twenty miles farther on, at Zverevo, the so-called front began. Private passengers were therefore not allowed to go to Zverevo.

It was evident that vast preparations were being made for a campaign against General Kornilov. There were many ammunition trains and large numbers of men concentrated there, waiting transportation. There was apparently no lack of money, and there was iron discipline, reminding one of the early days of the war. There was order everywhere.

The first problem confronting me was how to get to Zverevo. I went to the Commandant of the station, complained that I was penniless, that I could not wait indefinitely for the end of the fighting to return home to Kislovodsk, and urgently begged him to advise me what to do. I made such an appeal to him that he finally said, "A munition train is just about to leave for Zverevo. Come, get into it and go to Zverevo. Perhaps they will let pass you through the lines at the front. There is a second-class carriage attached to the train."

He led me to the carriage, in which were only the five soldiers who were in charge of the train. He introduced me to the chief of them as a stranded Sister of Mercy and asked for their indulgence. I thanked the obliging Commandant profusely and from the bottom my heart.

The train moved out of the station, but although I was satisfied with the first stage of my enterprise, I was by no means cheerful as to my prospects m Zverevo, the Bolshevik war zone. The head of the party sat down I opposite me. He was a dirty, ugly *muzhik.* I did not I encourage him to engage me in conversation, but he 1 was evidently wholly insensible to my feelings in the matter.

After the preliminary questions, he expressed his surprise that I should have chosen such an inopportune moment to go to Kislovodsk.

"But my mother is ill there," I lied, "perhaps she is dying now. It broke her heart when I went to the front."

"Ah, that's different," he declared, moving over to my side. "They will pass you in that case."

From an expression of sympathy he had no hesitation in proceeding to an attempt at

I warded off his advances with a smile and a coquettish glance. He treated me to a good meal, during which the conversation turned to general condiitions. He was, of course, a rabid Bolshevik and a savage opponent of Kornilov and all officers.

flirtation. He moved closer to me and even touched my arm. It was a delicate situation. I could not well afford to provoke his antagonism, so I warded off his advances with a smile and a coquettish glance. He treated me to a good meal, during which the conversation turned to general condiitions. He was, of course, a rabid Bolshevik and a savage opponent of Kornilov and all officers. My part in the conversation was confined to brief expressions of acquiescence, till suddenly he asked, "Have you heard of the Women's Battalion of Death?"

My heart thumped violently.

"What Battalion did you say?" I asked with an air of ignorance.

"Why, Bochkareva's Battalion!" he replied in a loud voice. "Bochkareva's?" I asked reminiscently. "Oh, yes, Bochkareva; yes, I have heard about her."

"The ——! She is a Kornilovka!" he exclaimed. "She is for the old regime."

"How do you know?" I asked." I thought she was non-partisan."

"We know them all, the counter-revolutionists! She is one of them," my companion declared emphatically.

"Well, but the Battalion of Death no longer exists, and Bochkareva has apparently vanished," I suggested.

"Yes, we know how they vanish. Many of them have vanished like that. Kornilov had vanished, too. Then they all pop up again somewhere or other and cause trouble," he declared.

"Now, what would you do to her if she were to pop up here?" I ventured to inquire.

"Kill her. She would never get away alive, you may stake an oath on that," he assured me. "We have the photographs of all the leading counter-revolutionaries, so that they can't conceal their identity if they are caught."

The conversation then took a more profitable turn for me. I learned all about the plans of the Bolshevik forces against Kornilov. The arrival of the train at Zverevo put an end to my association with my travelling companion. I thanked him warmly for all his kindness me.

"You know. Sister," he unexpectedly declared before parting, "I like you. Will you marry me?"

I was not prepared for this. It rather took me aback. He was such a dirty, repulsive-looking creature, and his proposal was so ludicrous that it was with difficulty that I controlled my desire to laugh. The situation was not one for merriment.

"Yes, with pleasure," I responded to his offer, with much graciousness as I could command, "but after have seen my mother."

He gave me his address and asked me to write to him, which I promised to do. Perhaps he is still waiting for a letter from me.

I left him at the train and went toward the station. There were Red Guards, sailors, soldiers, even Cossacks, who had joined the Bolsheviks, on the platform and inside the station. But there were no private citizens in sight. I sat down in a corner and waited. I was taken for a nurse attached to the Bolshevik army, and was not molested. One, two, three hours passed and still I could find no opportunity to proceed to my destination. A civilian, who somehow found his way into the station, was placed under arrest before my eyes without any preliminaries. I, therefore, preferred to sit quietly in my corner rather than move about.

Finally a pleasant looking young soldier became interested in me. He walked up and asked: "Why are you waiting here. Sister?"

"I am waiting for a comrade," I answered.

"What is his name?" he inquired, interested.

"Oh, that is a secret," I replied in a teasing manner.

He sat down near me, and asked me if I had worked at the front. I said that unfortunately I had been detailed only to hospitals in the rear.

"Why was that man arrested?" I ventured to ask.

"Because he had no papers from the Soviet," was the reply. "He will be shot immediately."

"Do you execute everybody who has no papers?" I asked.

"Everybody, without distinction."

"Even women?" I inquired.

"Yes, even women," was the reply. "This is a war zone."

"Holy Mother!" I exclaimed in horror. "How terrible! You really slay them all? Without even a trial?"

"There is little time for trials here. Once fallen here, there is no escape. Our firing squads make an end of all suspected persons on the spot," he informed me kindly. "Come, would you like to see the execution-grounds? They are quite near here."

I followed him reluctantly. A few hundred feet away from the station we stopped. I could go no further. The field in front of us was covered with scores of mangled, naked corpses. It made my flesh creep.

"There are about two hundred of them here, mostly officers who had joined or sought to join Kornilov," he explained.

I could not help shivering. The dreadful scene nearly shattered my nerves and it was all I could do not to collapse.

"Ah, you women, women," my escort nodded sympathetically. "You are all weak. You don't know what war is. Still," he admitted, "there are some who can compare with men. Take Bochkareva, for instance, she would not shudder at sights like this."

"Who is she, this Bochkareva?" I was curious.

"Haven't you heard of her?" he asked in surprise. "Why, she was a soldier of the old regime and organized the Women's Battalion of Death. She is for Kornilov and the bourgeoisie. They gave her an officer's rank and bought her over to their side, although she is of peasant blood."

It was all very interesting, this theory of my corruption. I had heard it before, but not stated in such definite terms. At the same time I was haunted by the picture of those mangled bodies, and the thought rankled in my mind of the treacherous Bolsheviks who had opposed capital punishment in the war against Germany but introduced it in the most brutal fashion in the war against their own brothers.

I then told my friend of the trouble in which I found myself, that I was penniless, that I had to get home to Kislovodsk and that I did not know how to get through the front. He explained to me that the so-called front was not a continuous line but a series of posts, maintained on this side by the Bolsheviks and on the opposite side by Kornilov.

"Sometimes," he added, "the peasants of the neighboring villages are allowed by both sides to pass through to Novocherkassk, Kornilov's headquarters. If you follow that road," and he pointed to it, "you will come to a village about three miles from here. One of the peasants may be willing to convey you across."

I thanked him for the valuable information, and we parted friends. The walk to the village was uneventful. On the outskirts of it I saw an old *muzhik* working outside of his hut. There was a stable and horses attached to it.

"Good day, grandfather!" I greeted the old man.

"Good day, little sister," he answered.

"Would you drive me to the city?" I asked.

"Great God! How is it possible? The Bolsheviks are fighting in front of the city, and they don't let anybody pass," he said.

"But people do go sometimes, don't they?"

"Yes, sometimes they do."

"Well, I will give you fifty rubles for driving me to the city," I offered.

The *muzhik* scratched his neck, reconsidering the matter.

"But aren't you a political?" he inquired cautiously.

"No," I assured him," I am not."

He went into the cabin to talk it over with his *baba*.

It was a tempting offer and her consent was apparently quickly obtained, for he soon returned and said, "All right, we will go. Come into the house. We will have tea and something to eat."

The invitation was welcome indeed, as I had grown hungry during my long wait at the station and the walk to the village. When we had finished our tea and lunch and the peasant harnessed his horse, I asked for a large apron, which I put on over my clothes. I then asked for the baba's winter shawl and wrapped it over my head and shoulders, almost completely covering my face, so that I no longer looked like a Sister of Mercy, but one of the local peasant-women.

Praying to God to grant me a safe journey, I seated myself in the cart. The horse started off along the road.

The Bolshevik front was still ahead of me. But I was making progress...

CHAPTER XVIII
CAUGHT IN A BOLSHEVIK DEATH-TRAP

"What shall I say to the sentries?" the *muzhik* asked me as we approached the front positions.

"Tell them that you are carrying your sick *baba* to a hospital in the city, as she is suffering from high fever," I answered, and I asked him to wrap me in the huge fur overcoat on which he was seated. I was warm enough without it, but I thought that it would raise my temperature even more, and I was not mistaken. Under all the wrappings I looked more like a heap than a human form. When we reached the outposts I began to moan as if in pain.

"Where are you going?" I heard a voice ask my driver sharply, as the horse stopped.

"To a hospital in the city," was the answer.

"What have you got there?" the inquirer continued.

"My *baba*. She is dying. I am taking her to a doctor," the peasant replied.

Here I groaned louder than ever. I was suffocating. My heart was thumping with dread of a sudden exposure and discovery. Every particle of time seemed an age.

The sentry who had stopped us apparently talked the matter over with some of his comrades, to the accompaniment of my loud moans. Without uncovering my face he issued a pass to the *muzhik*.

My heart beat joyfully as the horse started off at a rapid pace. For a while I still held my breath, hardly daring to believe that I had left Bolshevik territory behind me with so Uttle difficulty.

After some time we arrived at Komilov's front. The posts along it were held by officers, of whom his force was almost exclusively composed. At one such post we were stopped by an imperative "Halt!"

The driver was about to repeat the story of his sick baba when I surprised him by throwing off the fur coat, then the shawl, and jumping out of the vehicle, heaving a deep sigh of relief. I could not help laughing.

The *muzhik* must have thought me mad at first. The officers at the post could not understand it either.

"What the devil!" a couple of them muttered under their breath. I proceeded very coolly to pay the fifty rubles to the peasant, and thereupon to dismiss him, to his great amazement.

"I shall get to the city all right from here," I informed him.

"The deuce you will!" blurted out the officer in charge. "Who are you?"

"Why, can't you see, I am a Sister of Mercy," I answered impatiently.

"Where are you going?"

"I am going to see General Kornilov," I said, laughing.

The officers were getting furious.

"You will not go a step further," the chief officer ordered.

"Oh, yes, I will," I announced emphatically.

"You are arrested," was the reply.

I burst out laughing, while the officers turned white with fury.

"Don't you recognize me? I am Bochkareva," and I threw off my head-dress of the Sister of Mercy, revealing my own self. The officers gasped, and then immediately crowded round me congratulating me and shaking me by the hand. Kornilov was notified by telephone of my arrival and of the joke I had played on the sentries.

"How do you do, little sister?" he greeted me laughingly when I was brought to his headquarters. The story of my arrival and of the way I had got through the lines amused him very much. He looked very thin and somewhat aged, but as energetic as ever.

I reported to him that I was sent from Petrograd by General X and other officers, for the purpose of ascertaining his plans and exact situation. I also informed him that the Bolsheviks were making big preparations for an attack against him, that I had seen eleven cars with ammunition at Zverevo, and that the blow was planned to take place in a couple of days.

Kornilov replied that he knew of the impending offensive and that his condition was precarious. He had no money and no food, while the Bolsheviks were amply supplied with both. His soldiers were deserting him one by one. He was cut off from his friends and surrounded by enemies.

"Was it your intention to remain with me and join my force?" he asked me.

"No," I said, "I could not fight against my own people. The Russian soldier is dear to me, although he has been led astray for the present."

"It is also very hard for me to fight the men that I loved so much," he declared. "But they have turned beasts now. We are fighting for our lives, for our uniforms. The life of every Russian officer is at the mercy of the mob. It is a question of organizing for self-defense. One cannot hope to do much for the country, if the Bolsheviks are waging civil war when the Germans are advancing into Russia. This is a time for peace and union among all classes. It is a time for presenting a united front to the enemy of the Motherland. But Bolshevism has perverted the minds of the people. What is necessary, therefore, is to enlighten the masses. We can't hope to enlighten them by fighting. If it were possible to organize a counter-propaganda, to convince the Russian peasants that the Bolsheviks are rapidly driving our country to utter ruin, then they would rise and make an end of Lenin and Trotsky, elect a new Government, and drive the Germans out of Russia. This is the only solution that I can see, unless the Allies aid us in conciliating our soldiers and re-establishing a front against Germany."

This, in substance, was Kornilov's view of conditions in Russia, when I saw him in February, 1918. I remained only one day at his headquarters. From conversations with the men attached to his Staff, I learned that Kornilov's force comprised only about three thousand men. The Bolshevik army opposing it was about twenty times its strength. I left Novocherkassk in the evening, after an affectionate parting from Kornilov. He kissed me as he bade me farewell, and I wished him success for the sake of the country. But there was no success in prospect. We both knew it only too well. A heavy darkness had settled on Russia, stifling all that was still noble and righteous.

Encouraged by my success in reaching Kornilov's line, I determined to return by myself. I was taken to the outposts by a group of officers, and from there, accompanied by their blessings, I started out through the war zone alone. I crawled on all-fours as if through No Man's Land, and advanced a couple of versts without any mishap. The experience I had gained at the front stood me in good stead. I scented the approach of a patrol and, hid just in time to escape being observed.

The patrol turned out to be one of Kornilov's force, but I remained hidden. After some more crawling I caught the sound of voices coming from the direction of a coal-mine and judged the place to be one of the front positions. Exercising extreme caution, I managed to pass beyond it safely. Some distance away, dimly standing out against the horizon, was a wood.

A Bolshevik force got wind of the patrol I had encountered and went out to capture it by a flank operation. I decided to conceal myself behind a pile of coal and wait till quiet was restored. On my right and left were dumps of coal.

Keeping close against the coal-heap, I breathlessly awaited the result of the enterprise. After a little while the Bolsheviks returned with the prey. They had captured the patrol! There were twenty captives, fifteen officers and five cadets,

I discovered. They were led to a place only about twenty feet distant from the coal-heap behind which I was concealed.

The hundred Bolshevik soldiers surrounded the officers, cursed them, beat them with the butts of their rifles, tore off their epaulets and handled them in the most brutal fashion. The five youthful cadets must have suddenly seen an opportunity to escape, for they dashed off a few minutes afterwards. But they failed in their attempt. They were caught several hundred feet away and brought back.

The Bolshevik soldiers then decided to gouge out the eyes of the five youths in punishment for their attempt to run away. Each of the victims was held by a couple of men in such a position as to allow the bloody torturers to do their frightful work. In all my experiences of horror this was the most horrible crime I witnessed.

One of the officers could not contain himself and shrieked, "Murderers! Beasts! Kill me!"

He was struck with a bayonet, but only wounded. All the fifteen officers begged to be killed outright. But their request was refused.

"You must be taken before the Staff first," was the answer. Soon they were led away.

The five martyrs were left to expire in agony where they were.

My heart was petrified. My blood congealed. I thought I was going mad, that in a second I should not be able to control myself and should jump out, inviting death or perhaps similar torture.

I finally gathered strength to turn round and crawl away, in the opposite direction, toward the woods. At a distance of several hundred feet from the forest it seemed to me safe to rise and run for it. But somebody noticed me from the mine.

"A spy!" went up in a chorus from several throats, and a number of soldiers set off after me, shooting as they ran.

Nearer and nearer the pursuers came. I raced faster than I ever did before in my life. Here, within another hundred feet or so, were the woods. There, I might still hope to hide. I prayed for strength to get there. Bullets whistled by me, but firing as they ran the men could not take aim.

The woods! the woods! It was the one thought that possessed my whole being. Louder and louder grew the shouts behind me, "A female spy! A female spy!"

The woods were within my reach. Another bound, and I was in them. Onward I dashed like a wild deer. Was it because there were only a few soldiers left at the post and they could not desert it to engage in a hunt, or because the men decided that I could not escape from the forest anyhow, that my pursuers did not follow me into the woods? I know only that they were satisfied with sending a stream of bullets into the forest and then ceased to trouble about me.

I concealed myself in a hollow till everything was quiet again. Then I got out and tried to work out the right direction, but I made a mistake at first and returned to the edge at which I had entered. I then walked to the opposite side, struck a path and before taking it, I threw off my costume of a Sister of Mercy and hid it, drew out my soldier's cap, destroyed the passport of Smirnova, and appeared again in my own uniform. I realized that reports must have been sent out by my pursuers of a spy dressed as a nurse and determined that as Bochkareva I might still have a chance of life, but as Smirnova I was done for.

Day was breaking, but it was still dark in the woods. I met a soldier, who greeted me. I answered grufiiy, and he passed on, evidently taking me for a comrade. A little later I encountered two or three other soldiers, but again passed them without being suspected. I pulled out my direct ticket to Kislovodsk and the letter from Princess Tatuyeva. These were my two trump-cards. After walking for about thirteen miles I came in view of the station at Zverevo. A decision had to be adopted without delay. I felt that loitering would be fatal, and so I made up my mind to go straight to the station, announce my identity, claim that I had lost my way and surrender myself.

When I opened the door of the station, which was filled with Red Guards, and appeared on the threshold, the men gaped at me as if I were an apparition.

"Bochkareva!" they gasped.

Without stopping to hear them I walked up to the first soldier, with my legs trembling and my heart in my mouth, and said:

"Where is the Commandant? Take me to the Commandant!"

He looked at me with an ugly expression, but obeyed the order and led me to an office, also packed with Red Guards, where a youth of not more than nineteen or twenty was introduced to me as the head of the investigation committee, who was acting as chief in the absence of the Commandant. Again everybody gave vent to exclamations of surprise at my unexpected appearance.

"Are you Bochkareva?" the young man inquired, showing me to a seat. I was pale, weak and travel-worn and I sank into the chair gratefully. Looking at the young man, hope kindled in my breast. He had a noble, winning face.

"Yes, I am Bochkareva," I answered." I am going to Kislovodsk, to cure my wound in the spine, and I have lost my way."

"What were you thinking of? Are you in your senses? We are just preparing for an offensive against Kornilov. How could you take this route at such a time?

Didn't you know that your appearance here would mean your certain death?" the young man asked, greatly agitated over my fatal blunder.

"Why," he continued, "I just had a telephone call telling that a woman spy had crossed from Kornilov's side early this morning. They are looking for her now. You see the situation into which you have brought yourself!"

The youthful chief was apparently favorably inclined toward me. I decided to try to win him over completely.

"But I came of my own accord," I said, breaking into sobs. "I am innocent. I am just a sick woman, going to take a cure at the springs. Here is my ticket to Kislovodsk, and here is a letter from a friend of mine, my former adjutant, inviting me to come to the Caucasus. Surely you will not murder a poor, sick woman, if not for my own sake, at least for the sake of my wretched parents."

Several of the Red Guards present cut short my entreaties with angry cries:

"Kill her! What is the use of letting her talk! Kill her, and there will be one slut less in the world!"

"Now wait a minute!" the Acting Commandant interrupted. "She has come to us of her own free will and is not one of the officers that are opposing us. There will be an investigation first and we will ascertain whether she is guilty or innocent. If she is guilty, we will shoot her."

The words of the chief of the investigation committee gave me courage. He was evidently a humane and educated man. Subsequently I learned that he was a university student. His name was Ivan Ivanovich Petrukhin.

As he was still discoursing, a man dashed in like a whirlwind, puffing, perspiring, but rubbing his hands in satisfaction.

"Ah, I have just finished a good job! Fifteen of them, all officers! The boys got them like that," and he bowed and made a sign across the legs." The first volley peppered their legs and threw them in a heap on the ground. Then they were bayoneted and slashed to pieces. Ha, ha, ha! There were five others captured with them, cadets. They tried to escape and the good fellows gouged their eyes out!"

I was petrified. The newcomer was of middle height, heavily built, and dressed in an officer's uniform but without the epaulets. He looked savage, and his hideous laughter sent shudders up my spine. The bloodthirsty brute! Even Petrukhin's face turned pale at his entrance. He was no less a person than the assistant to the Commander-in-Chief of the Bolshevik Army. His name was Pugachov.

He did not notice me at first, so absorbed was he in the story of the slaughter of the fifteen officers.

"And here we have a celebrity," Petrukhin said, pointing at me.

The Assistant Commander made a step forward in military fashion, stared at me for an instant and then cried out in a terrifying voice: "Bochkareva!"

He was beside himself with joy.

"Ha, ha, ha!" he laughed diabolically." Under the old regime. I should have received an award of the first class for capturing such a spy! I will run out and tell the soldiers and sailors the good news. They will know how to take care of her. Ha, ha, ha!"

I arose horror-stricken. I wanted to say something but was speechless. Petrukhin was greatly horrified too. He ran after Pugach ov, seized him by the arm, and shouted, "What is the matter, have you gone mad? Madame Bochkareva came here of her own accord. Nobody captured her. She is going to Kislovodsk for a cure. She is a sick woman. She says that she lost her way. Anyhow, she has never fought against us. She returned home after we took power."

"Ah, you don't know her I," exclaimed Pugachov. "She is a Kornilovka, the right hand of Kornilov."

"Well, we are not releasing her, are we?" retorted Petrukhin." I am going to call the committee together and have her story investigated."

"An investigation!" scoffed Pugachov. "And if you don't find any evidence against her, will you let her go? You don't know her! She is a dangerous character! How could we afford to save her? I wouldn't even waste bullets on her. I would call the men and they would make a fine gruel of her!"

He made a motion toward the door. Petrukhin kept hold of him.

"But consider, she is a sick woman!" he pleaded. "What is the investigation committee for if not to investigate before punishing? Let the committee look into the matter and take whatever action it considers best."

At this point the Commandant of the station arrived. He supported Petrukhin." You can't act like that in such a case," he said. "This is clearly a matter for the investigation committee. If she is found guilty, we will execute her."

Petrukhin went to summon the members of the investigation committee, who were all, twelve in number, common soldiers. As soon as he told the news to each member, he told me later, the men became threatening, talking of the good fortune that brought me into their hands. But Petrukhin argued with every one of them in my favor, as he was convinced of the genuineness of my plea. In such a manner he won some of them over to my side.

Meanwhile Pugachov paced the room like a caged lion, thirsting for my blood.

"Ah, if I had only known it before, I would have had you shot in company with those fifteen officers!" he said to me.

"I should not have the heart to shoot at my own brothers, soldier or officer," I remarked.

"Eh, you are singing already," he turned on me. "We know your kind."

"Taking you all in all," I declared, "you are no better than the officers of the old regime."

"Silence!" he commanded angrily.

Petrukhin came in with the committee at that instant.

"I must ask you not to make such an uproar," he said, turning to Pugachov, feeling more confident with the committee at his back. "She is in our hands now, and we will do justice. It is for us to decide if she is guilty. Leave her alone."

There were only ten members of the committee within reach. The other two members were absent and the ten, as they made a quorum, decided to go on with the work.

"Whether you find her guilty or not, I will not let her get out of here alive!" Pugachov declared. "What am I?" he added. "I am no enemy either."

However, this threat worked in my favor, as it touched the committee's pride. They were not to be overridden like that. Pugachov demanded that I should be searched.

"I am at your disposal," I said, "but before you proceed further I want to hand over to you this package of money. There are ten thousand rubles in it, sent to me by Princess Tatuyeva, my former adjutant, to enable me to take the cure at the springs. I kept this money intact, because I hoped to return it to her upon reaching the Caucasus."

The money had in reality been given to me by Kornilov, to secure my parents and myself from starvation in the future.

The valuable package was taken away, without much questioning. I was then ordered to undress completely. Petrukhin protested against it, but Pugachov insisted. The dispute was settled by a vote, the majority being for my undressing.

The search was painstaking but fruitless. There was the ticket to Kislovodsk, the letter from Princess Tatuieva, a little bottle of holy water, given to me by my sister Nadia, and a scapular, presented to me before leaving for the front by one of the patronesses of the Battalion.

"Ah, now we have got it!" exclaimed Pugachov, seizing the sacred bag." There is the letter from Kornilov!"

The bag was ripped open and a scroll of paper was taken out on which a psalm had been written in a woman's hand. I declared that the sin of tearing it open would fall on their heads and that I would not sew it up again. One of the soldiers obtained a needle and thread and sewed up the bag again.

The members of the committee apologized for having been obliged to have me searched in such a manner.

"What shall you do with me now?" I asked.

"We shall have you shot!" answered Pugachov.

"What for?" I demanded in despair.

The brute did not reply. He merely smiled.

Petrukhin was afraid to defend me too warmly, lest he should be suspected of giving aid to a spy. He preferred to work indirectly for me, by influencing the members of the committee individually. It was decided, I believe, at the suggestion of Petrukhin, that the case should be submitted to the Commander-in-Chief, Sablin, for consideration and sentence. This was merely a device for preventing an immediate execution, but the feeling among the men was that my death was certain. Nevertheless, I was deeply grateful to Petrukhin for his humane attitude. He was a man of rare qualities, and among Bolsheviks he was almost unique.

I was ordered to a railway carriage used as a jail for captured officers and other prisoners. It was a death chamber. Nobody escaped from it alive. When I was led inside, there were exclamations, "Bochkareva! How did you get here? Coming from Kornilov?"

"No," I answered, "I was on my way to Kislovodsk."

There were about forty men in the car, the greater part of them officers. Among the latter there were two Generals. They were all shocked at my appearance among them. When my escort had departed, the prisoners talked more freely. To some of them I even told the truth, that I had actually been to Kornilov. None of them gave me any hope. All were resigned to death.

One of the Generals was an old man. He beckoned to me and I sat down beside him.

"I have a daughter like you," he said sadly, putting his arm round my shoulders. "I had heard of your brave deeds and had come to love you like my own child. But I never expected to meet you here, in this death-trap. Is it not dreadful? Here are we, all of us, the best men of the country, being executed, tormented, crushed by the savage mob. If it were only for the good of Russia! But Russia is perishing at this very moment. Perhaps God will save you yet. Then you will avenge us..."

I broke down, convulsed with sobs, and leaned against the General's shoulder. The old warrior could not restrain himself either and wept with me...

The other officers suddenly sang out in a chorus. They sang from despair, in an effort to keep from collapsing.

I cried long and bitterly. I prayed for my mother.

"Who would support her?" I appealed to Heaven. "She will be forced to go begging in her old age if I am killed." Life became very precious to me, the same life that I had exposed to a hundred perils. I did not want to die an infamous death, to lie on the field unburied, food for carrion crows.

"Why haven't you allowed me to die from an enemy's bullet?" I asked of God. "How have I deserved being butchered by the hands of my own people?"

The door swung open. About forty soldiers filed in. Their leader had a list of names in his hand.

"Bochkareva!" he called out first.

Somehow my heart leaped with joy. I thought that I was to be released. But the officers immediately disillusioned me with the statement that it was a call for execution. I stepped forward and answered, "I am here!"

"Take off your clothes!"

The order stupefied me. I remained motionless.

Some soldiers came up, pushed me forward and repeated the order several times. I awoke at last and began to undress.

The old General's name was read off the list next. Then a number of other officers were called out. Every one of them was ordered to cast off the uniform and remain in his undergarments.

The Bolsheviks needed all the uniforms they could get, and this was such an inexpensive way of obtaining them.

Tears streamed down my cheeks all the time. The old General was near me.

"Don't cry!" he urged me." We will die together."

Not all the prisoners were in our group. Those remaining kissed me farewell. The partings between the men were alone sufficient to rend one's heart.

"Well, we shall follow you in an hour or two," those who were left behind said bravely.

After I had taken off my boots, I removed the icon from my neck and fell before it on my knees.

"Why should I die such a death?" I cried. "For three years I have suffered for my country. Is this shameful end to be my reward? Have mercy. Holy Mother! If not for the sake of humble Maria, then for the sake of my destitute old mother and my aged father! Have mercy!"

Here I collapsed completely and became hysterical.

After a few moments an officer approached me, put his hand on my shoulder, and said, "You are a Russian officer. We are dying for a righteous cause. Be strong and die as it befits an officer to die!"

I made a superhuman effort to control myself. The tears stopped. I arose and announced to the guards, "I am ready."

We were led out from the car, all of us in our undergarments. A few hundred feet away was the field of slaughter. There were hundreds upon hundreds of human bodies heaped there. As we approached the place, the figure of Pugachov, marching about with a triumphant face, came into sight. He was in charge of the firing squad, composed of about one hundred men, some of whom were sailors, others soldiers, and others dressed as Red Guards.

We were surrounded and taken toward a slight elevation of ground, and placed in a line with our backs toward the hill. There were corpses behind us, in front of us, to our left, to our right, at our very feet. There were at least a thousand of them. The scene was a horror of horrors. We were suffocated by the poisonous stench. The executioners did not seem to mind it so much. They were used to it.

There were corpses behind us, in front of us, to our left, to our right, at our very feet. There were at least a thousand of them. The scene was a horror of horrors.

I was placed at the extreme right of the line. Next to me was the old General. There were twenty of us altogether.

"We are waiting for the committee," Pugachov remarked, to explain the delay in the proceedings.

"What a pleasure!" he rubbed his hands, laughing. "We have a woman today."

"Oh, yes," he added, turning to us all, "you can write letters home and ask that your bodies be sent there for burial, if you wish. Or you can ask for similar favors."

The suspense of waiting was as cruel as anything else about the place. Every officer's face wore an expression of implacable hatred for that brute of a man, Pugachov. Never have I seen a more bloodthirsty scoundrel. I did not think that such a man was to be found in Russia.

The waiting wore me out soon and I fell again on my knees, praying to the little icon, and crying to Heaven, "God, when have I sinned to earn such a death? Why should I die like a dog, without burial, without a priest, with no funeral? And who will take care of my mother? She will expire when she learns of my end."

The Bolshevik soldiers burst out laughing. My pleading appealed to their sense of humor. They joked and made merry.

"Don't cry, my child," the General bent over me, pattmg me. "They are savages. Their hearts are of stone. They would not even let us receive the last sacrament. Let us die like heroes, nevertheless."

His words gave me strength. I got up, stood erect and said, "Yes, I will die as a hero."

Then, for about ten minutes I gazed at the faces of our executioners, scrutinizing their features. It was hard to distinguish in them signs of humanity. They were Russian soldiers turned inhuman. The lines in their faces were those of brutal apes.

"My God! What hast Thou done to Thy children?" I prayed.

All the events of my life passed before me in a long procession. My childhood, those years of hard toil in the little grocer's shop of Nastasia Leontievna; the affair with Lazov; my marriage to Bochkarev; Yasha; the three years of war; they all passed through my imagination, some incidents strangely gripping my interest for a moment or two, others flitting by hastily. Somehow that episode of my early life, when I quarrelled with the little boy placed in my charge and the undeserved whipping I got from his mother stood out very prominently in my mind. It was my first act of self-assertion. I had rebelled and escaped... Then there was that jump into the Ob. It almost seemed that it was not I who sought relief in its cold, deep waters from the ugly Afanasy. But I wished that I had been drowned then, rather than die such a death...

CHAPTER XIX
SAVED BY A MIRACLE

The investigation committee finally appeared in the distance. Petrukhin was leading it. There were all the twelve members present, the two absentees apparently having joined the other ten.

"You see, how kind we are," some of the soldiers said. "We are having the committee present at your execution."

Not one of us answered.

"We have all been to see Sablin, the Commander-in-Chief," Petrukhin announced as soon as he approached near enough to Pugachov. "He said that Bochkareva would have to be shot, but not necessarily now and with this group."

A ray of hope was kindled in my soul.

"Nothing of the sort!" Pugachov bawled angrily. "What's the matter here? Why this delay? The list is already made up."

The soldiers supported Pugachov.

"Shoot her! Finish her now! What's the use of bothering with her again!" cried the men.

But just as Pugachov guessed that Petrukhin had obtained the delay in the hope of saving me, so the latter had realized that spoken words would not be sufficient to secure the fulfilment of his order. He had provided himself with a note from Sablin.

"Here is an order from the Commander-in-Chief," Petrukhin declared, pulling out a paper. "It says that Botclikareva shall be taken to my compartment in the railway carriage and kept there under guard."

Pugachov jumped up as if he had been stung. But the committee now rallied to the support of Petrukhin, maintaining that orders were orders, and that I should be executed later.

Not the least interested spectator of the heated discussion was myself. The officers followed the argument breathlessly, too. The soldiers grumbled. The forces of life and death struggled within me. Now the first would triumph, now the second, depending on the turn of the quarrel.

"That won't do!" shouted Pugachov, thrusting aside the order of the Commander-in-Chief. "It's too late for orders like that. We will shoot her! Enough talk!"

At this moment I became aware that one of the two newly-arrived members of the committee was staring at me intently. He took a couple of steps toward me, bent his head sideways and fixed his eyes on me. There was something about that look that electrified me. As the man, who was a common soldier, craned his neck forward and stepped out of the group, a strange silence gripped everybody, so affected were all by the painful expression on his face.

"Are you Yashka?" he sang out slowly.

"How do you know me?" I asked quickly, almost overpowered by a presentiment of salvation.

"Don't you remember how you saved my life in that March offensive, when I was wounded in the leg and you dragged me out of the mud under fire? My name is Peter. I should have perished there, in the water, and many others like me, if not for you. Why do they want to shoot you now?"

"Because I am an officer," I replied.

"What conversations are you holding here?" Pugachov thundered." She will have to be shot, and no arguments!"

"And I won't allow her to be shot!" my God-appointed savior answered back firmly, and walked up to me, seized my arm, pulled me out of my place, occupying it himself.

"You will shoot me first!" he exclaimed. "She saved my life. She saved many of our lives. The entire Fifth Corps knows Yashka. She is a common peasant like myself, and understands no politics. If you shoot her, you will have to shoot me first!"

This speech put new life into me. It also touched the hearts of many in the crowd.

Petrukhin went up, took a place beside Peter and myself, and declared, "You will shoot me, too, before you execute an innocent, suffering woman!"

The soldiers were now divided. Some shouted, "Let's shoot her and make an end of this squabble! What's the use of arguments?"

Others were more human. "She is not of the bourgeoisie, but a common peasant like ourselves," they argued. "And she does not understand politics. Perhaps she really was going to seek a cure. She was not captured, but came to us of her own accord, we must not forget that."

For some time the place was transformed into a debating-ground. It was a strange scene for a debate. There were the hundreds of bodies scattered round us. There were the twenty of us in our undergarments awaiting death. Of the twenty only I had a chance for life. The remaining nineteen held themselves stoically erect. No hope stirred within them. No miracle could save them. And amidst all this a hundred Russian soldiers, a quarter of an hour before all savages, now half of them with a spark of humanity in their breasts, were debating!

The members of the committee finally recovered their wits and took charge of the situation. Turning to Pugachov, they declared, "Now we have an order here from the Commander-in-Chief, and it shall be obeyed. We are going to take her away."

They closed about me and I was marched out of the line and off the field. Pugatchov was in a white rage, raving like a madman, grinding his teeth. As we walked away, his brutal voice roared, "Fire at the knees!"

A volley rang out. Immediately cries and groans filled the air. Turning my head, I saw the savages rush upon the heap of victims with their bayonets, digging them deep into the bodies of my companions of a few minutes before, and crushing the last signs of life out of them with their heels.

It was frightful, indescribably frightful. The moans, w'ere so penetrating, so blood-curdling that I staggered, fell to the ground my full length, and swooned.

For four hours I remained unconscious. When I came to, I was in a compartment of a railway coach. Petrukhin sat by me, holding my hand, and weeping.

When I thought of the circumstances that had led to my fainting, the figure of Pugachov swam up before my eyes, and I took an oath there and then to kill him at the first opportunity, if I escaped from the Bolshevik trap.

Petrukhin then told me that Peter had aroused such compassion for me among the members of the Investigation Committee that they had agreed to go with him to Sablin, and petition the Commander-in-Chief to send me to Moscow for trial by a military tribunal. About fifty soldiers were also won over to my side by Peter's accounts of Yashka's work in the trenches and No Man's Land, and of my reputation among all the men. Petrukhin had remained at my bedside till I recovered consciousness, but he now wished to join the deputation. I thanked him gratefully for his kindness towards me and his desperate efforts to save my life.

Before he left, word reached him that Pugachov had incited some of the men against me, threatening to kidnap and lynch me before I was taken away. Petrukhin placed five loyal friends of his at my compartment, with orders not to surrender me at any cost.

I prayed to God for Petrukhin, and hearing my prayer he said, "Now, I, too, believe in God. The appearance of this man, Peter, was truly miraculous. In spite of all my efforts, you would have been executed but for him."

"But what are my chances of escaping death now?" I asked.

"They are still very small," he answered. "Your record is against you. You do not deny being a friend of Kornilov. Your strict discipline in the Battalion and your fighting the Germans at a time when the whole front was fraternizing, are known here. Besides, the death penalty has become so customary here that it would be very unusual for one to escape it. Only the other day a physician and his wife, on their way to Kislovodsk to the springs, somehow arrived in Zverevo. They were arrested, attached to a party about to be shot, and executed without any investigation. Afterwards papers from their local Soviet were found in their clothes, certifying that they were actually ill, the physician suffering from a cancer, and requesting that they should be allowed to proceed to Kislovodsk."

Petrukhin kissed my hand, and left, warning me:

"Wait here till I return. Nobody will harm you in my absence."

He locked the door behind him. I took out the little bottle of holy water, given to me by my youngest sister, Nadia, and drank it. On my knees before the little icon, I prayed long and devoutly to God, Jesus, and the Holy Mother. My ears caught a noise outside the car; it came from several menacing soldiers who wanted to get in and kill me on the spot. I prayed with greater fervor than before, pleading for my life in the name of my mother, my father and my little sister. My heart was heavy with sorrow and despair.

As I was hugging the little icon, tears streaming from my eyes, I suddenly heard a voice, a very tender voice, say to me, "Your life will be saved."

I was alone in the compartment. I realize that it is a daring statement to make. I do not seek to make any one believe it. It may be accepted or not. But I am satisfied that I did hear the voice of a divine messenger. It was soothing, elevating. Suddenly I felt happy and calm. I thanked the Almighty for His boundless grace and vowed to have a public prayer offered at the Moscow Cathedral of Christ the Savior[48] at the first opportunity, in commemoration of His miraculous message to me.

Then I fell asleep, and rested calmly till the arrival of Petrukhin. His face was wreathed in smiles, he clasped my hand joyfully, saying, "Thank God! Thank God! You are at least saved from the mob. Sablin has ordered you to be sent to, Moscow. The necessary papers are being prepared now."

At this point Peter came in, followed by some members of the investigation committee. All were happy. It was a wonderful moment. How an act of humanity transforms men's countenances! Peter and his comrades congratulated me, and I was too overcome to express all the gratefulness that I felt toward these men.

---

48. Razed in 1931 on the orders of Josef Stalin.

Petrukhin then narrated how he had dealt with the infuriated soldiers, who had clamored for my life. He told them that I was being led away to Moscow in the hope that I would there deliver up several counterrevolutionary Generals associated with Kornilov.

"Will she be shot afterwards?" they inquired.

"Of course," Petrukhin declared. The lynchers went away satisfied.

"I was curious to know what would be done to me in Moscow. Petrukhin replied to my inquiries that among the papers relating to my case, which my escort would take with them to Moscow, the chief document was the protocol. That protocol had been drawn up by himself, in the capacity of chairman of the Investigation Committee. He described in it how I had lost my way while going to Kislovodsk, getting stranded at Zverevo, and how I had reported of my own free will to the authorities, adding that I had with me a ticket to Kislovodsk, an invitation from Princess Tatuyeva to come to the Caucasus, and a certificate from a physician certifying to my ill-health. The last was, of course, an invention. Petrukhin sent the ticket and the letter from Tiflis, adding that he had misplaced the physician's certificate and would send it on later.

"It is unlikely," he said to me," that you would be punished with death in the face of such evidence. I should expect your release, sooner or later. But in any event, here is a poison pill. I prepared it for you originally to take in case the mob got their way, so that you should escape torture at the hands of these savages. I hope you will not need to resort to it in Moscow."

I still carry with me that poison pill wherever I go...

Petrukhin gave me forty rubles for expenses, as I was penniless. I thanked him and asked him to write a letter to my people, telling them where I was. We then took leave of one another. Petrukhin and Peter exchanged kisses with me, and I again and again reiterated how much I owed to them, swearing that in any future emergency, whatever happened, I would always be ready to do everything within my power for them. We all realized that many a change was still in store for Mother Russia, before she settled down to a peaceful existence.

Accompanied by my friends and surrounded by four armed guards, forming my escort, I was led to an empty railway coach, attached to an engine. On this train, consisting of cattle-trucks and my coach, I was taken to Nikitino. There I was brought before the Commandant, with a request to provide accommodation for the party on an ordinary train. It was the very Commandant who had helped me so generously to get to Zverevo on the munition train. Of course, he did not recognize the Sister of Mercy in Bochkareva.

On the platform I had another striking encounter. The news that Bochkareva had been seized and was being taken to Moscow became known in the station and a number of Red Guards and soldiers gathered about me, showering upon me insults, curses and threats. Among these, in the foremost rank, was the repulsive-looking man who was in charge of the train on which I went to Zverevo and who had proposed marriage to me!

The beast did not recognize me now. He sneered im my face, and repeated my name syllable by syllable, taking a peculiar joy in distorting it and railing generally at my appearance and reputation.

"The slut! We have got her, the harlot!" he raved. "Only I can't understand why they didn't shoot her there. Why bother with such a slut!"

I could not help laughing. I laughed long, without restraint. It was so amusing. I was almost tempted to disclose to him how I had duped him. He still has no idea that Alexandra Smirnova, whose fictitious address at Kislovodsk he, in all probability, cherishes yet, was Maria Bochkareva!

For three days I travelled with my escort from Nikitino to Moscow. I was treated with consideration, but always as a prisoner. The guards would get food for me and themselves at the stations on the way. Upon our arrival at Moscow I was taken in a motor-car to the Soldiers' Section of the Soviet, established in what was formerly the Governor's mansion. My guards delivered me to a civilian, with all the documents of the case, and left.

"What, coming from Kornilov?" the official asked me gruffly.

"No, I was on my way to take the cure at Kislovodsk," I replied.

"Ah, yes, we know those cures! What about the epaulets? Why did you take them off?"

"Because I am a plain peasant woman. I have defended my country bravely for three years. I am not guilty."

"Well, we will see about that later," he interrupted and ordered me to be led away to prison.

I was locked up in a small cell, in which there were already about twenty prisoners, officers and civilians, all arrested by agents who had overheard them talk against the Bolshevik regime! A fine reincarnation of the worst methods of Tsarism.

The cell was in a frightful condition. There was no lavatory in it, and the inmates were not permitted to leave the room! The stench was indescribable. The men smoked incessantly. The prisoners were not even allowed to take the short, daily promenade outside, which was granted by the old regime.

Apparently in order to make me confess, I was subjected to a new form of torture, never practiced by the Tsar's jailers. I was denied food! For three days I did not receive even the niggardly ration given to the other prisoners. My companions were all kind to me, but the portions that they received were barely enough to sustain life in their own bodies. So for three days and three nights, I lay on the bunk, in a heap under a cover, on the point of suffocation, starved, feverish, and thirsty, as no water was allowed me.

During these days the Commandant of the prison, a sailor, would come in several times daily to torment me with his tongue.

"What are you going to do to me?" I asked.

"What? You will be shot!" was his answer.

"Why?"

"Ha, ha. Because you are a friend of Kornilov's."

Those were the hours when I hugged the pill given me by Petrukhin, expecting every moment an order to face a firing squad.

Soon one of the arrested officers, who had been caught cursing Bolshevism while drunk, was set free. Before he went, some of his companions intrusted him with messages to their relatives. I thought of the Vasilyevs, who had so kindly taken me from the hospital to their home in the autumn of 1916, and begged the officer to visit them and tell them of my plight. He promised to do so and carried out his pledge. I sent them a message that I expected to be executed and asked their help.

When Daria Maximovna got the message she was horrified and immediately set out to get permission to see me. But when she called at the Soldiers' Section for a pass to see Bochkareva, she was taken for a friend of Kornilov's and would have been badly mauled if not for the fact that her son Stepan, who had belonged to my Company and who had brought about the friendship between his mother and myself, was now one of the Bolshevik chiefs. Daria Maximovna cried out that she was the mother of Stepan Vasilyev, of such and such a department, and he was brought to identify his mother.

This rescued her from a severe punishment. She appealed to her son to intervene in my behalf, but he refused, saying that he could not come to the aid of an avowed friend of Kornilov's. He, however, obtained a pass to my cell for his mother. Later he responded to her entreaties and did say a few good words for me, telling the proper authorities that I was a simple peasant woman with no understanding of politics.

On the fourth day of my imprisonment I received a quarter of a pound of bread, some tea and two cubes of sugar. The bread was black, consisting partly of straw. I could not even touch it and had to satisfy myself with three cups of tea. Later in the day a sailor came in, and, addressing me as comrade, informed me that one Vasilyeva was waiting to see me. I was weak, so weak that I could not move a few feet without assistance. As soon as I got up and made a step, I sank back on the bed in a helpless condition.

"Are you ill?" the sailor asked.

"Yes," I murmured.

He took me by the arm and led me to a chair in the office. I was bathed in perspiration after the little walk and so dizzy that I could not see anything. When Daria Maximovna saw me she fell on my neck and wept. Turning to the officials, she cried out bitterly, "How could you ever have such a woman arrested and subjected to torture? A woman who was so kind to the soldiers, and suffered so much for your own brothers!"

She then opened a package, took out some bread and butter, and handed them to me with these words:

"Manka, here is a quarter of a pound of bread. All we got today was three-eighths of a pound. And this is a quarter of a pound of butter, our entire ration."

I was full of gratitude to this dear woman and her children, who had sacrificed their own portions for me. The bread was good. The difficulty was, according to Daria Maximovna, to get enough for them all. Even their meager ration was not always obtainable.

I then told her my troubles and the punishment I was expecting, begging her to write to my mother in case of my execution.

I spent two weeks in that abominable cell before I was taken before the tribunal. I was marched along the Tverskaya, Moscow's chief thoroughfare, and recognized on the way by the crowds. The tribunal was quartered in the Kremlin. For a couple of hours I waited there, at the end of which time I was surprised to see Stepan Vasilyev come in and approach me.

"Marusia, how did you ever get into this?" he asked me, shaking my hand and inviting me to sit down.

I told him the story of my going to Kislovodsk to take the cure.

"But how did you ever get to Zverevo?" he inquired.

"I had a ticket to Kislovodsk. I did not know that Zverevo was such a forbidden place. Once they sold me a ticket, I thought it all right to follow the regular route," I answered excitedly.

"I spent a couple of hours yesterday examining your case and the documents relating to it, but I could not quite understand how you got to Zverevo," Stepan said."Perhaps you really did go to see Kornilov?"

"I do not deny my friendship for Kornilov," I declared, glad at heart that Stepan had turned up in such a position of authority." But you know that I am almost illiterate and understand no politics and do not mix with any party. I fought in the trenches for Russia and it is Mother Russia alone that interests me. All Russians are my brothers."

Stepan answered that he knew of my ignorance of political matters. He then went out to report to the tribunal, and shortly afterwards I was called in. There were six men, all common soldiers, seated at a long table covered with a green cloth, in the middle of a large hall, richly decorated. I was asked to sit down and tell my story, and how I got into Zverevo. The six judges were all young men, not one of them over thirty.

I was about to rise from the chair to tell my story, but was very courteously asked to remain seated. I then told of my wound in the back, of the operation that I still needed for the extraction of a piece of shell, and of my consulting a Petrograd physician who had advised me to go to the springs at Kislovodsk. I said that I had heard of the fighting between Kornilov and the Bolsheviks, at Novocherkassk, but had no idea what a civil war was like and had never thought of a front in such a struggle. I, therefore, continued my journey to Nikitino, where the Commandant had sent me on to Zverevo. Of course, I failed to mention the fact that the Commandant had sent on to Zverevo not Bochkareva but Smirnova, a Sister of Mercy. I concluded with the statement that as soon as I reached Zverevo I realized that I was in a dangerous situation, and had surrendered to the local authorities.

I was informed that it would take a week for my case to be cleared up and a decision reached. Instead of sending me to the Butyrka, the prison in which I had spent the last two weeks, I was taken to the military guard house, opposite the Soldiers' Section. Drunken sailors and Red Guards were usually confined there. The room in which I was put was narrow and long, the windows were large but closely grated. There were about ten prisoners in it.

"Ah, Bochkareva! Look who's here!"

I was met with these words as soon as I crossed the threshold. They quickly turned into phrases of abuse and ridicule. I was quiet, and sought seclusion and rest in a corner, but in vain. The inmates were Bolsheviks of the lowest sort, degenerates and former criminals. I was the object of their constant ill-treatment, so that torturing me day and night became their diversion. If I tried to sleep, I soon found some one near me. When I ate or drank, the beasts assembled about me, showering insults on me and playing dirty tricks. Weeping had no effect on them. Night after night I was forced to stay awake, sometimes throwing myself upon an intruder with my teeth in an effort to drive him away. I implored the warder to give me a cell to myself.

"Let it be a cold, gloomy hole. Give me no food. But take me away from these drunken brutes!" I would plead.

"We will take you away soon – to shoot you!" the warder would joke in reply, amid the uproarious laughter of my tormentors.

The appointed week elapsed and still there was no decision in my case. The days – long, cruel, agonizing days – passed slowly by. The impossibility of sleeping was above all so torturing that it drove me to a state actually bordering on insanity. Two and a half weeks I lived in that inferno, seventeen days without a single full night's sleep!

Then one morning the warder, who had delighted daily in telling me stories of what would be done to me, very vivid stories of frightfulness, came in with some papers in his hand.

"Bochkareva!" he called out to me. "You are free." And he opened the door facing me.

I was so surprised that I thought at first that this was another trick to torture me.

"Free?" I asked. "Why?" I had grown to believe the warder's tales of what awaited me, and I could not imagine him as the carrier of such tidings.

"Am I free for good?" I asked.

"Yes," was the answer. "You will go with a guard to the Soldiers' Section, where you will get the necessary papers."

I bade farewell, with a sigh of relief, to the chamber of horrors, and went immediately to get the document from the tribunal, which stated that I had been arrested but found innocent of the charge and that, as I was ill, I was to be allowed complete freedom of movement in the country. With this passport in my pocket I was set at liberty.

CHAPTER XX
I SET OUT ON A MISSION

The Vasilyevs were the only people I could go to in Moscow. They lived on the outskirts of the city. I made an attempt to walk to their house, but was too weak to proceed more than two blocks. There was a cabman near at hand, but he wanted twenty-five rubles to take me to my friends. I tried to bargain, offering fifteen, but he would not hear of it. As I had no money, I finally hired the cab in the hope that Daria Maximovna would pay for it. The alternative was to remain where I was.

Madame Vasilyeva received me as if I were her own daughter. She was overwhelmed with joy at my release. I was too weak and worn out to appreciate fully my miraculous deliverance from torture and death. I was given some light food, and Daria Maximovna began to prepare a bath for me. I had not changed my undergarments for several weeks, and my body was blacker than it ever had been during my life in the trenches. My skin was in a terrible condition from vermin. The bath was a greater relief at the moment than my release itself. And the long hours of sleep following it were even more welcome. I doubt if sleep ever tasted sweeter to any one.

It was impossible to remain long as a guest in Moscow in those early days of March, 1918. Stepan lived away from his home, as he and his parents held v/ idely divergent views in regard to the political situation. The family consisted of Daria Maximovna, her husband and the younger son. The daughter, Tonetchka, was married and lived elsewhere. The three Vasilyevs received daily a pound and one-eighth of bread! The weekly meat ration was a pound and a half. I, therefore, promptly realized what a burden I was bound to be. But I could not make up my mind where to go and what to do. The Vasilyevs offered to buy me a ticket home, but the document I had from the Soldiers' Section was in itself a ticket.

I recalled that some of my wounded girls had been sent to Moscow, to be quartered in the Home for Invalids, and I thought of looking them up. I took a walk to the city. When I approached the block in which the Home was situated,

I noticed a crowd in the street, largely composed of soldiers, holding meetings of indignation. When I reached the Home I saw a number of wounded soldiers, some of them without legs or arms, dispersed about the front grounds.

On inquiry I learned that the Bolshevik authorities had turned the hundreds of crippled inmates of the Home into the street. Many of them, including my girls, had already disappeared, some no doubt being forced to beg, others being cared for by charitable people and societies. But still a goodly number remained, crying, cursing Lenin and Trotsky, and asking passersby for food and shelter. It was a pathetic sight. The cruelty of the order made one's blood boil. It was evidently an act of wanton brutality. The excuse that the Government needed the building was certainly no justification for it.

There were about two hundred soldiers in the crowd, and I stopped to listen to their conversation. All of them had been attracted to the place by the complaints of the ejected invalids. Their talk came as a revelation to me. They were in a mutinous spirit, stirred up against the regime of Lenin and Trotsky. For several hours I lingered round the various groups, sometimes taking part in the discussions.

"See what you have brought about by your own acts. You have shamefully beaten and killed your officers. You have forgotten God and destroyed the Church. Now, this is the result of your deeds." In some such manner I would address the men, and they would answer somewhat as follows:

"We believed that by overthrowing our officers and the wealthy class, we should have plenty of bread and land. But now the factories are demolished and there is no work. We are terrorized by the Red Guards, who are recruited mostly from drunkards and criminals. If there are any honest soldiers among them, it is because hunger and poverty force them to enlist in order to escape starvation. If we demand justice and fair play, we are shot down by the Red executioners. And all the while the Germans are advancing into Russia, and nobody is sent to fight them, our real enemies."

At these words I crossed myself, thanking the Almighty for the deep change He had wrought in the minds of the people.

The crowd became so excited that the authorities were notified and a detachment of the Red Guard was sent to suppress it. It arrived suddenly and warned us to disperse by firing a volley into the air. The gathering separated and vanished from the street. A group of about ten soldiers, including myself, rushed into a neighboring courtyard and continued the conversation there behind the gates.

"See, what you get now! If you were armed, they would not dare to treat you like that. They made you surrender your arms and now oppress you worse than the Tsar. Who ever heard of a thousand sick persons being thrown out into the street under the old regime?" I asked.

"Yes, we have been betrayed. It is clear now. The Germans are taking away all our bread, occupying our land, destroying our country, demanding all our money and possessions. We have been betrayed," nodded several men.

"Ah, so you are beginning to see the truth!"

"Yes, we are," declared one fellow." A month ago I wouldn't have talked to you. I was then the chairman of a local Soviet. But I see what it all means now. We are being arrested, searched, robbed, terrorized by the Red Guard mercenaries. I would, myself, shoot Lenin and Trotsky for this outrageous treatment of the hospital patients. A month ago I was a fool, but I see now that I was all wrong in my ideas about you and other opponents of the Bolsheviks. You are not an enemy of the people, but a friend."

Accompanied by a couple of soldiers I walked away. One of them told me he had seen one of my girls begging, after she had been turned out of the Home. My heart ached at the thought, but I was absolutely without means. What could I have done for her? We reached the Cathedral of Christ the Saviour and I remembered the vow I had made to have a public mass celebrated in commemoration of my miraculous escape from death.

I took leave of my companions and entered the church. There were about five or six hundred people there. On that very day, I believe, the order was promulgated separating the Church from the State. All the devout members of the Cathedral came to the Communion service that afternoon.

I went to see the deacon in the vestry and told him of the miracle that had been vouchsafed me and the vow I had made. I did not fail to mention the fact that I was penniless and could not pay for the service. At the conclusion of the Communion, the priest announced :

"There has just come here a Christian woman who has suffered greatly for the country and whose name is known throughout the land. A miracle saved her in a desperate moment. God listened to her prayers and sent her an old friend, whose life she had once saved, on the eve of her execution. The execution was postponed. She then prayed to God again, and a divine voice informed her that her life would be spared. She vowed to offer public prayers in this Cathedral in the event of her release. The Lord mercifully granted her freedom, and she is now here to fulfil the vow."

The priest then asked the deacon to bring me up to the altar. When I was led there, a murmur went through the assembly:

"Heavens! It's Bochkareva!"

Candles were lit and for fifteen minutes prayers of praise to the Lord were read, glorifying His name.

I returned to the Vasilyevs by tram. On the car there were many soldiers, and again their conversation cheered me up.

"A fine end we have come to! The Germans are moving nearer and nearer, and here they are shooting and arresting the people!" the men said to one another. "Why don't they send the Red Guard to resist the enemy? We are being sold to the Germans."

This was my second encounter with sober-minded soldiers in one day. I arrived at Daria Maximovna's in high spirits. The awakening of the Russian soldier had begun!

I had left my medals and crosses in Petrograd before starting out on the fateful errand. Borrowing some money from Madame Vasilyeva I went to Petrograd to fetch them. The railway carriage in which I travelled was packed with about a hundred and fifty soldiers. But they were no longer the cut-throats, the incensed and revengeful ruffians of two months ago. They did not threaten. They did not brag. The kindness of their true natures had again asserted itself. They even made a place for me, inviting me to sit down.

"Please, Madame Bochkareva," they said," take this seat."

"Thank you, comrades," I answered.

"No, don't call us comrades any more. It's a disgrace now. The comrades are at present fleeing from the front, while the Germans are threatening Moscow," some of them remarked.

I felt among friends. This comradeship was what endeared the Russian soldier to my heart. Not the comradeship of the agitators, not the comradeship so loudly proclaimed in the Bolshevik manifestos and proclamations, but the true comradeship that had made the three years in the trenches the happiest of my life. That old spirit again filled the air. It was almost too good to be true. After the nightmare of revolutions and terror, it seemed like a dream. The soldiers were actually cursing Bolshevism, denouncing Lenin and Trotsky!

"How has it come about that you all talk so sensibly?" I asked.

"Because the Germans are advancing on Moscow, and Lenin and Trotsky don't even raise a finger to stop them," came the answer. "A soldier has escaped from Kiev and has just telegraphed that the Germans are seizing Russians and sending them to Germany to help to fight against the Allies. Lenin and Trotsky told us that the Allies were our enemies. We now see that they are our friends."

Another soldier, who had been home on leave, told of an armed Red Guard detachment that had descended on his village one fine day and robbed the peasants of all the bread they had, the product of their sweat and toil, exposing them to starvation.

"The people are hungry, that's why they join the Red Guard," one of the men remarked. "At least then they get food and arms with which to plunder. It is getting so that no one is safe unless he belongs to the Red Guard."

"But why don't you do something?" I addressed myself to them. "Everywhere I see the people are indignant, but they do nothing to cast off the yoke."

"We have demanded more than once the resignation of Lenin and Trotsky. There were large majorities against them at several elections. But they are supported by the Red Guard and keep themselves in power in spite of the will of the people. The peasants are against them almost to a man."

"The more reason why you should act," I said. "Something ought to be done!"

"What? Tell us what!" several inquired.

"Even to get together, for instance, and re-establish the front!" I suggested.

"We would, but we have nobody we can trust to lead us. All our good people are fighting among themselves," they argued. "Besides, we should need arms and food."

"You just said that the Allies were our friends. Suppose we asked them to send us arms and food and help us to reorganize the front, would you be willing to fight the Germ.ans again?" I inquired.

"Yes," answered some, "we would."

"No," replied others, "what if the Allies got into Russia and wanted to take advantage of us, like the Germans?"

"Well, you must elect your own leader to cooperate with the Allies only on condition that we fight till we defeat the enemy and finish the war," I proposed.

"But whom could we choose as our leader?" the men persisted. "All our chiefs are divided. Some are reputed to be monarchists. Others are said to be exploiters of the poor working people. Others are declared to be German agents. Where could we find a man who did not belong to one or other of these parties?"

"What if I, for instance, took charge, and became your leader?" I ventured to ask. "Would you follow me?"

"Yes, yes!" they cried. "We could trust you. You are a peasant yourself. But what could you do?"

"What could I do? You know that these scoundrels are destroying Russia. The Germans are seizing everything they can lay hold on. I would try to restore the front!"

"But how?" they asked.

At this moment the idea of going to America originated in my mind. We had all heard that America was now one of the Allies.

"What if I should go to America to ask there for help?" I ventured.

My companions all burst out laughing. America is so remote and so unreal to the Russian peasant. It did not sound like a practical proposition to the soldiers. But they raised only one objection.

"How would you ever get there? The Bolsheviks and Red Guards will never let you out of the country," they said.

"But if I did get there and to the other Allies," I insisted, "and came back with an army and equipment, would you join me then, and would you persuade all your friends to come with you?"

"Yes, we would! Yes! We know that you could not be bought. You are one of us!" they shouted.

"In that event, I will go to America!" I announced resolutely, there and then making up my mind to go. The soldiers would not believe me. When we reached Petrograd, and I parted from them affectionately, with their blessings following me, I did not forget to warn them to remember their pledge upon hearing of my return from foreign lands with troops.

I spent only a few hours in Petrograd and did not go to see General X. I got my war decorations from the woman friend with whom I had left them, and saw only a few of my acquaintances. I told all of them of the great change in the state of mind of the soldiers, and they were delighted.

"Thank God!" they exclaimed. "If the soldiers are waking up, then Russia will yet be saved."

After dinner I took a train back to Moscow. As usual, soldiers formed the bulk of the passengers. I listened to their discussions attentively, although this time I took no part in them, as there were a few Bolsheviks among the men, and I did not wish to divulge my plans. I heard many curse Lenin and Trotsky, and all expressed their willingness to go to fight the Germans.

One fellow asked, "How could you fight them, without leaders and organization?"

"Ah, that's the trouble," answered several at once. "We have no leaders. If some appeared and only appealed to us, we would make short work of the Bolsheviks and drive the Germans out of Russia."

I said nothing, but I took good note of their words.

The people were groping for light. It strengthened my determination to go to the Allied countries in search of help for Russia. But it was necessary to evolve some plan whereby I could get out of the country. A happy thought then occurred to me. I would make my destination the home of my valued friend, Mrs. Emmeline Pankhurst in London.

Upon my arrival at Moscow, I announced to the Vasilyevs my decision to go to London. It was explained to me that the only way out of Russia lay through Vladivostok, and that I should have to cross America before coming to England. That suited me perfectly.

Before taking the necessary steps for the departure I resolved to look up my girls and I visited a hospital to which my poor little soldiers were said to have been taken. When I arrived at the address I found the building closed and was referred to a certain professor, whom I finally traced. He told me that those of the girls who were not severely wounded had left for their homes. Only about thirty invalids remained. Five of these were suffering from shell shock and were either hysterical or insane. Many of the others were nervous wrecks. He had worked hard to get them into the Home for Invalids, but hardly had they arrived there when the building was requisitioned by the Bolsheviks and the inmates turned out into the streets. Vera Mikhailovna, a wealthy woman, had rescued them from the streets and sheltered them in her house, but just before my visit she had telephoned to him that the Bolsheviks had now requisitioned her own house, and she was at a loss to know how to dispose of the girls. He concluded with the suggestion that both of us should go over to Vera Mikhailovna.

With a heavy heart I entered the large house in which my unfortunate girls, momentarily awaiting the word to get out, were kept. My visit was a complete surprise to them. But there was no joy in my heart as I crossed the threshold of their room. It was not a happy reunion. I had no means with which to help them, no power, no influential friends.

"The Commander! the Commander!" the women exclaimed joyously as soon as they saw me, rushing toward me, throwing themselves upon my neck, kissing me, hugging me.

"The Commander has come! She will save us! She will get us money, bread, a home!"

They danced about me in high glee, making me feel even more bitter and miserable.

"My dear girls!" I said, in order to disillusion them at once, "I am myself penniless and hungry. You mustn't expect any help of me now."

"No matter! You know how to get everything!" they said confidently." You will take us to fight the Bolsheviks as we fought the Germans!"

There was a conference between Vera Mikhailovna, the professor and myself on the problem confronting us. Vera Mikhailovna suggested that I should take the girls along with me to my village. I rejected the idea at first, both because

I did not intend to remain at Tutalsk, but only to pass through it on the way to Vladivostok and because of my lack of funds. Vera Mikhailovna, however, insisted that the wisest thing in the circumstances would be to take them away from Moscow. She told me that several of the girls had been enticed away and maltreated by the Bolshevik soldiers and that the result of leaving them in Moscow would be their ruin. She offered to provide tickets for them all to my village and a thousand rubles in ready money. I finally consented to take my invalids with me, hoping to obtain sufficient funds in America to ensure them a life of peace and comfort.

I had resolved to go to America. But I had no funds. As my destination was to be London, for the reasons mentioned, I thought of seeking assistance from the British Consul in Moscow. With the aid of the Vasilyevs, I succeeded in finding the Consul's offices and went to see him. There were many people waiting to see the Consul, and I was informed that he could not be seen. His secretary came out and asked me the purpose of my call. I gave him my name, told him of my plight and of my decision to go to London, to visit Mrs. Pankhurst, and asked for aid on the ground that I had fought and sacrificed much for the cause of Russia and the Allies. He reported my presence to the Consul, who received me almost immediately.

The Consul was very courteous. He met me with a smile and a cordial handshake, said that he had read in the papers of my arrest at Zverevo and inquired what he could do for me. I showed him the document from the Soviet, but did not reveal to him the fact of my mission to Kornilov, adding, "Consul, this paper, as you see, allows me freedom of movement, I want to take advantage of it and go to London, to visit my friend, Mrs. Pankhurst. But I am without means. I came to ask you to send me, as a soldier, who had fought for the Allied cause, to England. If Russia should awake, I shall eagerly resume my service on behalf of this cause."

The Consul explained that the Bolsheviks would not allow him to draw on the Consulate's deposits in the banks, but, in view of my circumstances, he could supply me with some money for expenses. As to my visit to London, he said there were almost insuperable difficulties in the way, even for his own countrymen, let alone Russians.

But I would not alter my mind, and persisted in begging him to send me to his country. He promised to consider the matter and give a definite answer that night. He then invited me to dine with him at eight o'clock that evening.

When I returned for dinner the Consul informed me that he had already telegraphed to the British Consul at Vladivostok of my going to London by way of America, requesting him to aid me in every way he could. At dinner I told the Consul how Mrs. Pankhurst had come to know me, but kept to myself the real purpose of my journey, as I feared that the Consul would not want to antagonize the Bolsheviks by extending his protection to me. He gave me five hundred rubles, and I decided to leave immediately. A Siberian express was leaving at 12:40 that night. I had a few hours left to get my girls to the station and to bid farewell to the Vasilyevs.

My immediate destination was Tutalsk, on the Great Siberian Line. I was uneasy about the treatment our party might receive from the soldiers, who occupied three-quarters of the space on the train. But here again the mental transformation was obvious. The passengers discussed affairs sensibly. There were many officers on the train, but they were not molested. The soldiers were friendly to them and to us. The all-absorbing topic was the advance of the Germans. Lenin and Trotsky were cursed and denounced as despots worse even than the Tsar. There were many refugees from the newly invaded provinces, and their tales further increased the mutinous spirit of the men.

"We were promised bread and land. Now the Germans are taking both away."... "We wanted an end to the war, but Lenin has got us into a worse position than before."

"We were promised bread and land. Now the Germans are taking both away."

"We wanted an end to the war, but Lenin has got us into a worse position than before."

"We went to the Bolshevik offices and told them of our hunger, and they advised us to enlist in the Red Guard."

"It is impossible to find work, all the factories are shut down or disorganized."

These and similar sentiments were expressed on every side. Underlying them all was a greater hatred for the Germans than ever. There was no doubt in my mind that those men were ready to follow any trusted leader, with arms and food, against the Germans.

At Chelyabinsk the train stopped for a couple of hours.[49] There were two regiments stationed there, and there were several hundred soldiers on the express. A meeting was quickly organized quite near the station, within a short distance of the place where I had been thrown off the train some three months ago. But how different was the mood of the masses now! There

---

49. Just a few months later at Chelyabinsk train station, on May 14, 1918, a dispute between Czech legion-naires heading east and Magyars heading west ended violently. It precipitated Czech troops to eventually seize the entire Trans-Siberian Railway line, altering the course of the Civil War.

were thousands at the meetings. A refugee addressed the crowd. He made a stirring, sarcastic speech.

"Every one of us," he began, "has something at stake in Russia. We all want to defend our country. We have all made our sacrifices. For three years I fought in this war. Then I was set free to return home. But I found my home in the hands of the Germans. I could not return. I lost my parents, my wife, my sisters! What do I now get for all my sacrifices?

"Liberty! I came to Petrograd. For three days I went hungry. I was not alone. There were many other soldiers who suffered the same fate. They gave us no bread. What have we gained?

"Liberty!

"I went to see the chief of the Government in Petrograd. But I was not admitted to him. I was nearly beaten to death and thrown out of the building. Why?

"Liberty!

"The Germans are taking everything they can lay hands on, and at the same time the Red Guard is being strengthened in order to fight – whom, the Germans? – no, the so-called bourgeoisie! But are they not our own brethren, our own blood? In whose name are we urged to slaughter our own people while the Germans ravish our land?

"In the name of Liberty!

"Our country has been disgraced and ruined and still we are being called upon to destroy our own educated and intelligent classes.

"Is this liberty?

"I hear that in Moscow a thousand invalids were thrown out into the street. These invalids are soldiers like yourselves and myself, only maimed and crippled for life. Why were they thrown out?

"For the sake df liberty!"

We were all deeply impressed by this speech. Not a single voice was raised in protest. Every heart felt that the liberty we had received was not the kind of liberty we had dreamed of. We wanted peace, happiness, brotherhood, not civil war, foreign invasions, strife, starvation and disease.

Another speaker arose and said, "He is right. We have been deceived and disgraced. We go hungry and no one cares. But how can we get out of this shameful situation? We should have to overthrow the present leaders, and re-establish the front. The Japanese are already moving into Siberia, and the Germans are occupying Russia, all because we are divided. We shall be under some foreign yoke if we don't join our forces. We quarrelled with our officers, but how can we ever hope to do anything without officers? We might make peace with them, but where can we get arms to overthrow our present leaders, who have surrounded themselves with bands of Red Guards?"

For a moment the vast gathering remained silent. It was a pathetic calm. There was a painful sense that our much-cherished freedom had turned into an oppressive bondage.

Suddenly a couple of men raised their voices, shouting protests, denouncing the speaker, even threatening him. They were promptly seized and placed under arrest, and quiet was restored.

"Allow me to answer the question!" I shouted to the chairman from the distant place I occupied.

"Bochkareva! It's Bochkareva!" a number of voices passed the word to the platform, and immediately I was lifted up and carried on to the platform.

"It's a pleasure to speak to you now," I began, "only a few weeks ago you would have torn me to pieces."

"Yes, it's true! We killed many!" several men interrupted. "But we were told that the officers wanted to enslave us, that's why we killed them. We now see that our real enemies are not the officers, but the Germans."

"Before I answer the question put by the previous speaker, let me ask you what your attitude is toward the Allies?" I said.

"America, England, and France we trust. They are our friends. They are free countries. But we distrust Japan. Japan wants Siberia," came in reply from many directions.

Here a soldier interrupted and asked permission to ask a question. It was granted.

"I can't understand why our Allies do not defend us," he said. "Not even one of them has come to our help at a time when Germany is devouring our land. The Allied envoys are running away from Russia, and those that remain do not listen to the voice of the masses, but to the representatives of Lenin and Trotsky. At Moscow I saw an official of the Soviet escort an Englishman to a train. I was hungry. There were hundreds of soldiers like me at the station. Our hearts were aching. We wanted to give him a message, but he did not even turn to us. Instead, he warmly shook hands with the Soviet official."

"What if we should appeal to the Allies, to America, England, and France, to furnish us with bread, arms and money for the reconstruction of the front?" I resumed.

"How can we trust them?" I was interrupted again. "They will come here and work in league with Lenin and his band of bloodsuckers."

"Why not join forces and elect a Constituent Assembly, and let your own leaders co-operate with the Allies?" I suggested.

"But whom could we choose?"

"That we would decide later. There are plenty of good men still left in Russia," I answered. "But what if I, for instance, should want to do something, would you trust me?"

"Yes, yes! We know you! You are of the people!" hundreds of voices cried out.

"Well, let me tell you then, I am going to America and England. If I should succeed and come back with an Allied force, would you come to aid me in saving Russia?"

"Yes, we will! Yes, yes!" the crowd roared.

With this the meeting ended. The train was now about to start and we hurried towards it, singing on the way. I felt happy and hopeful. Several thousand soldiers were not to be disregarded. They were almost unanimous in their new view of the country's condition. Taken in conbination with what I had observed in Moscow and on the way to Petrograd, this meeting further reinforced my hopes for Russia's salvation. It was obviously a phenomenon of widespread occurrence, this awakening of the soldiers.

My mother had received Petrukhin's letter, and for six weeks had mourned me as dead. She was overwhelmed with joy upon my return, but became a little uneasy as she perceived a long line of girls, many of them almost barefoot, file after me into the little hut. She took me aside and asked what it meant, confiding to me that she had only fifty rubles left of the money I had brought home on my previous visit. I begged her to be patient and assured her that I would arrange matters promptly. I immediately went to the owner of the hut and several others of the leading peasants of the community, got them together, explained to them the situation, informed them that I had only one thousand rubles to spend toward the support of the girls, and asked if they would undertake to feed and house them on credit till my return from America.

"I swear that I will pay every kopek due to you. I will get enough money to pay not only the debts, but to ensure for them sustenance and shelter to the end of their lives. Now I want you to keep a record of all your expenses. Will you trust me?"

"Yes," replied the peasants. "We know that you have done a great deal for Russia, and we have confidence in you."

This was the arrangement under which the thirty invalids of my Battalion of Death were left by me in the village of Tutalsk in March, 1918. The thousand rubles I gave to my mother with instructions to buy shoes for the most destitute of the girls. Of the five hundred rubles given to me by the Consul, I gave three hundred to my mother. I decided to take my youngest sister, Nadia, with me to

America. Accompanied to the station by my parents, the thirty girls, and half the community, I started eastward, for Irkutsk and Vladivostok, dressed once more as a woman.

At the station in Irkutsk I noticed a young girl, with two tiny children in her arms. Somehow her face looked familiar to me, but I could not recall who she was. She was evidently in trouble, poor and ragged. For a while she stared at me. Then she ran up and cried out breathlessly, "Manya'!"

She was the younger daughter of the woman Kitova, whose husband had killed the dog-catcher and who had accompanied him into exile, at the same time that I had gone into exile with Yasha. Then, she was only a little girl, not more than eleven or twelve years old. Now she was the mother of two children.

For three days, she told me, her mother and herself had been living on the floor of the station. They had only seventy kopeks left in their possession. With this money the mother had gone to the town to find lodging! More than three months they had been travelling from Yakutsk, where this girl had married a political. All the money in my purse was two hundred rubles. I gave forty and then another twenty to the poor girl.

While I was holding one of the two babies, an official approached me.

"Are you Bochkareva?" he asked.

"Yes," I answered.

He wanted to detain me, but some of the soldiers I had travelled on the same train with me hurried to my defense. There was a hot argument. I drew out my pass from the Soviet and claimed the freedom to go wherever I pleased. I was finally left in peace.

I waited for the return of old Kitova to the last minute, desirous to see her and especially to learn about Yasha and other friends in North Siberia. Her daughter could only tell me that Yasha had married a Yakut woman, after the local fashion, and was still in Amga when last she heard...

We resumed the journey eastward. At Khabarovsk, about 460 miles from Vladivostok, we changed trains and had to accommodate ourselves for the night at the station in the women's waiting room. When I was about to settle down for the night, the door opened and a voice behind me called out sharply, "Commander Bochkareva?"

"Yes," I replied, alarmed at this form of address.

"Are you going to England?" was the next question.

"No."

"Where, then, are you going?"

"To Vladivostok, to stay with some relatives."

The official then demanded my baggage in order that he might search it. He found a letter from the Moscow Consul to his Vladivostok colleague. I explained that the Consul had helped me in Moscow and now asked the English representative at Vladivostok to help me also. The official told me in a whisper that he was only fulfilling orders, but did not sympathize any longer with Lenin's regime. He had left four soldiers outside the room in order to facilitate matters for me. His eyes then fell on a photograph of me in the trunk. It showed me in full uniform and was the last copy in my possession. He asked for it and my autograph, and to win his good will I gave it to him without demur. He then advised me to conceal the letter from the Consul, and I sent it by Nadia to Ivanov, one of my fellow-travellers outside. One of these was a member of a provincial Soviet, an ex-Bolshevik. He and other soldiers aided me while I was on the train to evade the Red Guards, who used to search it daily, at various stations, for officers going to join General Semyonov. More than once, in an emergency, I was concealed under their overcoats. When the Guard asked, "Who's there?"

"A sick comrade," was the answer, and they passed on.

The official had received orders to take me to the town and detain me. Escorted by the four Guards, Nadia and I were taken to the police station. I was locked up, while the official went to call a meeting of the local Soviet. Nadia remained outside the cell, and I suddenly heard her cry for help. Rushing to the door, I saw through the keyhole that the Red Guards were annoying her. I banged at the door, shouting to the rascals to leave her alone, appealing to their sense of shame, but they only jeered and continued to torment her. My helplessness behind the locked door infuriated me. I dare not think of what the ruffians would have done to Nadia had not my friend Ivanov come in with two other soldiers to plead for me.

They found Nadia crying and me banging at the door in a white fury. I told them of the behavior of the four Red Guards toward my sister, and a sharp quarrel ensued. Presently the chairman of the local Soviet and the majority of its members arrived. My case was taken up. It appeared that orders had been received from Moscow or Irkutsk to detain me. As the search had not led to the discovery of any incriminating evidence against me, my claim that I was going to Vladivostok could not be refuted.

Ivanov and the two soldiers put up a valiant defense, arguing that I was a sick woman, that they had come to know me during our companionship on the train as a real friend of the people, and that it would be a disgrace to arrest me and send me back with no evidence against me.

But for these three defenders, I should in all probability have been dispatched under escort to Moscow or Tutalsk. With their aid, I was able to make such a favorable impression on the Khabarovsk Soviet that I was permitted to proceed to Vladivostok, where I arrived about the middle of April, 1918, with five rubles and seventy kopeks in my purse.

The Soviet in Vladivostok kept a close watch over all the people who were arriving and departing. As soon as Nadia and I reached a lodging house, our documents were demanded in order that they might be sent to the Soviet for inspection. Nadia had a regular passport, while I made use of the paper from the Moscow Soldiers' Section. It is usual for such documents to be returned to their owners with the stamp of the local Soviet on the back. But ours were slow in arriving – not a good omen.

I went to the English Consul and was received in his office by an elderly Russian Colonel, who served there in the capacity of secretary and interpreter. He recognized me at once, as a telegram from Moscow announcing my coming had preceded me. The Consul was very kind and cordial when I was shown into his study, but declared that his position was such that he could not take it upon himself to obtain a passport for me from the Soviet, as he was suspected of counter-revolutionary activities.

Without revealing to the Consul the true purpose of my journey, I explained to him that my journey to London was undertaken not merely as a social visit to Mrs. Pankhurst, but as an escape from the terror of Bolshevism, which made life perilous for me anywhere in Russia. He advised me to go to the local Soviet, tell them of my desire to go to Mrs. Pankhurst, of whom the Bolsheviks had certainly heard, and ask for passports.

The Consul thought that the Soviet could not find anything suspicious about my journey to his country, and would allow me to proceed unmolested. I replied with an account of some of the things I had endured at the hands of Lenin's government and said that I was certain that my formal application for a passport would be the end of my adventure. He then telephoned to the American Consul at Vladivostok, informed him of my arrival and my plight, and enlisted his interest.

I returned to the hotel, with three hundred rubles in my purse, given me by the Consul. The place was dirty and without conveniences, but it was almost impossible to obtain decent accommodation in the city. However, the proprietor of the inn was very helpful and later saved me from trouble.

The following day the Consul told me that all efforts to win the goodwill of the Soviet toward me had not only failed but had been met with threats. The Bolsheviks might even send me back, I learned. I renewed my entreaties to the Consul to send me away, even without the Soviet's passport. He would not promise to do so, but under the pressure of my appeals finally showed an inclination to consider the matter.

Upon leaving the Consulate I was stopped in the street by a soldier.

"Bochkareva?" he asked.

"Yes," I answered.

"Why did you come here to tramp the streets?" was the next question.

"I came to visit my relatives, but found that they had moved, so I am going back soon."

He let me go my way. As soon as I arrived at the inn, the proprietor took me aside to tell me that representatives of the Soviet had called in my absence, and inquired as to my doings and my plans. He had informed them that I had come to visit some relatives, but was unable to find where they were living. They had left with the threat that they would return to arrest me. I did not intend to wait for their arrival and allow myself to be detained and sent back. I telephoned to the Consul and told him of the latest development. Fortunately he had some good news for me. An American transport was to arrive in Vladivostok two days later!

Nadia and I hurried to the Consulate. The Consul declared that the Bolsheviks had threatened him if he should be found aiding me to get away. Meanwhile he proceeded to have all the necessary foreign passports prepared for us, and we were photographed for that purpose. The difficulty of leaving Vladivostok without a pass from the Soviet still confronted us. The harbor was under strict supervision, and the boats that were used to ferry passengers from the shore to the steamships were manned and inspected by Bolsheviks.

For nearly two days I remained in my room, in constant dread of the appearance of Red Guards to arrest me. They did not come, however, apparently convinced that I could not escape them anyway. They had ample reason afterwards to change their minds about this. I then went to the Consul again. The American transport *Sheridan* was due that night, he said, but he was not sure yet if the Captain would be willing to take me on board.

Meanwhile we sought a means to elude the inspectors at the port. A large traveling basket was tried, and I managed to pack myself into it, but the Consul decided that I might be suffocated in case the basket should be left at the pier for a couple of hours. So I got out of the basket.

The transport arrived in the evening, and the Captain expressed his willingness to carry me across the Pacific.

At the request of the Consul, I remained in his house, while my sister, accompanied by an officer, went to the inn to get my things, and with them left for the vessel. Two hours later I called up the inn to find out whether Nadia had been there with the officer. The proprietor informed me that about fifty Red Guards had just been there looking for me, and had been disagreeably surprised to learn that I had departed already.

"Where did she go?" they asked the proprietor.

"To the railway station, to take a train," he lied.

"What train?" they shouted indignantly. "There are no trains leaving tonight." With that they went away, presumably to search for me.

I communicated to the Consul what I had learned, and he hid me in a closet. Shortly afterwards several Red Guards arrived, asking for Bochkareva. The Consul denied knowledge of my whereabouts, declared that I had come to him only once, as a result of which he had applied to the Soviet for a passport for me, but since he was refused he washed his hands of my case. The Red Guards said that I had been observed entering the Consulate, but had not been seen to leave it. They glanced about for me and then left, after the Consul's denial of my visit.

The old Colonel returned, after taking Nadia aboard the transport, with the news that I should have company on the way, as eight Russian officers were to be passengers on the same vessel. Hundreds of Russian officers had arrived in Vladivostok in the belief that they could join the British army there and be transported to France. Unfortunately, the Allies would not accept their services and they found themselves in difficult circumstances, without means to return to European Russia and with no desire to do so, as long as Bolshevism was still rampant there. Some of them succeeded by various means in making their way to the United States or Canada.

The Colonel asked me if I wanted to meet my fellow travellers. I answered in the affirmative, and as they were at the moment at the Consulate, he took me into the room, in which they were waiting. Scarcely had I crossed the threshold, when, glancing at the small group of officers, my eyes suddenly fell on Leonid Grigoryevich Filippov, my former battle adjutant, who had carried me unconscious under German fire to safety in that unhappy advance of the Battalion.

"What are you doing here?" both of us asked each other simultaneously, astonished at this unexpected meeting.

I had always felt that I owed my life to Lieutenant Filippov after I had been stunned by a shell and injured while running from the enemy at the end of the fruitless offensive launched by the Battalion. He had taken charge of the Battalion after I had been sent to the Petrograd hospital, and later left for Odessa to train as an aviator.

From a short private conversation I learned that Lieutenant Filippov was in the same plight as all the other officers who had come to Vladivostok under the impression that they would be accepted by the Allies. I decided to ask the Consul to allow him to assume his former post of adjutant to me and let him become a member of my party. The Consul graciously consented, and I was happy at the thought of journeying to foreign lands in the company of an educated friend, with a knowledge of languages, peoples and geography, who was also devoted to Russia with all his heart.

After another conference with the Consul, it was decided that I should be dressed as an Englishwoman and as such make an effort to get to the American transport. The necessary clothes were obtained, and in fifteen minutes I appeared no longer as a soldier, but as a veiled foreign lady who did not understand a word of Russian. Accompanied by the Colonel, I left for the harbour, after having expressed my deepest thanks to the Consul for his great sacrifices in my behalf.

I was supposed to play a speechless role and leave everything to my escort. This I did, although more than once my heart jumped when a guard seemed to scrutinize me closely, and now and then I had to suppress an impulse to laugh when the Colonel, in reply to questions, said that I was an Englishwoman returning home. It was dark when I was ferried to the transport, and everything went off without mishap. But that was not the end of the adventure.

The transport had to remain for another day in the harbor, and it was expected that the Soviet would search it for me. To baffle all attempts to discover me, I was placed in a cabin, the entrance and all approaches to which were guarded. Nobody was allowed to come near the room, all inquirers being told that an important German general was detained there on his way to an American prison camp. Even Lieutenant Filippov did not know of the trick and was greatly worried over my non-arrival as the hour for the departure of the ship drew near. If any Bolshevik emissary was sent on board the vessel to look for me, he was stopped in front of a certain cabin by American soldiers and informed that no one would be permitted to get within so many feet of the imprisoned enemy general.

When the anchors of the *Sheridan* were raised and the ship began to move, I came out of the cabin, to the liveliest merriment of everybody who had expected to see a stern Teuton general emerge from the door.

I was free!

It was April 18, 1918, when I left Russian soil for the first time in my life. Under the American flag, on an American transport, I was heading for that wonderful land – America – carrying in my breast the message of the Russian peasant-soldier to the Allies:

"Help Russia to release herself from the German yoke and become free – in return for the five million lives that she has sacrificed for your safety, the security of your liberties, the preservation of your own lands and lives!"

AFTERWORD
BOCHKAREVA'S FATE

Maria Bochkareva arrived in San Francisco in April 1918. Aided by the socialite and suffragette Florence Harriman, she traveled across the United States.

On July 10, 1918, she met with President Woodrow Wilson in the White House (she had also met in New York with former president Teddy Roosevelt). Witnesses to the meeting say her recounting of her harrowing life story to the president was profoundly emotional. She spoke too fast for the translator to keep up, and at one point fell to her knees, begging Wilson to supply troops, food and aid. The appeal reportedly brought tears to Wilson's eyes, and he promised her swift aid. While cause and effect is difficult to establish, we know that, by his own account, in July 1918 Wilson was "sweating blood over the question of what is right and feasible to do in Russia."[50] Nonetheless, that same month Wilson agreed to send 5,000 American soldiers to join in the Allied campaign in Arkhangelsk and Murmansk, while another 8,000 were sent to Vladivostok.

Maria's sister Nadyezhda decided to stay behind in America and enrolled in Washington Missionary College (now Washington Adventist University) in Tacoma Park, Maryland. It is believed she joined a Red Cross mission to Siberia the following year, but returned to the US, as she had become an American citizen.

Bochkareva meanwhile sailed for London, where she had an audience with King George V, which she recounted in later testimony to investigators:

"I entered the hall and, a few minutes later, the door opened and the King of England walked in. He greatly resembled Tsar Nicholas II. I approached the King. He said that he was very glad to meet the second Joan of Arc and, as a friend of Russia, 'I welcome you as a woman who

---

50. Carl J. Richard, *When the United States Invaded Russia: Woodrow Wilson's Siberian Disaster*, Lanham: Rowman & Littlefield, 2013, page 17.

has done much for Russia.' In response, I told him that it gave me great happiness to see the King of free England. The King asked me to sit, and then sat across from me… The King said, 'You are a Russian officer.' I answered, 'Yes.' Then the King said that 'It is your duty in four days to go to Russia, to Arkhangelsk, and I am counting on you, on the fact that you will work.' I said to the King of England, 'Yes sir!'"[51]

On August 27, 1918, Bochkareva arrived in Arkhangelsk with British expeditionary forces, and sought to raise a women's battalion

Nadya Frolkova, Maria's sister, in the US in 1918.

to do battle with the Bolsheviks. Yet the White General in charge of anti-Bolshevik forces in the city and the North, Vladimir Marushevsky, had other ideas. On December 27, 1918, after meeting with Bochkareva, he issued an order declaring that calling up women to serve in a role "for which they were not suited" would "bring shame upon the people of the North" and he forbade Bochkareva from even wearing her officer's uniform.[52]

Bochkareva bided her time for a year in Arkhangelsk, where her efforts and personal habits were less welcome than they had been two years previous in Petersburg. In August 1919, she was given R1000 and passage on the *Kolguyev*, which took her to the Ob River and on to Tomsk, where she arrived on October 19. Finding her parents still in a very difficult fiancial situation, Bochkarev resolved to petition Admiral Kolchak, then the head of White Forces in Siberia, to be allowed to resign and receive an army pension. On November 10, in Omsk, she met with Kolchak, who said, "You ask to resign, but people like you are essential to us now. I entrust you with the formation of a volunteer female sanitary brigade… We have many wounded or suffering from typhus, and there is no one to look after them. I hope you will do it."

51. Sergei Drokov, "Мария Бочкарева: краткий биографический очерк русского воина."

52. Ibid.

She accepted Kolchak's proposal and within two days had recruited 200 people to be volunteers in the brigade of the Holy Cross and Green Banner.[53] But Kolchak and his retinue was in the process of leaving Omsk, the capital of White Siberia. On November 15, 1920, the city fell to the Reds.

Transferring her Omsk brigade to the supervision of the hospital doctor, Bochkareva returned to Tomsk. As she reported in her later testimony:

I lived in Tomsk under the Whites for five days. Then Soviet power arrived. I appeared before the Tomsk commandant, handed over my revolver, and said who I was and what I had done with the Whites. I proposed my services to Soviet power. The commandant said that he did not need my services, but if they were necessary, he would send for me. The commandant obtained a signed statement from me that I would not leave the city and let me go, saying I would not be arrested.

I lived at home, threw off my military uniform, dressed in a woman's dress and decided not to do anything more, sewing a soldier's overcoat with my sister. On Christmas, at two in the morning, near Stary Cathedral, I was arrested, and later sent to Tomsk prison, from where I was taken to Krasnoyarsk.[54]

Bochkareva was held for three months in Krasnoyarsk and in the final protocol of her case, dated April 5, 1920, investigator Pobolotin wrote:

Bochkareva, being an implacable enemy of Soviet power, and a supporter of the policies of General Kornilov, traveled to America, where she had meetings with the American President Wilson, her appearance in San Francisco raising a ruckus among American workers as a martyr for the ideal of justice, while in reality she is a friend of imperialists and capitalists. From America, Bochkareva traveled to England and through the assistance of a rich suffragette attained an audience with the British war minister, who in turn arranged her meeting with the King of England... Bochkareva's criminal activity against the RSFSR has been proven... I recommend she be handed over to the head of the Special Department of the VChK [Cheka] of the 5th Army.

53. Ibid.

54. Ibid.

On April 21, it was decided to transfer Bochkareva to the Special Department of the Cheka in Moscow. But on May 15 that decision was reversed and the order was given that she be executed. On May 16, 1920, in Krasnoyarsk, Maria Bochkareva was shot on the order of the Siberian Cheka head, Ivan Pavlunovsky, and Omsk Regional Cheka Secretary Isaak Shimanovsky.

On the cover of her case file, in blue pencil, are written the words, "Fulfilled. May 16."

Yet it may be that Bochkareva's story did not end there. In the 1992 prosecutor's statement that posthumously rehabilitated her, it was noted that there were no witnesses to her May 1920 execution.

Further, historian Sergei Drokov, in his short biography of Bochkareva, avers that she was not shot in May 1920, but was somehow spirited out of Krasnoyarsk by Isaac Don Levine, who was in Russia covering the Civil War for the *Chicago Daily News* and had been granted permission to travel east from Moscow by Lenin himself. Drokov asserts that Levine and Bochkareva made it over the border to Kharbin, China, where Bochkareva met a widowed soldier she had served with; the two were married and she changed her name and lived in Kharbin until 1927, when she shared the fate of many Russian families, being forcibly repatriated to Soviet Russia. Cryptically, Drokov cites as his source an interview with another Russian historian, who claims to have met the elderly Bochkareva on a Moscow trolleybus at the end of the 1950s.[55]

In any event, on October 22, 2016, a marble memorial plaque with Bochkareva's image engraved on it was unveiled in the village of Novo-Kuskovo, Asinovsky rayon, in Tomsk Oblast, the town where Maria's family resettled to just over a century before, when she was six or seven years old.

– Paul E. Richardson

---

55. Ibid.

Printed in Great Britain
by Amazon